2 to 22 DAYS IN GERMANY, AUSTRIA, AND SWITZERLAND

THE ITINERARY PLANNER

1993 Edition

RICK STEVES

John Muir Publications
Santa Fe, New Mexico

Thanks to my hardworking team at Europe Through the Back Door, Steve Smith for research assistance, the many readers who shared tips and experiences from their travels, my wife, Anne, and the many Europeans who make travel such good living.

JMP travel guidebooks by Rick Steves
Asia Through the Back Door
Europe Through the Back Door
Europe 101: History and Art for Travelers (with Gene
    Openshaw)
Kidding Around Seattle
Mona Winks: Self-Guided Tours of Europe's Top Museums
    (with Gene Openshaw).
2 to 22 Days in Europe
2 to 22 Days in Norway, Sweden, and Denmark
2 to 22 Days in Spain and Portugal
2 to 22 Days in Great Britain
2 to 22 Days in Germany, Austria, and Switzerland
2 to 22 Days in France (with Steve Smith)
2 to 22 Days in Italy

John Muir Publications, P.O. Box 613, Santa Fe, NM 87504

ISSN 1058-6059
ISBN 1-56261-020-1

Distributed to the book trade by
W.W. Norton & Company, Inc.,
New York, New York

Design Mary Shapiro
Maps Dave Hoerlein
Typography Copygraphics
Printer McNaughton & Gunn
Cover photo Leo de Wys Inc./Fridmar Damm

CONTENTS

Europe

22 Days Itinerary Route

HOW TO USE THIS BOOK

This book is the tour guide in your pocket. It lets you be the boss by giving you the best 22 days in Germany, Switzerland, and Austria and a suggested way to use that time most efficiently.

The 2 to 22 Days series is for do-it-yourselfers who would like the organization and smoothness of a tour without the straitjacket. It's almost having your strudel and eating it, too.

This flexible plan is maximum thrills per mile, minute, and dollar. It's designed for travel by rental car or train (as each chapter explains). The pace is fast but not hectic. It's designed for the American with 2 to 22 days who wants to see everything but doesn't want the "if it's Tuesday, this must be Salzburg" craziness. The plan includes the predictable "required" biggies (Rhine castles, Mozart's house, and the Vienna Opera) with a good dose of "Back Door" intimacy mixed in (cozy Danube villages, thrilling mountain luge rides, Swiss chocolate factories, a Black Forest mineral spa, and traffic-free Swiss Alp towns).

2 to 22 Days in Germany, Austria, and Switzerland is balanced and streamlined, avoiding typical tourist burnout by including only the most exciting castles and churches. I've been very selective. For example, you won't visit both the Matterhorn and the Jungfrau—just the best of the two. The "best," of course, is only my opinion. But after twelve busy years of travel writing, lecturing, and tour guiding, I've developed a sixth sense of what tickles the traveler's fancy. I love this itinerary. Just thinking about it makes me want to slap dance and yodel.

Of course, connect-the-dots travel isn't perfect, just as color-by-numbers painting isn't good art. But this guide is your friendly Franconian, your German in a jam, your handbook. It's a well thought out and tested itinerary. I've done it—and refined it—many times on my own and with people who join me on my "Back Door Europe" tours. Take advantage of it, but don't let it rule you.

Read this book before you begin your trip. Use it as a

rack to hang more ideas on. As you plan, study, travel, and talk to people, you'll fill the book with notes. It's your tool. It is completely modular and adaptable to any trip. You'll find 22 units, or days, each with the same sections:

1. **Introductory Overview** for the day.

2. A daily hour-by-hour **Suggested Schedule** (using the European 24-hour clock).

3. **Orientation** information (with practical details like tourist information numbers, telephone codes, and so on).

4. **Transportation tips** and instructions for both car and train travel.

5. List of the most important **Sightseeing Highlights** (rated: ▲▲▲ Don't miss; ▲▲ Try hard to see; ▲ Worthwhile if you can make it; no pyramid—worth knowing about).

6. **Food and Lodging**: How and where to find the best budget places, including addresses, phone numbers, and my favorites.

7. **Itinerary Options** for those with more or less than the suggested time or with particular interests. This itinerary is rubbery!

8. Practical and easy-to-read **maps** locating recommended places. (Map-maker Dave Hoerlein has traveled this entire itinerary. His maps fit the text intimately and point out the major landmarks, streets, and accommodations mentioned. They're designed to help you follow the text, orient you, and direct you until you pick up something better at the tourist information office.)

At the end of the book are "Practical Extras" such as tips on telephoning and sample train timetables and itineraries.

Travel Smart

This itinerary works great for well-organized travelers who lay departure groundwork upon arrival in a town, read a day ahead in this book, use the local tourist information offices (abbreviated "TI" and listed with phone numbers for every town in this book), and enjoy the hospitality of the Germanic people. Ask questions. Most locals are eager to point you in their idea of the right direction. Use the telephone, wear a money belt, use a small pocket notebook to organize your thoughts, and make simplicity a virtue. If you insist on being confused, your trip will be a mess. Those who expect to travel smart, do. (My book, *Europe Through the Back Door*, 11th edition, 1993, is packed with the skills and tricks of budget travel.)

Cost

This trip's cost breaks down like this. A basic round-trip U.S. to Frankfurt flight is $600 to $900, depending on the season and where you fly from. A three-week car rental (split between two people; and including tax, insurance, and gas) or a three-week first-class railpass comes to about $550 per person. For room and board, figure $50 a day, double occupancy: $1,100 each. This is more than feasible. (Students or older bohemians could eat and sleep for $35.) Add $300 for admissions and fun money and you've got a great European adventure for around $2,800 per person.

When to Go

Summer is peak season—best weather, snow-free Alpine trails, and the busiest schedule of tourist fun but crowded and most expensive. Most of us travel during this period anyway, so this book tackles the only serious peak-season problem—finding a room. Arrive early, call ahead (nearly every place will hold a room until late afternoon if you call that morning), and utilize local information sources as explained throughout this book.

"Shoulder season" travel (May, early June, September, and early October) is ideal. Shoulder season travelers enjoy minimal crowds, decent weather, sights and tourist fun spots still open, and being able to just grab a room almost whenever and wherever they like.

Winter travelers find absolutely no crowds, but many sights and accommodations are closed or run on a limited schedule. The weather can be cold and dreary, and nighttime will draw the shades on your sightseeing

before dinnertime. The weather is predictably unpredict-
able, but you may find the climate chart in the back of
this book helpful.

Prices in this Book

Accommodations prices are generally for two people in
peak (most expensive) season and include a continental
breakfast (usually just a roll and coffee). Most cheap listings are around $10 per person in dormitory accommo-
dations. Cheap and inexpensive places provide a bed and
sink, with toilet and hot showers down the hall. Moder-
ate and expensive rooms usually include private showers.
Many hotels have a few rooms below the price range
listed but consider them "primitive" and are not likely to
push them. Many will also have less expensive beds in triples or quads. Third beds are often available (and cheap)
on request. Remember, "expensive" in this book is
"budget" in most other guidebooks.

I haven't cluttered this book with many minor prices
(specific admission fees and student discounts and so
on). When you keep the large picture in mind, admission
fees shouldn't affect your sightseeing plans. But remember to get your discounts if you're a senior or student.
Students are recognized as such only with the official
ISIC card (from your foreign study office).

Prices as well as hours and telephone numbers are
accurate as of mid-1992. Things are always changing, and
I've tossed timidity out the window knowing you'll
understand that this book, like any guidebook, starts to
yellow before it's even printed. These countries are more
stable than most European countries, but do what you
can to double-check hours and times when you arrive.

This book is best consumed by 1994. If past its pull
date for your tour, it's the prices, details about accommodations, along with some times and phone numbers that
will have changed. Basic sightseeing ideas should be
good well into the next millennium—barring unforeseen
military or volcanic activity.

Money

Currency Conversion

I've priced most things in local currencies throughout the book. Figure about 1.5 deutsche marks (DM) per dollar, 10.5 Austrian schillings (AS) per dollar, and 1.4 Swiss francs (SF) per dollar: 1 DM = $.67, 1 AS = $.10, and 1 SF = $.73 (as of August 1992).

To convert prices to dollars in your head, keep it approximate. Subtract a third off DM prices (e.g., 60 DM = $40). For SF, take off a quarter (e.g., 60 SF = $45). Divide AS by 10 to get dollars (e.g., 450 AS = about $45). So that 30 DM cuckoo clock is about $20, the 15 SF lunch is about $12, and the 800 AS taxi ride through Vienna is. . .uh oh.

Telling Time

I've used the 24-hour clock (or "military" time) throughout. Everything's the same until noon. Then, instead of "p.m." times, you'll see 13:00, 14:00, and so on (to convert, just subtract 12 and add "p.m."). Sooner or later you'll need to get comfortable with this standard European time system.

The hours listed are for peak season. Many places close an hour earlier off-season. Some are open only on weekends or are closed entirely in the winter. Confirm your sightseeing plans locally—especially when traveling between October and May. Many sights stop selling tickets 30 to 45 minutes before closing.

Borders, Passports, Visas, Shots, and Culture Shock

Traveling throughout this region requires only a passport. No shots and no visas. Border crossings between Germany, Switzerland, and Austria are extremely easy, often just a wave through. When you change countries, however, you do change money, postage stamps, and *unterhosen*.

You'll be dealing with cultural diversity. Work to adapt. The United States is huge, but it's one country with one language. The cultural stew of Europe is wonderfully complex. I always assumed Germany was "Germany";

but Germany is *Tedesco* to the Italians, *Allemagne* to the French, and *Deutschland* to the people who live there. While we think shower curtains are logical, many countries just cover the toilet paper and let the rest of the room shower with you. In Europe, what we call the second floor is the "first" and Christmas is 25-12-93. When writing numbers Europeans give their 1's an upswing and cross their 7's. If you don't adapt, your 7 will be mistaken for a sloppy 1 and you'll miss your train.

Keeping in Touch

The *International Herald Tribune* comes out almost daily via satellite from many places in Europe. *USA Today* is available, if you're in the mood for a slice of pie chart, and *The European* is trying to do for Europe what *USA Today* has done to America. European editions of *Time* and *Newsweek* hit the stands each Tuesday. Remember, news in English will only be sold where there's enough demand—in big cities and tourist centers. If you're concerned about how some event might affect your safety as an American traveling abroad, call the U.S. consulate or embassy in the nearest big city for advice. The best way to keep in touch with loved ones back home is to periodically call home direct. Most phone booths allow international calls. (See "Telephoning" in Practical Extras.)

Ugly Americanism

We travel all the way to Europe to experience something different—to become temporary locals. Americans have a knack for finding certain truths to be God-given and self-evident—things like cold beer, a bottomless coffee cup, long hot showers, free public toilets, and bigger being better. One of the beauties of travel is the opportunity to see that there are logical, civil, and even better alternatives. You'll be traveling in countries with people who consume less while enjoying a higher standard of living than we do and who have a broader understanding of the world beyond their borders. Most Europeans like Americans, but they don't envy us and wouldn't trade places.

If there is a European image of you and me, it is that we are big, loud, a bit naive, aggressively friendly, and rich. Still, I find warmth and friendliness throughout the Continent. An eagerness to go local and an ability—when something's not to my liking—to change my liking ensures that I'll enjoy a full dose of this European hospitality. I work to fit in. If the bed's too short, the real problem is that I'm too long.

Scheduling
Your overall itinerary is a fun challenge. To give you a little rootedness, I've minimized one-night stands. Two nights in a row, even with a hectic travel day before and after, is less grueling than changing lodging daily.

Try to alternate intense and relaxed periods. Every trip (and every traveler) needs at least a few slack days. I followed the biblical "one in seven" idea religiously on my last trip. If you can stretch this trip to 28 or 30 days, you won't need a vacation when you get home.

Read through this book and note special days (festivals, colorful market days, days when sights are closed). Sundays have pros and cons as they do for travelers in the U.S.A. (special events, limited hours, shops and banks closed, limited public transportation, no rush hours). Saturdays are virtually weekdays. Popular places are even more popular on weekends. Most sights are closed during one weekday.

The daily suggested schedules and optional plans take many factors into account. I don't explain most of these, but I hope you take the schedules seriously. I've listed many more sights than can be seen in the allotted time. Assume you will return!

Driving
This route is ideal by car. Every long stretch is autobahn (super freeway), and nearly every scenic backcountry drive is paved and comfortable. Drivers over 21 need only their U.S. license and the insurance that comes automatically with the rental car. Besides the rare insurance card

check, there are no border formalities to worry about.

The local rules of the road are much like ours. Learn the universal road signs (charts explain them in most road atlases and at service stations). Seat belts are required, and two beers under those belts is enough to land you in jail.

Use good local maps and study them before each drive. Familiarize yourself with which exits you need to look out for, which major cities you'll travel in the direction of, where the ruined castles lurk, and so on. Pick up the "cardboard clock" (*Parkscheibe*, available free at gas stations, police stations, and Tabak shops) and display your arrival time on the dashboard so parking attendants can see you've been there less than the posted maximum stay (blue lines indicate 90-minute zones on Austrian streets).

To understand the complex but super-efficient autobahn (no speed limit, toll-free) pick up the "Autobahn Service" booklet at any autobahn rest stop (free, listing all intersection signs, stops, services, road symbols, and more). Use a good map, and study the intersection signs: *Dreieck* means three corners, a "Y" in the road; *Autobahnkreuz* is a "cross" or intersection. Gas stations are spaced about every 30 miles, normally with a restaurant, a small shop, and sometimes a tourist information desk. Unleaded (*Bleifrei*) is now everywhere. Exits are often 20 miles apart. Know what you're looking for—*nord, süd, ost, west,* or *mittel*—miss it and you're long autobahn gone. When driving slower than 120 kph, stay out of the left-hand passing lane. Remember, in Europe, the shortest distance between any two points is the autobahn. Signs directing you to the autobahn are green in Austria and Switzerland, blue in Germany.

Get used to metric. A liter is about a quart, four to a gallon; a kilometer is 6/10 of a mile. I figure kilometers to miles by cutting them in half and adding back 10 percent of the original (120 km is 60 + 12 miles, 300 km is 150 + 30 miles).

Try to rent a car with a trunk so you can leave "deep storage" things safely out of sight. I keep a box in the trunk for things I don't need to cart in and out of hotels. My pantry box sits on the back seat, and I equip it for

easy and enjoyable, time- and money-saving car picnics
(either at the very pleasant autobahn picnic areas or as I
drive—if my navigator can play cook). I stock up with
plenty of orange juice in liter boxes, paper towels, plastic
cups, and so on. Copy the car key as soon as possible for
safety and so two people have access to the car.

Car Rental
If you plan to drive, it's cheapest to rent a car through
your travel agent well before departure (not in Germany).
You'll want a weekly rate with unlimited mileage. For
three weeks or longer, it's cheaper to lease the car (a
scheme that can save you money on taxes and insurance).
Plan to pick up the car at the Frankfurt airport and drop it
off there at the end of your trip. Remember, if you drop it
early or keep it longer, you'll be credited or charged at a
fair, prorated price. Every major car rental agency has a
Frankfurt airport office. Comparison shop through your
agent. Expect to pay $500 to $600 for a small car for three
weeks with unlimited mileage, plus around $60 a week
for the collision damage waiver full insurance option.

I normally rent the small inexpensive model (e.g., Ford
Fiesta). For a bigger, roomier, and more powerful inexpensive car, move up to the Ford 1.3-liter Escort or VW
Polo category. For peace of mind, I splurge for the CDW
(collision damage waiver insurance supplement,
ridiculously high because the base rental price doesn't
really allow a reasonable profit), which gives a zero
deductible rather than the standard $1,000+ deductible.
With the luxury of CDW you can enjoy the autobahns
knowing you can bring back the car in an unrecognizable
shambles and just say, "S-s-s-sorry."

By Train
While this itinerary is designed for car travel, it can be
adapted for train and bus. The trains are punctual and
cover all the cities very well, but frustrating schedules
make a few out-of-the-way recommendations (such as
the concentration camp at Mauthausen) just not worth
the time and trouble.

This itinerary covers enough ground to make a 3-week first-class Eurailpass worthwhile—especially for a single traveler (about $550, available from your travel agent or by mail from Europe Through the Back Door—see catalog). You can save $100 by managing with the "any 9 days out of 21" Eurail Flexipass. But this small saving requires some serious streamlining.

Eurailers should know what extras are included on their pass—like any German buses marked "Bahn" (run by the train company), city S-bahn systems, boats on the Rhine, Mosel, and Danube rivers and the Swiss lakes, and the Romantic Road bus tour. While this itinerary justifies a 21-day train pass, if you decide to buy tickets as you go, look into local specials. Seniors (women over 60, men over 65) and youths (under 26, Transalpino or BIGE tickets) can enjoy substantial discounts. While Eurail gives you first-class travel, individual second-class tickets provide the same transportation for 33 percent less per kilometer.

Hundreds of local train stations rent bikes for about $5 a day (less for train pass holders, ask for a *Fahrrad am Bahnhof* brochure at any station).

Car or Train?
This tour is a little better by car. But, with a few exceptions, trains cover the entire itinerary just fine. (See chart in Practical Extras for recommended train itinerary and times, frequency, and prices of individual train journeys.) A 3-week first-class Eurailpass is best for single travelers, those who'll be spending more time in big cities, and those who don't want to drive in Europe. While a car gives you the ultimate in mobility and freedom, enables you to search for hotels more easily, and carries your bags for you, the train zips you effortlessly from city to city, normally dropping you in the center and near the tourist office. Cars are great in the countryside but a worthless headache in places like Munich, Bern, and Vienna.

Eating

The local cuisine is heavy and hearty. While it's tasty, it can get monotonous if you fall into the schnitzel or wurst and potatoes rut. To eat well, use a phrase book or menu translator and be adventurous. The *Marling German Menu Master* is the best phrase book for galloping gluttons. Each region has its local specialties, which, while not the cheapest, are often the best values on the menu.

There are many kinds of restaurants. Hotels often serve fine food. A *Gaststatte* is a simple, less expensive restaurant. The various regions' many ethnic restaurants provide a welcome break from the basic Germanic fare. Foreign food is either from the remnants of a crumbled empire (Hungarian and Bohemian—where Austria gets its goulash and dumplings) or a new arrival to serve the many hungry but poor guest workers (Italian, Turkish, Greek, and Yugoslavian food is commonplace and a good value). The cheapest meals are found in department store cafeterias, *Schnell-Imbiss* (fast-food) stand-up joints, university cafeterias (*mensas*), and youth hostels. For a quick, cheap bite, have a deli or butcher make you a *Wurstsemmel*, or hearty meat sandwich.

Most restaurants tack a menu onto their door for browsers and will have either an English menu or someone who can translate for you. Even so, sooner or later you'll be rudely surprised as I was when my *pepperoni* pizza arrived covered with green peppers. Only a rude waiter will rush you. Good service is relaxed (slow to an American). When you want the bill, ask, *Die Rechnung, bitte*. Service is included although it's customary to round the bill up after a good meal. Wish others happy eating with a cheery *Guten Appetit*.

A basic Continental-style breakfast of coffee and rolls almost always comes with your hotel or *Zimmer* (room in a private home). A breakfast roll and a tiny tub of cheese tucked away before you leave your hotel make a handy snack or light lunch later.

For most visitors, the rich pastries, the wine, and the beer provide the fondest memories of Germany's cuisine. The wine (85% white) is particularly good from the Mosel, Rhine, Danube, eastern Austria, and southwestern Switzerland areas. Order wine by the *Viertel*, or quarter liter. You can say *ein Viertel suss* (sweet), *halbe trocken* (medium) or *trocken* (dry), *weiss* (white) or *rot* (red) *Wein* (wine) *bitte* (please). *Sekt* is German champagne. Mosel and Saar wines come in a slender green bottle, Rhine wines in a tall brown one, and Franconian in a jug-shaped bottle.

The Germans enjoy a tremendous variety of great beer. The average German, who drinks forty gallons of beer a year, knows that *dunkel* is dark, *hell* is light, *Flaschenbier* is bottled, and *vom fass* is on tap. *Pils* is barley based, *Weize* is wheat based, and *Malzbier* is the malt beer that children learn on. When you order beer, ask for *ein Halb* for a half liter or *ein Mass* for a whole liter. Some beer halls only serve it by the liter (about a quart).

Accommodations

While accommodations in Germany, Switzerland, and Austria are fairly expensive, they are normally very comfortable and a good value. Plan on spending $70 per hotel double in big cities, $50 in towns.

The more people you put in a hotel room, the cheaper it gets. While hotel singles are most expensive, private accommodations (Zimmer) have a flat per-person rate. Hostels and dorms always charge per person. People staying several nights are most desirable. One-night stays are sometimes charged extra.

In recommending a hotel, I like places that are in a convenient, central, quiet, and safe location, small, family run with local character, simple facilities not catering to American "needs," inexpensive, friendly, English-speaking, clean, and not listed in other guidebooks. Obviously a friendly, clean, quiet, central, cheap room is virtually impossible to find, and all of my recommendations fall short of perfection—sometimes miserably. But I've listed the best values for each price category that I could find, given the above criteria.

While you'll see lots of No Vacancy signs in July and
August and during a few scattered holiday periods, reservations are not normally necessary. During peak times, or
if you have a particular place you want, call ahead or try
to arrive early. It's best to call between 9:00 and 10:00 on
the day you plan to arrive, when the hotel knows who's
checking out and just which rooms will be available. I've
taken great pains to list telephone numbers with long distance instructions (see Practical Extras). Use the telephone and the new convenient telephone cards. A hotel
receptionist will trust you and hold a room until 17:00.
Don't let these people down. I promised you'd call and
cancel if for some reason you won't show up. Don't need-
lessly confirm rooms through the tourist office; they'll
take a commission.

Accommodations categories in descending order of
price are: Hotel, Hotel Garni (room and breakfast only, no
other meals), Pension, Gasthaus, Fremdenzimmer, Zimmer frei (private home), youth hostel, camping, and park
bench. Room lists are always available at local tourist
offices, and remaining vacancies are often posted there
after hours. Normally the cost of a room includes a continental breakfast, taxes, service, and showers and toilet
either in the room or down the hall. This price is usually
posted in the room. Before accepting, confirm your
understanding of the complete price. The only tip the
hotels I've listed would like is a friendly, easygoing guest.

Those camping should get a camping guide for the
area. Listings are available in each country, and your
hometown travel bookstore has guidebooks for camping
Europe. You'll find campgrounds just about wherever
you need them. Look for *Campingplatz* signs. Camping
is a popular middle-class family way to go among Germans. You'll find that campgrounds are cheap ($4-$5 per
person), friendly, safe, more convenient than rustic, and
very rarely full.

Youth hostelers can take advantage of the wonderful
network of hostels. Follow the signs marked *Jugendherberge*. Triangles and the "tree next to a house" are also
youth hostel symbols. Generally, you must have your

membership card ($25 per year, sold in most U.S. cities),
though sometimes nonmembers are admitted for an extra
charge.

Hostels are open to members of all ages (except in
Bavaria where a maximum age of 26 is strictly enforced).
They usually cost $6 to $14 per night (cheaper for those
under 27, plus $4 sheet rental if you don't have your own)
and serve good cheap meals or provide kitchen facilities.
While many have couple's or family rooms available upon
request for a little extra money, plan on beds in segregated
dorms—five to twenty per room. Hostels can be idyllic
and peaceful, or school groups can raise the rafters.
School groups are most common on summer weekends
and on school year weekdays. I like small hostels best.
While many hostels may say they're full over the telephone, most hold a few beds for people who drop in, or
they can direct you to budget accommodations nearby.

The accommodations prices listed in this book should
be good through 1993.

Recommended Guidebooks
This small book is your itinerary handbook. While many
do great with this book alone, I'd supplement it with a
directory-type guidebook and some good maps. I know
it hurts to spend $30 or $40 on extra books and maps,
but when you consider the improvements they'll make in
your $2,800 vacation—not to mention the money they'll
save you—not buying them would be perfectly penny-
wise and pound-foolish. Consider the following books.

A general low-budget directory-type guidebook—a
fatter book than this one, listing a broader range of
accommodations, restaurants, and sights. Which one you
choose depends on your budget and style of travel. My
favorite is *Let's Go: Germany, Austria, and Switzerland*,
written and updated every year by Harvard students (new
editions come out around January). *Let's Go* covers big
cities, villages, the countryside, art, entertainment,
budget room and board, and transportation. It's written
for students on student budgets, and even though I'm
neither, I use it every year. Here, I virtually ignore hostel-

ing, camping, and the local youth and nightlife scene. *Let's Go* covers that better than I can. If their youthful approach isn't yours, and you've got plenty of money, then try Arthur Frommer's *Dollarwise* guides to Germany, Switzerland, and Austria.

A cultural and sightseeing guide—the tall green Michelin guides (Germany, Austria, and Switzerland) have nothing about room and board but everything else you'll ever need to know about the sights, customs, and culture. They are excellent (especially for drivers) and available in English in Europe. A small German phrase book and dictionary (such as my new Europe Through The Back Door German phrase book, published by JMP) is also helpful.

My *Europe Through the Back Door* (Santa Fe, N.M.: John Muir Publications, 11th edition, 1993) gives you the basic skills, the foundations that make this demanding 22-day plan possible. Chapters include minimizing jet lag, packing light, driving versus train travel, finding budget beds without reservations, changing money, theft, travel photography, long-distance telephoning in Europe, Ugly Americanism, traveler's toilet trauma, laundry, and itinerary strategies and techniques. The book also includes special articles on forty exciting nooks and undiscovered European crannies that I call "Back Doors."

Other Rick Steves "2 to 22 Day" Itinerary Planners—if your trip is bigger than this book, consider my guides to Europe, Britain, France, Italy, Spain/Portugal, and Norway/Sweden/Denmark (all published annually by John Muir).

Europe 101: History and Art for Travelers (Santa Fe, N.M.: John Muir Publications, 1991; by Rick Steves and Gene Openshaw) tells you the story of these cultures in a practical, fun-to-read, 360-page package. It's ideal for those who want to be able to step into a Gothic cathedral and excitedly nudge their partner, saying, "Isn't this a marvelous improvement over Romanesque!"

Mona Winks: Self-Guided Tours of Europe's Top Museums (Santa Fe, N.M.: John Muir Publications, 1993; by Rick Steves and Gene Openshaw) gives you fun, easy-to-follow, self-guided tours of Europe's twenty most exhausting and frightening museums, including (for this tour) the top museums in Munich and Vienna.

Most European bookstores, especially in tourist areas, have good selections of maps. For this tour, I picked up the *Bundesrepublik Deutschland Auto Atlas* (by RV Reise und Verkehrsverlag, 1:200,000 scale) for Germany and the *Osterreich Strassen Atlas* (also by RV Reise und Verkehrsverlag, 1:300,000 scale) for Austria. Each of these atlases has good coverage of the entire country with an extensive index and handy maps of all major cities. For Switzerland, I got by with Michelin maps 216 and 217 (or *Die General Karte* maps 1 and 2) with 1:200,000 scale. Throughout the tour you'll be picking up free maps of cities and regions at local tourist offices.

Back Door Manners

I have heard over and over how 2 to 22 Days readers were the most considerate and fun-to-have-as-guests travelers my recommended accommodations dealt with. Thank you for traveling sensitive to the culture and as temporary locals. It's fun to follow you in my travels.

Vagabondage or Freedom

This book's goal is to free you, not chain you. Defend your spontaneity as you would your mother. Use this book to sort the region's myriad sights into the most interesting, representative, diverse, and efficient 2 or 22 days of travel. Use it to avoid time- and money-wasting mistakes, to get more intimate with Europe by traveling without a tour. Remember, you're traveling as a temporary local person. And use it as a point of departure for shaping your best possible travel experience. Only a real dullard would follow this entire plan exactly as I've laid it out.

Anyone who's read this far has what it takes intellectually to do this tour on their own. Be confident, militantly positive, relish the challenge and rewards of doing your own planning. Judging from all the positive feedback and happy postcards we get from our traveling readers, it's safe to assume you're on your way to a great European vacation—independent, inexpensive—with the finesse of an experienced traveler. Europe—here you come!

Send Me a Postcard, Drop Me a Line

While I do what I can to keep this book accurate and up-to-date, things are always changing. If you enjoy a successful trip with the help of this book and would like to share your discoveries, please send any tips, recommendations, criticisms, or corrections to me at Europe Through the Back Door, Box C-2009, Edmonds, WA 98020. To update the book before your trip or share tips, tap into our free computer bulletin board travel information service (206/771-1902:1200 or 2400/8/N/1). All correspondents will receive a two-year subscription to our "Back Door Travel" quarterly newsletter (it's free anyway). Tips actually used will get you a first-class railpass in heaven. Thanks, and *Gute Reise*!

BACK DOOR PHILOSOPHY
AS TAUGHT IN *EUROPE THROUGH THE BACK DOOR*

Travel is intensified living—maximum thrills per minute and one of the last great sources of legal adventure. Travel is freedom. It's recess, and we need it.

Experiencing the real Europe requires catching it by surprise, going casual...."Through the Back Door."

Affording travel is a matter of priorities. (Make do with the old car.) You can travel—simple, safe, and comfortable—anywhere in Europe for $50 a day plus transportation costs. In many ways, spending more money only builds a thicker wall between you and what you came to see. Europe is a cultural carnival, and time after time, you'll find that its best acts are free and the best seats are the cheap ones.

A tight budget forces you to travel close to the ground, meeting and communicating with the people, not relying on service with a purchased smile. Never sacrifice sleep, nutrition, safety, or cleanliness in the name of budget. Simply enjoy the local-style alternatives to expensive hotels and restaurants.

Extroverts have more fun. If your trip is low on magic moments, kick yourself and make things happen. If you don't enjoy a place, maybe you don't know enough about it. Seek the truth. Recognize tourist traps. Give a people the benefit of your open mind. See things as different but not better or worse. Any culture has much to share.

Of course, travel, like the world, is a series of hills and valleys. Be fanatically positive and militantly optimistic. If something's not to your liking, change your liking. Travel is addicting. It can make you a happier American, as well as a citizen of the world. Our Earth is home to six billion equally important people. It's humbling to travel and find that people don't envy Americans. They like us, but with all due respect, they wouldn't trade places.

Globe-trotting destroys ethnocentricity. It helps you understand and appreciate different cultures. Travel changes people. It broadens perspectives and teaches new ways to measure quality of life. Many travelers toss aside their "hometown blinders." Their prized souvenirs are the strands of different cultures they decide to knit into their own character. The world is a cultural yarn shop. And Back Door Travelers are weaving the ultimate tapestry. Come on, raise your travel dreams to their upright and locked position, and join in!

DAY 1 Start in Frankfurt, usually the most direct and least expensive German destination from the U.S.A. Pick up your rental car and drive to the famous medieval fairy-tale town of Rothenburg for your first night.

DAY 2 Spend all day medievaled in Germany's best-preserved walled town. Walk the wall, visit the exquisite carved altar and the strangely enjoyable medieval crime-and-punishment museum. Be careful . . . this cobbled mall is Germany's best shopping town.

DAY 3 Drive south today, exploring the Romantic Road through picturesque villages, past farmhouses and onion-domed churches deep into Bavaria's medieval heartland. After hiking up to the Ehrenberg ruined castle and screaming down a nearby ski slope in an oversized skate-board, catch your breath for an evening of slap dancing and yodeling in the Tirolean town of Reutte, Austria.

DAY 4 Bavaria's the cookie jar, and no one's looking. After touring "Mad" Ludwig's fairy-tale Neuschwanstein Castle, Europe's most spectacular, stop by the Wies Church, a textbook example of Bavarian rococo bursting with curly curlicues, and visit Germany's wood-carving capital, Oberammergau, to window shop and tour the great Passion Play Theater.

DAY 5 Work your way north to Munich, possibly riding the lift up the Zugspitze, Germany's tallest mountain, and stopping at Andechs Monastery for Germany's finest beer. Orient yourself in Munich's old center with its colorful pedestrian mall.

DAY 6 Today is spent immersed in Munich's art and history—crown jewels, baroque theater, Wittelsbach palaces, great art, beautiful parks, and gardens. Munich evenings are best spent in frothy beer halls—belching oompah music, rowdy Bavarian atmosphere, big beers,

big pretzels, and no-nonsense buxom beer maids who
pull mustard packets from their cleavages.

DAY 7 And on the seventh day you'll rest—but only until
noon, when you travel south to Salzburg, visiting Hitler's
mountain hideaway, Berchtesgaden, on the way. Put on
an old miner's outfit (freshly laundered) and tour a salt
mine, riding the tiny train into the mountain to slide
down long, hopefully splinter-free banisters, cruise subterranean lakes, and learn about old-fashioned salt mining.

DAY 8 After enjoying the sights and castle of Salzburg,
leave Mozart's hometown for "Sound of Music" country.
Spend a very scenic afternoon in the Salzkammergut Lake
District (through hills alive with the S.O.M.), then check
into a private home in the postcard-pretty, fjord-cuddling
town of Hallstatt.

DAY 9 Take a short intermission from fairy-tale Austria
for a pilgrimage to the powerful Mauthausen concentration camp. Then follow the Danube through its most
romantic section, lined with ruined castles, glorious
abbeys, vineyard upon vineyard, and small towns, on into
Vienna.

DAY 10 Vienna, the easternmost and most exciting historic and cultural city of this tour, was the Habsburg capital. It excels in art, tombs, palaces, pastries, coffee shops,
and music. In other words, you'll be very busy today.

DAY 11 After another Vienna morning and the afternoon
at the Schönbrunn Palace, Versailles's eastern rival, drive
the autobahn five hours west to Innsbruck, sleeping in
the nearby village of Hall in Tirol.

DAY 12 Joyride through the Alps into Switzerland.
Appenzell—traditional and cozy—is the best first taste of
Heidi-land. This is cowbell country. Only a few staggering mountains, but a fine chance to savor Switzerland's
small-town ambience.

DAY 13 Today you'll visit the Ballenberg Open-Air Folk
Museum. Historic buildings from every corner of the
country have been moved to this huge park to give you

an intimate walk through Switzerland's diverse culture. Thirty minutes away is the grand old resort of Interlaken, gateway to the scenic Jungfrau region. South of there, a gondola will lift you high above the valley into the terrific traffic-free Alpine village of Gimmelwald.

DAY 14 You learn why they say, "If Heaven isn't what it's cracked up to be, send me back to Gimmelwald." You're free all day to frolic and hike, high above the stress and clouds of the real world. Take a vacation from your busy vacation. Recharge your touristic batteries.

DAY 15 After breakfast at 10,000 feet and a morning hike, you'll visit Bern, the stately but human, classy but fun, Swiss capital, and the most enjoyable look at urban Switzerland. Then it's on into French-speaking Switzerland where you'll settle down in Murten . . . Morat, if you're speaking French.

DAY 16 Using Murten, Switzerland's best-preserved medieval walled town as home base, tour the highlights of French Switzerland. It'll be a busy day exploring the romantic Château Chillon on Lake Geneva, seeing Gruyère cheese made in its spectacularly sited hometown, and trying to get lost in a nearby Swiss chocolate factory.

DAY 17 After an easy morning in Murten and a look at the ruins of the Roman capital city of Avenches, drive into Germany's Black Forest, through spa towns and vineyards to the charming and overlooked village of Staufen.

DAY 18 The Black Forest is filled with tourists and cuckoo clocks. It's also swimming with soothing mineral spas, Germany's healthiest air and sunniest climate, traditional villages and folk fests, and wonderful wooded drives. After a quick look at the city of Freiburg, enjoy a scenic drive through the heart of this legendary forest, and find your hotel in Baden-Baden. Today's grand finale is a two-hour "Roman Irish" bath complete with massage. No wonder this place was Europe's leading spa one hundred years ago.

DAY 19 Tour the Baden-Baden casino, drive to Roman Trier, Germany's oldest city, and meander with the peaceful Mosel River from there to the pleasant village of Zell.

DAY 20 Explore more of the misty, swan-speckled Mosel, so much more relaxing than the busy and industrial Rhine. Tour Germany's most exciting medieval castle, Burg Eltz, then drive to Bonn.

DAY 21 Today you'll break again from storybook Germany to sample two real, live, no-nonsense cities. Bonn, the home of Beethoven and a colorful modern university city, was West Germany's postwar capital. Köln, which, like most German cities, rose gleaming and muscular from the ashes of World War II, is a cheery, modern city with some world-class art and Germany's finest Gothic cathedral. Sleep in a small Rhine village in castle country.

DAY 22 Your grand finale is a day of cruising the Rhine and climbing through its castles. Cruise from Koblenz to Mainz and tour the mighty Rheinfels Castle above the town of St. Goar. When you return to Frankfurt, the circle is complete and you've experienced the best 22 days Germany, Austria, and Switzerland have to offer. Of course, next year you may want 22 more.

ARRIVE IN FRANKFURT, SET UP IN ROTHENBURG

How much you do today depends on what time your flight arrives. It's best to plan an easy first day or two in Europe. Today's goal is to arrive safely, travel to Rothenburg (pronounced ROE-ten-burg), and get settled. Since most flights will get you in by midday, figure on a couple hours of sightseeing along Germany's Romantic Road before reaching Rothenburg.

Suggested Schedule

Arrive at Frankfurt airport.
Pick up reserved car, hit the autobahn.
If early, visit Würzburg.
Take Romantic Road from Bad Mergentheim to Rothenburg.
Check into Rothenburg hotel. Quiet evening.

When flying to Europe, you lose a day; if you leave on a Tuesday, you'll land on Wednesday. Call before going to the airport to confirm departure time as scheduled. Expect delays. Bring something to do—a book, a journal, some handwork—to make any waits easy on yourself. Remember, no matter what happens en route, if you arrive in Europe safely on the day you hoped to, consider the flight a smashing success.

To minimize jet lag (body clock adjustment stress):

• Leave healthy and well rested. Pretend you're leaving a day earlier than you really are. Plan accordingly and enjoy a peaceful last day at home.

• During the flight, minimize stress by eating lightly and avoiding alcohol, caffeine, and sugar. Drink juice ("Two glasses, no ice please"). Take walks.

• After boarding the plane, set your watch ahead to European time. Start adjusting mentally before you land.

• Sleep through the in-flight movie, or at least close your eyes and fake it.

• On the day you arrive, keep yourself awake until a reasonable local bedtime. Jet lag hates fresh air, bright light, and exercise. A long evening city walk is helpful.

• You'll probably wake up very early the next morning—but ready to roll.

Landing in Frankfurt

Frankfurt's airport (*Flughafen*), just an 11-minute train ride from downtown (6 trips per hour, 5 DM, ride included in the 4 DM all-day transit pass), is very efficient and user-friendly. It has everything an airport could need: showers, baggage check, banks with fair rates open 7:30 to 22:00, a grocery store, a handy train station, a decent waiting lounge where you can sleep overnight, easy rental car pickup, plenty of parking, a hard-to-miss big green meeting point sign, an information booth, a McDonald's that serves beer, and lots of Yankee soldiers. McWelcome to Germany.

Upon arrival in Frankfurt, change a couple of hundred dollars into deutsche marks, call your Rothenburg hotel to reserve or reconfirm your room, and leave. If you're driving, pick up your car and follow the blue autobahn signs for Würzburg.

Train travelers can validate your Eurailpasses or buy tickets at the airport station where you'll catch a train directly to Würzburg and connect to Rothenburg via Steinach. (The Romantic Road bus leaves Frankfurt at 8:15. If you're coming in from the Rhine, the morning train arrives a few minutes late. They say they'll hold the bus a few minutes for those who call in a request and reservation.)

Picking Up Your Car

Your rental car orientation is always rushed, but be sure to understand the basics. Locate the car manual, know how to change a tire and what kind of gas to use, and understand the breakdown policy and how to use the local automobile club membership (like our AAA) if it comes with your car rental. Ask the attendant for a list of drop-off offices, any map he can give you, an autobahn

Germany

handbook, a list of standard road signs, directions to Rothenburg, and a spare key (or get one copied ASAP). Before you leave, drive around the airport parking lot and get to know your car for five minutes. Work the keys, try everything, and find problems before you leave.

Transportation: Frankfurt to Rothenburg

The 3-hour drive from the airport to Rothenburg is something even a jet-lagged zombie can handle. The airport is on the Würzburg freeway. It's a 75-mile straight shot to Würzburg; just follow the blue (for autobahn) signs. The

Spessart rest stop at Rohrbrunn (tel. 06094/220, open 10:00-13:00 and 14:00-19:00) has a tourist information office (TI), where friendly Herr Ohm can telephone Rothenburg (and speak German) for you. Pick up "Let's Go Bavaria," brochures on Würzburg, Rothenburg, and the Romantic Road, and a Munich map, all free and in English.

Leave the freeway at the Würzburg/Stuttgart/Ulm road 19 exit and follow 19 south to just before Bad Mergentheim where a very scenic slice of the Romantic Road will lead you directly into Rothenburg. If you're plugging in a stop at Würzburg, take the later Heidingsfeld-Würzburg exit and follow the signs to Stadmitte, then to the Residenz. (*Wo ist. . . ?* means "Where is?") Signs will direct you from downtown Würzburg south to Stuttgart/Ulm on road 19.

Train travelers may have missed the Romantic Road bus on the day of their arrival, so they'll have to go straight to Rothenburg with a possible stop in Würzburg (the Residenz is a 15-minute walk from the station). The three-and-a-half-hour train ride from the airport to Rothenburg goes airport–Frankfurt Hauptbahnhof (central station)–Würzburg–Steinach–Rothenburg with trains departing from the airport at 7:00, 9:00, 10:00, 11:00, 13:00, 15:00, and 16:00, from Frankfurt Central 21 minutes later, arriving in Würzburg in about 2 hours, and on to Rothenburg (after a change in Steinach). The tiny Steinach–Rothenburg train often leaves from the "B" section of track, away from the middle of the station, shortly after the Würzburg train arrives. Don't miss it. Steinach is very sleepy.

The Romantic Road bus tour leaves from Europa bus stops next to the Frankfurt station (south side, daily 8:15 departure, mid-March through October) and at the Würzburg station (daily 9:00, mid-May through September, never full).

Sightseeing Highlights between Frankfurt and Rothenburg

Frankfurt—Probably a nice place to live, but I wouldn't want to visit. Don't visit Frankfurt unless your only alternative is killing time at the airport before flying home. If that happens, pick up a city map at the TI in the station (long hours, tel. 069/212-3-8849), walk down sleazy Kaiserstrasse past Goethe's house (great man, mediocre sight) to Römerberg, Frankfurt's lively market square. A string of museums is just across the river along Schaumainkai (open Tuesday-Saturday, 10:00-17:00). Try to avoid driving or sleeping in Frankfurt. Pleasant Rhine towns are just a quick drive or train ride away.

If you must spend the night in Frankfurt, you can sleep near the station at **Pension Lohmann** (70 DM, Stuttgarterstr. 31, tel. 069/232534), **Hotel Goldener Stern** (70-90 DM, Karlsruherstr. 8, tel. 069/233309) or at the youth hostel (cheap, bus 46 from station to Frankenstein Place, Deutschherrnufer 12, tel. 069/619058).

▲▲ **Würzburg**—A historic city, though freshly rebuilt since World War II, Würzburg is worth a stop to see its impressive Prince Bishop's Residenz, bubbly baroque chapel (Hofkirche), and sculpted gardens. This is a Franconian Versailles with grand stairways, 3-D art, and a tennis court-sized fresco by Tiepolo. Tag along with a tour if you can find one in English, or buy the fine little guidebook. (Open 9:00-17:00 April-September, and 10:00-15:30 October-March; closed Monday. Last entry one-half hour before closing, admission 3.50 DM.) Easy parking is available right there. (TI tel. 0931/37436.)

Romantic Road (Romantische Strasse)—The best way to connect Frankfurt with Munich or Füssen is via the popular Romantic Road. This path winds you past the most beautiful towns and scenery of Germany's medieval heartland. Any tourist office can give you a brochure listing the many interesting baroque palaces, lovely carved altarpieces, and walled medieval cities you'll pass along the way. From Frankfurt or Würzburg in the north to Munich or Füssen in the south, the route includes these highlights:

▲ **Weikersheim**—Palace with fine baroque gardens (luxurious picnic spot), folk museum, and picturesque town square.

▲ **Herrgottskapelle**—Tilman Riemenschneider's

greatest carved altarpiece in a peaceful church (one mile from Creglingen). Fast and fun Fingerhut (thimble) Museum just across the street. Both open until 18:00.

▲▲▲ **Rothenburg ob der Tauber**—See tomorrow.

▲ **Dinkelsbühl**—Rothenburg's little sister. Twenty towers and gates surround this cute, beautifully preserved walled town. Kinderzeche children's festival turns Dinkelsbühl wonderfully on end each mid-July. (TI tel. 09851/3031.)

Rottenbuch—Impressive church, nondescript village in lovely setting.

▲▲ **Wieskirche**—Germany's most glorious baroque-rococo church. In a sweet meadow. Newly restored. Heavenly!

▲▲▲ **Neuschwanstein**—"Mad" King Ludwig's Disneyesque castle, described later.

The drive gives you a good look at rural Germany. My favorite sections are from Weikersheim to Rothenburg and from Landsberg to Füssen. By car, simply follow the green *Romantische Strasse* signs.

By train . . . take the bus. The Europa Bus Company makes this trip twice a day in each direction (Frankfurt–Munich mid-May through October, Würzburg–Füssen mid-May through September). The 11-hour ride costs about $60 but is free with a Eurailpass. Each bus makes stops in the towns of Rothenburg (2 hours) and Dinkelsbühl (45 minutes) and briefly at a few other attractions, and has a guide who hands out brochures and narrates the journey in English. There is no quicker or easier way to travel across Germany and get such a hearty dose of its countryside.

Romantic Road Bus Schedule				
Frankfurt	8:15	—	19:55	—
Würzburg	10:15	9:00	18:10	19:20
Rothenburg	11:35	12:00	15:15	15:35
Dinkelsbühl	14:45	14:30	12:35	13:10
Augsburg	17:40	16:55	10:20	11:00
Munich	18:55	—	9:00	—
Füssen	—	19:35	—	8:15

Bus reservations are free but rarely necessary (except possibly on a summer weekend; call 069/7903240 three days in advance). You can stop over where you like. Study the timetable to see how you can start and end in different towns and switch buses if you like along the way.

Germany (Deutschland)

* United Germany is 136,000 square miles (the size of Montana).
* Population is 77 million (about 650 per square mile, declining slowly).
* The West was 95,000 square miles (like Wyoming) with 61 million people.
* The East was 41,000 square miles (like Virginia) with 16 million people.
* One deutsche mark (DM) is about $.67; $1 is about 1.5 DM.

Deutschland is energetic, efficient, organized, and Europe's economic muscleman. Eighty-five percent of its people live in cities; and average earnings are among the highest on earth. Ninety-seven percent of the workers get a one-month paid vacation, and during the other eleven months, they create a gross national product of about one-third that of the United States, and growing. Germany has risen from the ashes of World War II to become the world's fifth biggest industrial power, ranking fourth in steel output and nuclear power and third in automobile production. Its bustling new cities are designed to make people feel like they belong. It shines culturally, beating out all but two countries in production of books, Nobel laureates, and professors. And think of the Olympic gold medals coming their way next time around.

While its East-West division lasted about forty years, historically, Germany has been and continues to be divided north and south. While northern Germany was barbarian, is Protestant, and assaults life aggressively, southern Germany was Roman, is Catholic, and enjoys a more relaxed tempo of life. The southern German, or Bavarian, dialect is to High (northern) German what the dialect of Alabama or Georgia is to the speech of the northern United States. The American image of Germany is Bavaria (probably because that was "our" sector immediately after the war) where the countryside is most traditional. This historic north-south division is less pronounced these days as Germany becomes a more mobile society. Of course, the big chore facing Germany today is integrating the rotten and wilted economy of what was East Germany into the powerhouse economy of the West.

Germany's most interesting tourist route today— Rhine, Romantic Road, Bavaria—was yesterday's most important trade route, along which its most prosperous and important medieval cities were located. Germany as a nation is just 120 years old. In 1850, there were 35 independent countries in what is now one Germany. In medieval times, there were over 300, each with its own weights, measures, coinage, king, and lotto. Many were surrounded by what we would call iron curtains. This helps explain Germany's many diverse customs.

Germans eat lunch from 11:30 to 14:30 and dinner between 18:00 and 21:00. Each region has its own gastronomic twist, so order local house specials whenever possible. Pork, fish, and venison are good, and don't miss the bratwurst and sauerkraut. Potatoes are the standard vegetable. Great beers and white wines abound. Try the small local brands. Go with whatever beer is on tap. "Gummi Bears" are a local gumdrop candy with a cult following (beware of imitations—you must see the word "Gummi"), and Nutella is a chocolate nut spread specialty that may change your life.

Banks are generally open from 8:00 to 12:00 and 14:00 to 16:00, other offices from 8:00 to 16:00. Beware: some banks charge per traveler's check. August is a holiday month for workers, but that doesn't really affect us tourists (unless you're on the road on the 15th, when half of Germany is going over the Alps one way and half returning the other).

ROTHENBURG ON THE TAUBER

Today you stay put, get over jet lag, and enjoy Germany's most exciting medieval town. Rothenburg is well worth two nights and a whole day. In the Middle Ages, when Frankfurt and Munich were hick towns, Rothenburg was Germany's second-largest free imperial city with a whopping population of 6,000. Today it's her best-preserved medieval walled town, enjoying tremendous tourist popularity without losing its charm.

Suggested Schedule	
7:00	Walk the wall.
8:30	Breakfast.
9:00	Stop at the TI to confirm plans. Climb the tower, visit the city museum and the Medieval Crime and Punishment museum. Buy a picnic.
12:00	Picnic in the castle garden, rest.
13:30	City walking tour.
16:00	More museums, shop, or walk through the countryside.
Sleep	Rothenburg.

Orientation—Rothenburg

To orient yourself in Rothenburg, think of the town map as a human head. Its nose—the castle garden—sticks out to the left, and the neck is the skinny lower part, with the youth hostel and my favorite hotels.

Rothenburg's heyday was from 1150 to 1400 when it was the crossing point of two major trade routes: Tashkent–Paris and Hamburg–Venice. Most of the buildings you'll see were built by 1400. The city started around the long-gone castle (built in 1142, destroyed in 1356). You can see the shadow of the first town wall, which defines the oldest part of Rothenburg in today's street plan. A few gates from this wall survive. The richest and therefore biggest houses were in this central part. The

commoners built higgledy-piggledy (read picturesquely)
farther from the center near the present walls. Today, the
great trade is tourism; two-thirds of the townspeople are
employed serving you.

Too often, Rothenburg brings out the shopper in visitors before they've had a chance to appreciate the historic
city. True, this is a great place to do your German shopping, but first see the town. The TI on the market square
has guided tours in English (daily in summer at 13:30
from the market square, 5 DM including church and
altar). If none are scheduled, you can hire a private guide.
For 70 DM, a local historian—who's usually an intriguing
character as well—will bring the ramparts alive. Eight
hundred years of history are packed between the cobbles.
(Find a guide through the TI, or call Manfred Baumann,
tel. 09861/4146, or Frau Gertrud Wagner, tel. 09861/2288).

Start your visit by picking up a map, the "sights worth
seeing and knowing" brochure (a virtual walking guide to
the town; read it all), and information at the TI on the
main square (Monday through Friday 9:00-12:00 and
14:00-18:00, Saturday 9:00-12:00 and 14:00-16:00,
closed Sunday, tel. 09861/40492). The TI's "Hotels and
Pensions of Rothenburg" map has the most detail and
names all streets. Confirm sightseeing plans and ask
about the daily 13:30 walking tour and evening entertainment. The best town map is available free at the Friese
shop, two doors toward the nose. Telephone code:
09861.

Sightseeing Highlights—Rothenburg
▲▲ **Walk the Wall**—Just over a mile around, with great
views, and providing a good orientation, this walk can be
done by those under 6 feet tall in less than an hour and
requires no special sense of balance. Photographers will
go through lots of film, especially before breakfast or at
sunset when the lighting is best and the crowds are least.
The best fortifications are in the Spitaltor (south end).
Walk from there counterclockwise to the forehead.
Climb the Rödertor en route.

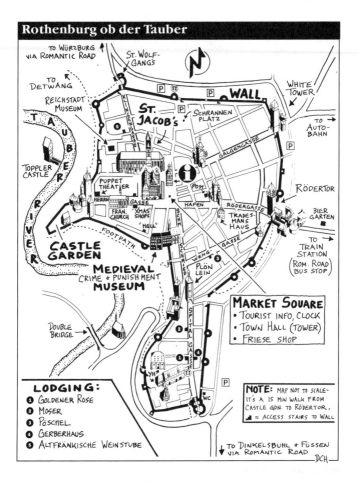

Rothenburg ob der Tauber

TO WÜRZBURG VIA ROMANTIC ROAD

ST. WOLF-GANGS

TO DETWANG

REICHSTADT MUSEUM

ST. JACOB'S

SCHRANNEN PLATZ

WALL

WHITE TOWER

TO AUTO-BAHN

GALGENGASSE

TOPPLER CASTLE

RÖDERTOR

PUPPET THEATER

HERRN GASSE

POST

HAFEN

RÖDERGASSE

BIER GARTEN

FRAN CHURCH

XMAS SHOPS

HELL

TRADES-MANS HAUS

TO TRAIN STATION (ROM. ROAD BUS STOP)

CASTLE GARDEN

FOOTPATH

WENG GASSE

PLÖN LEIN

MEDIEVAL CRIME & PUNISHMENT MUSEUM

DOUBLE BRIDGE

SPITAL GASSE

YH

WC

MARKET SQUARE
• TOURIST INFO, CLOCK
• TOWN HALL (TOWER)
• FRIESE SHOP

LODGING:
❶ GOLDENER ROSE
❷ MOSER
❸ PÖSCHEL
❹ GERBERHAUS
❺ ALTFRÄNKISCHE WEINSTUBE

NOTE: MAP NOT TO SCALE-IT'S A 15 MIN WALK FROM CASTLE GDN. TO RÖDERTOR. ◢ = ACCESS STAIRS TO WALL

TO DINKELSBUHL & FÜSSEN VIA ROMANTIC ROAD

DCH

▲ **Rödertor**—The wall tower nearest the train station is the only one you can climb. It is worth the hike up for the view and a fascinating rundown on the bombing of Rothenburg in the last weeks of World War II (the northeast corner of the city was destroyed; photos, English translation, 1 DM, 9:00-17:00, closed off-season).

▲▲ **Climb Town Hall Tower**—The best view of Rothenburg and the surrounding countryside and a closeup look at an old tiled roof from the inside (open 9:30-12:30 and 13:00-16:00, weekends 13:00-16:00, off-

season open Saturday and Sunday 12:00-15:00) is yours
for a rigorous (214 steps, 180 feet) but interesting climb
and 1 DM. Ladies, beware, some men find the view best
from the bottom of the ladder just before the top.

▲▲ **Herrengasse and the Castle Garden**—Any
town's Herrengasse, where the richest patricians and merchants (the *Herren*) lived, is your chance to see its finest
old mansions. Wander from the market square down Herrengasse (past the old Rothenburg official measurement
rods on the city hall wall), drop into the lavish front
rooms of a ritzy hotel or two, and continue on down
through the old gate (notice the tiny after-curfew door in
the big door and the hole from which hot tar was poured
onto attackers) into the garden that used to be the castle.
(Great Tauber Riviera views at twilight.)

▲▲▲ **Medieval Crime and Punishment Museum**—
It's the best of its kind, full of fascinating old legal bits
and *Kriminal* pieces, instruments of punishment and torture, even a special cage—complete with a metal gag—
for nags. Exhibits are in English. There are fun cards and
posters and a goofy photo opportunity in the stocks outside. (Open daily 9:30-18:00, in winter 14:00-16:00, 4 DM.)

▲▲ **St. Jacob's Church**—Here you'll find a glorious
500-year-old wooden altarpiece by Tilman Riemenschneider, located up the stairs and behind the organ.
Riemenschneider was the Michelangelo of German
woodcarvers. This is the one required art treasure in
town. (Open daily 9:00-17:00, off-season 10:00-12:00,
14:00-16:00, 2 DM.)

Meistertrunk Show—Be on the main square at 11:00,
12:00, 13:00, 14:00, 15:00, 20:00, 21:00, or 22:00 for the
ritual gathering of the tourists to see the less than
breathtaking reenactment of the Meistertrunk story.

In 1631, the Catholic army took the Protestant town
and was about to do its rape, pillage, and plunder thing
when the mayor said, "Hey, if I can drink this entire
3-liter tankard of wine in one gulp, will you leave us
alone?" The invading commander, sensing he was dealing with an unbalanced people, said, "Sure." Mayor
Nusch drank the whole thing and the town was saved.

(I've often wondered how the mayor celebrated.)

Hint: for the best show, don't watch the clock; watch the open-mouthed tourists gasp as the old windows flip open. At the late shows, the square flickers with flash attachments.

Historical Vaults—Under the town hall tower is a city history museum that gives a good look at medieval Rothenburg and a good-enough replica of the famous Meistertrunk tankard (well described in English, open 9:00-18:00, closed off-season, 2 DM).

Museum of the Imperial City (Reichsstadt Museum) — This stuffier museum, housed in the former Dominican Convent, gives a more in-depth look at old Rothenburg with some fine art and the supposed Meistertrunk tankard, labeled *Kürfurstenhumpen* (open 10:00-17:00, in winter 13:00-16:00, 3 DM).

St. Wolfgang's Church—This fortified Gothic church is built into the medieval wall at Klingentor (near the "forehead"). Explore its dungeonlike passages below and check out the shepherd's dance exhibit to see where they hot-oiled the enemy back in the good old days. (Open 10:00-12:00 and 14:00-18:00, closed off-season.)

Alt Rothenburger Handwerferhaus—This 700-year-old tradesman's house shows the typical living situation of Rothenburg in its heyday (Alter Stadtgraben 26, near the Markus Tower, daily 9:00-18:00 and 20:00-21:00, closed off-season, 3 DM).

▲ **Walk in the Countryside**—Just below the Burggarten (castle garden) in the Tauber Valley is the cute, skinny, 600-year-old castle/summer home of Mayor Toppler (open 13:00-17:00, 2 DM). It's furnished intimately and well worth a look. Notice the photo of bombed-out 1945 Rothenburg on the top floor. Then walk on past the covered bridge and huge trout to the peaceful village of Detwang. Detwang is actually older than Rothenburg, with another great Riemenschneider altarpiece in its church (from 968, the second oldest in Franconia). For a scenic return, loop back to Rothenburg through the valley along the river past a café with outdoor tables, great desserts, and a town view to match.

A Franconian Bike Ride—For a fun, breezy look at the countryside around Rothenburg, rent a bike from the train station (12 DM per day, 7 DM with a train pass or ticket, open 5:00-18:30). For a pleasant half-day pedal, bike south down to Detwang via Topplerschloss and Fuchesmill (an old water mill across the street). Go north along the level bike path to Tauberscheckenbach, then uphill about twenty minutes to Adelshofen and south back to Rothenburg.

Swimming—Rothenburg has a fine modern recreation center, with an indoor/outdoor pool and a sauna, a few minutes walk down the Dinkelsbühl Road (open from 8:00 or 9:00 to 20:00, past the bottom of the neck, tel. 09861/4565).

Franconian Open-Air Museum—Twenty minutes drive from Rothenburg in the undiscovered "Rothenburgy" town of Bad Windsheim is a small, open-air folk museum that, compared with others in Europe, isn't much. But it's trying very hard and gives you the best look around at traditional rural Franconia. (Open 9:00-18:00, closed off-season, 5 DM.)

Shopping

Rothenburg is one of Germany's best shopping towns. Do it here, mail it home, and get it out of your hair. Lovely prints, carvings, wine glasses, Christmas tree ornaments, and beer steins are popular.

The Kathe Wohlfahrt Christmas trinkets phenomenon is spreading across the half-timbered reaches of Europe. In Rothenburg, tourists flock to the Kathe Wohlfahrt Kris Kringle Market and the Christmas Village (on either side of Herrengasse, just off the main square). This is a Christmas wonderland filled with enough twinkling lights to require a special electric hookup, instant Christmas spirit mood music (best appreciated on a hot day in July), and American and Japanese tourists filling little woven shopping baskets with 5 to 10 DM goodies to hang on their trees. (Okay, I admit it, my Christmas tree dangles with a few KW ornaments.)

The Friese shop (just off the market square, west of the tourist office on the corner across from the public W.C.)

is a charming contrast. It's very friendly and gives shoppers with this book tremendous service: a 10 percent discount, 14 percent tax deducted if you have it mailed, and a free Rothenburg map. Anneliese, who runs the place with her sons, Frankie and Berni, charges only her cost to ship things, changes money at the best rates in town with no extra charge, and lets tired travelers leave their bags in her back room for free.

For good prints and paintings, visit friendly Wilma Diener's shop at Untere Schmiedgasse 2. For less coziness, but a free shot of schnapps, visit the larger Ernst Geissendörfer print shop where the main square hits Schmiedgasse.

Those who prefer to eat their souvenirs shop the *Bäckerei* (bakeries). Their succulent pastries, pies, and cakes are pleasantly distracting. Skip the good-looking but badtasting "Rothenburger Schneeballs."

Evening Fun and Beer Drinking

The best beer garden for balmy summer evenings is just outside the wall at the Rödertor (red gate). If this is dead, as it often is, go a few doors farther out to the alley (left) just before the Sparekasse for two popular bars and the hottest disco in town.

For a rare chance to mix it up with locals who aren't selling anything, bring your favorite slang and tongue-twisters to the English conversation club (Wednesdays, 20:00) at Mario's Altefränkische Weinstube. This dark and smoky pub is an atmospheric hangout any night but Tuesday, when it's closed (Klosterhof 7, off Klingengasse, behind St. Jacob's church, tel. 6404).

For mellow ambience, try the beautifully restored Alte Keller's Weinstube on Alterkellerstrasse under walls festooned with old toys.

Sleeping in Rothenburg (about 1.5 DM = US$1)

Rothenburg is crowded with visitors, including probably Europe's greatest single concentration of Japanese tourists, but when the sun sets, most go home to big city high-rise hotels, and room finding is easy. The first five listings are at the south end of town, a 7-minute (without shopping) walk downhill from the marketplace (which has a tourist office with room-finding service). Walk downhill on Schmiedgasse (*gasse* means lane) until it becomes Spitalgasse (Hospital Lane).

I stay in **Hotel Goldener Rose** (60 DM doubles without shower, classy 78 DM doubles in the annex behind the garden, Spitalgasse 28, 8803 Rothenburg, tel. 09861 / 4638, closed in January and February) where scurrying Karin serves breakfast and stately Henni causes many monoglots to dream in fluent Deutsche. The hotel has only one shower for two floors of rooms and the street-side rooms can be noisy, but the rooms are clean and airy and you're surrounded by cobbles, flowers, and red tiled roofs. The Favetta family also serves good, reasonably priced meals. Remember to keep your key to get in after they close (at the side gate in the alley).

For the best real with-a-local-family, comfortable, and homey experience, stay with **Herr und Frau Moser** (28 DM per person, one double and one triple, Spitalgasse 12, tel. 5971). This charming retired couple speaks little English but try very hard. Speak slow, clear, simple English.

Pension Pöschel (60 DM doubles and 30 DM singles, Wenggasse 22, tel. 09861/3430) is also friendly with bright rooms and a little closer to the marketplace. Just across the street, the **Gastehaus Raidel** (58 DM doubles, Wenggasse 3, tel. 3115), with bright rooms but cramped facilities down the hall, works in a pinch (it's run by grim people who make me sing the "Addams Family" theme song).

Hotel Gerberhaus (80-140 DM doubles, all with private showers, Spitalgasse 25, 8803 Rothenburg, tel. 09861/3055, fax 86555), a new hotel in a 500-year-old building, is warmly run by Ingra, who mixes modern comforts into bright and airy rooms while keeping the traditional flavor. Great breakfasts and pleasant garden in back.

Rothenburg's fine youth hostel, the **Rossmühle** (16 DM beds, 5 DM sheets, 8 DM dinners, tel. 09861/4510, reception open 7:00-9:00, 17:00-19:00, 20:00-22:00, will hold rooms until 18:00 if you call, lockup at 23:30) has about three double bunks per room and is often filled with school groups. This droopy-eyed building is the old town horse mill (used when the town was under siege and the river-powered mill was inaccessible). They also run the simpler and 4 DM cheaper **Spitalhof** hostel, next door. Remember, this is Bavaria, which has an age limit of 26 for hosteling except for families traveling with children under 16.

Gasthof Marktplatz (55 DM doubles overlooking the town square and 80 DM doubles with showers, Grüner Markt 10, tel. 09861/6722) has simple rooms, a cozy atmosphere, and is right on the town square. Its cheap rooms are the only rooms listed in this book that have access to absolutely no shower, just a sink in the room.

Bohemians with bucks enjoy the **Hotel Altfränkische Weinstube am Klosterhof** (85-100 DM, all with showers, Klosterhof 7, tel. 09861/6404). A young couple, Mario and Erika, run this dark and smoky pub in a 600-year-old building. Upstairs they rent *gemütliche* rooms with up-scale Monty Python atmosphere, TVs, modern showers, open beam ceilings, and "himmel beds" (canopied four-posters, called heaven beds). It's located just off Klingengasse behind St. Jacob's church. Their pub is a candle-lit classic, serving hot food until 22:00, closing at 1:00. You're welcome to drop by on Wednesday evenings (20:00) for the English conversation club.

If money doesn't matter, the **Burg Hotel** (200 DM doubles, Klostergasse 1, on the wall near the castle garden, tel. 09861/5037), with elegance almost unimaginable in a medieval building with a Tauber Valley view and a high-heeled receptionist, offers a good way to spend it.

To get away from the tourism, stay out of town. **Willi Then** (60 DM doubles, near Rothenburg's train station, across from the laundromat at 8 Johannitergasse, tel. 5177) rents inexpensive rooms, speaks flawless English, and is very helpful. He'll even do your laundry. The town of Detwang, a fifteen-minute walk below Rothenburg, is loaded with quiet Zimmer. The clean, quiet, and comfortable old **Gasthof zum Schwarzen Lamm** in Detwang (about 80 DM per double, tel. 6727) serves good

food, as does the popular and very local-style **Eulen-
stube** next door. **Gastehaus Alte Schveinerei** (8801
Bettwar, tel. 09861/1541) offers good food and quiet,
comfy, reasonable rooms a little farther down the road in
Bettwar.

(Reminder: Hotel prices, unless otherwise indicated,
are for double rooms with breakfast. More expensive listings are generally with a private shower.)

Eating in Rothenburg
It can be tough to find a reasonable meal (or a place serving late) in the town center. Most places serve meals only
from 11:30 to 13:30 and 18:00 to 20:00. Galgengasse (Gal-
lows Lane) has two cheap and popular standbys: **Pizzeria Roma** (19 Galgengasse, 11:30-24:00) serves 10 DM
pizzas and normal schnitzel fare; **Gasthof zum Ochen**
(26 Galgengasse, 11:30-13:30, 18:00-20:00, closed Thursday) offers decent 10 DM meals. **Zum Schmolzer** (corner of Stollengasse and Rosengasse) is a local favorite for
its cheap beer and good food. If you need a break from
schnitzel, the **Hong Kong China Restaurant**, outside
the town near the train tracks (1 Bensenstr., tel.
09861/7377), serves good Chinese food. There's a big
grocery store just outside the wall at Rodertor.

Itinerary Options
This "two nights and a full day" plan assumes you have a
car. Eurailers taking the Romantic Road bus tour must
leave around 13:30, so you'll have to decide between half
a day or a day and a half here. For sightseeing, half a day is
enough. For a rest after jet lag, a day and a half sounds better.

Countless renowned travelers have searched for the
elusive "untouristy Rothenburg." There are many con-
tenders (Michelstadt, Miltenberg, Bamberg, Bad Windsheim, Dinkelsbühl, and others I decided to forget), but
none holds a candle to the king of medieval German cute-
ness. Even with crowds, overpriced souvenirs, Japanese-
speaking night watchmen, and yes, even with schneeballs, Rothenburg is best. Save time and mileage, and be
satisfied with the winner.

ROMANTIC ROAD TO THE TIROL

Wind through Bavaria's Romantic Road, stopping wherever the cows look friendly or a village fountain beckons. After a glimpse of Europe's most fairy-tale castle, you'll cross into Tirol in Austria to explore the desolate ruins of a medieval castle and finish the day with an evening of slap dancing, yodeling, and local music.

Suggested Schedule

7:30	Breakfast.
8:30	Romantic Road, head for Austria.
9:30	Stop in Dinkelsbühl, buy picnic.
10:00	Drive south on Romantic Road, picnicking en route.
14:00	Cross into Austria, check into a hotel in Reutte.
15:00	Hike to Ehrenberg ruins.
16:30	Luge ride down the ski slope.
18:00	Rest and dinner.
20:30	Tirolean folk evening.
Sleep	Reutte.

Transportation: Rothenburg to Reutte, Austria

Get an early start to enjoy the quaint hills and rolling villages of what was Germany's major medieval trade route. After a quick stop in Dinkelsbühl, cross the baby Danube River (*Donau* in German) and continue south along the Romantic Road to Füssen. Drive by Neuschwanstein Castle just to sweeten your dreams before crossing into Austria to get set up at Reutte.

Reutte (pronounced ROY-teh, rolled r), population 5,000, is a relaxed town, far from the international tourist crowd but popular with Germans and Austrians for its climate. Doctors recommend its "grade 1" air. If the weather's good, hike to the mysterious castle ruins and ride the luge. Finish your day off with a slap-dancing bang at a Tirolean folk evening.

Train travelers catch the Romantic Road bus tour from the Rothenburg train station (departures at 11:35 and 12:00). You can catch one bus into Munich (arrives at 18:55) or the other direct to Füssen (arrives at 19:35, long after the last bus to Reutte). Ask about exact times in Rothenburg at the train station or tourist office. Be early! If you stake out a seat when the bus arrives, you'll have a better chance of being on it when it leaves two hours later.

Today and tomorrow, you'll cross the German-Austrian border several times. The plan calls for sleeping tonight and tomorrow night just a few miles south of Germany in the Austrian town of Reutte and making a loop tomorrow from Austria back through Germany, returning to your Austrian home base.

Sightseeing Highlights

▲ **Dinkelsbühl**—Just a small Rothenburg without the mobs but cute enough to merit a short stop. Park near the church in the center, buy a picnic, and just browse. You'll find an interesting local museum, a well-preserved medieval wall, towers, gates, and a moat.

▲▲ **Sommerrodelbahn, the Luge**—From Oberammergau, you can drive through Garmisch, past Germany's highest mountain, the Zugspitze, into Austria via Lermoos. Or you can take the small scenic shortcut to Reutte past Ludwig's Linderhof and along the windsurfer-strewn Plansee.

The Innsbruck–Lermoos–Reutte road passes the ruined castles of Ehrenberg (just outside of Reutte) and two rare and exciting luge courses. In the summer, this ski slope is used as a luge course, or Sommerrodelbahn. To try one of Europe's great $5 thrills, take the lift up, grab a sledlike go-cart, and luge down. The concrete bobsled course banks on the corners, and even a novice can go very, very fast. Most are cautious on their first run and speed demons on their second. (Recently, a woman showed me her journal illustrated with her husband's dried five-inch-long luge scab. He disobeyed the only essential rule of luging—keep both hands on your stick.) No one emerges from the course without a windblown hairdo and a smile-creased face. Both places charge a steep 65 AS per run with discount cards for 5 or 10 trips and run from about mid-May through September and into October if weather permits, from 9:00 or 10:00 until about 17:00. Closed in wet weather.

The small and steep luge: The first course (100-meter drop over 800-meter course) is 6 kilometers beyond Reutte's castle ruins; look for a chair lift on the right and exit on the tiny road at the yellow Riesenrutschbahn sign (call ahead, tel. 05674/5350, the local TI at 05674/5354 speaks more English).

The longest luge: The Biberwihr Sommerrodelbahn, 15 minutes closer to Innsbruck, just past Lermoos in Biberwihr (the first exit after a long tunnel), is a better luge, the longest in Austria—1,300 meters—but has a shorter season. It opens at 9:00, a good tomorrow morning alternative if today is wet. Tel. 05673/2111, local TI tel. 05673/2922.

Just before this luge, behind the Sport und Trachtenstüberl shop is a wooden church dome with a striking Zugspitze backdrop. If you have sunshine and a camera, don't miss it.

▲▲ **Reutte's Ehrenberg Ruins**—The brooding ruins of Ehrenberg, just outside of Reutte on the road to Lermoos, await survivors of the luge. These thirteenth-century rock piles are a great contrast to tomorrow's "modern" castles. Park in the lot at the base of the hill and hike up; it's a 20-minute walk to the small (*kleine*) castle for a great view from your own private ruins. Imagine how proud Count Meinrad II of Tirol (who built the castle in 1290) would be to know that his castle repelled 16,000 Swedish soldiers in the defense of Catholicism in 1632.

You'll find more medieval mystique atop the taller neighboring hill in the big (*gross*) ruins. You can't see anything from below and almost nothing when you get there, but these bigger, more desolate and overgrown ruins are a little more romantic (and a lot harder to get to).

The easiest way down is via the small road from the gully between the two castles. The car park is just off the Lermoos–Reutte road with a café/guest house. Reutte is a pleasant 90-minute walk away. Back in town, most hotels have sketches of the intact castle.

▲▲ **Tiroler Folk Evening**—Ask in your hotel if there's a Tirolean folk evening tonight. About two evenings a week in the summer, Reutte or a nearby town puts on an evening of yodeling, slap dancing, and Tirolean frolic— usually worth the charge and a few kilometers drive. Off-season, you'll have to do your own yodeling.

Reutte, Füssen, Neuschwanstein, and Accommodations in the Region
See tomorrow.

Itinerary Options
Train travelers may prefer skipping Reutte and taking advantage of the better train and bus connections in Füssen or doing tomorrow's "castle day" as a side trip from

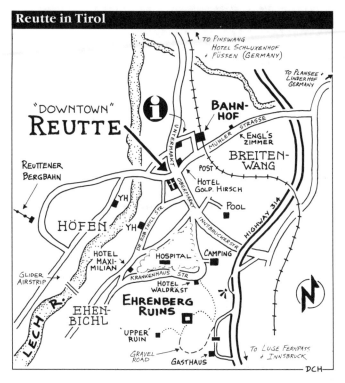

Reutte in Tirol

TO PINSWANG
HOTEL SCHLUXENHOF
& FÜSSEN (GERMANY)

TO PLANSEE &
LINDERHOF
GERMANY

"DOWNTOWN"
REUTTE

BAHN-
HOF

UNTERMARKT

MÜHLER STRASSE

ENGL'S
ZIMMER

BREITEN-
WANG

REUTTENER
BERGBAHN

POST

HOTEL
GOLD. HIRSCH

OBERMARKT

YH

POOL

HIGHWAY 314

HÖFEN

YH

INNSBRUCKER STR.

DR. ROB. TIROL STR.

HOTEL
MAXI-
MILIAN

HOSPITAL

CAMPING

GLIDER
AIRSTRIP

KRANKENHAUS STR.

HOTEL
WALDRAST

LECH R.

EHEN-
BICHL

EHRENBERG
RUINS

`UPPER`
RUIN

GRAVEL
ROAD

GASTHAUS

TO LUGE FERNPASS
& INNSBRUCK

N

—DCH—

Munich. Organized tours do the Bavarian biggies in a day.
The Grey Line, tel. 089/5904248, does Neuschwanstein,
Linderhof, Oberammergau, and the Wies Church in a
busy 10-hour day for 50 DM, departing daily at 8:30 from
near the Munich station. Staying in Reutte may not be
worth the transportation headaches for those without
wheels.

Remember, the luge experience is possible only on dry
days. It fits easily into Day 3, 4, or 5.

If for some reason you do Munich on your way to
Reutte, the autobahn from Reutte through Innsbruck to
Salzburg takes 5 hours. Stay on it. The small roads basi-
cally repeat what you've already seen. You could stop at
Hall just past Innsbruck to reserve and pay for your night
there for your late arrival after Vienna.

If you're skipping Vienna, do Munich first, then Reutte,
then follow the lovely Lech River Valley into Switzerland.

BAVARIA AND CASTLE DAY

Today you'll circle through the nutcracker and castle corner of Bavaria. After touring Europe's most ornate castle, Ludwig's fantasy called Neuschwanstein, visit Germany's most ornate church, a rococo riot. After a quick look at Oberammergau, Bavaria's wood-carving capital and home of the famous passion play, you can tour another of Ludwig's extravagant castles—the more livable Linderhof Palace.

Suggested Schedule—by Car (Home Base Reutte)

7:30	Breakfast.
8:15	Leave Reutte.
8:45	Tour Neuschwanstein Castle.
11:30	Picnic by the lake (Alpsee).
12:15	Drive to Wies Church and on to Oberammergau.
13:45	Park at Passion Play Theater, take tour.
15:30	Tour Linderhof Castle (or shopping in Oberammergau).
17:15	Drive home to Reutte via Plansee.
18:30	Tirolean folk evening (if not last night).
Sleep	Reutte.

Suggested Schedule—by Train (Home Base Füssen)

7:30	Breakfast.
8:00	Bus or bike to Neuschwanstein, tour Ludwig's castles (one or both).
11:00	Lakeside picnic under the castle.
12:00	Bike (along lake, tiny road over border) or bus (via Füssen) to Reutte.
14:00	Hike up to the Ehrenberg ruins. Bike or bus back to Füssen.

Transportation (60-mile circle)
This day is designed for drivers (instructions are worked into the sightseeing descriptions). More than a day's worth

Bavaria and Tirol—The Castle Loop

of travel fun is laid out in a circular drive starting in Reutte.

Without your own wheels, it won't all be possible. Local bus service is inexpensive but spotty for sightseeing. Buses from the Füssen station to Neuschwanstein run hourly. Füssen to Wies Church buses go twice a day. Oberammergau to Linderhof buses run fairly regularly. Hitchhiking is possible, but hitting everything is highly improbable. Without a car, I'd consider home basing in Munich and take an all-day bus tour or sleep in Füssen or Reutte and skip the Wies Church and Oberammergau. There are four Reutte-to-Füssen buses a day, the last at about 18:00. This is great biking country. Most train stations (including Reutte and Füssen) and many hotels rent bikes quite cheap.

From Reutte, you can bus directly to the castle at Neuschwanstein (11:25-12:00) and return (15:45-16:10).
Hourly trains make the 2-hour trip connecting Munich
and Füssen.

Reutte

You won't find Reutte in any American guidebook. Its
charms are subtle. It never was rich or important, and the
carvings on the buildings are all painted on. Its castle is
ruined, its churches are full, its men yodel for each other
on birthdays, and its energy lately is spent soaking its Austrian and German guests in gemütlichkeit.

Because most guests stay for a week, the town's attractions are more time-consuming than thrilling. The mountain lift swoops you high above the tree line to an Alpine
flower park with special slow-down-and-smell-the-
many-local-varieties paths. The town Heimatmuseum
(10:00-12:00, 14:00-17:00, closed Monday, in the Green
House on Untermarkt, around the corner from Hotel
Golden Hirsch) offers a quick look at the local folk culture and the story of the castle, but so do the walls and
mantels of most of the hotels.

Reutte has an Olympic-sized swimming pool open
from 10:00 to 21:00, which might be a good way to cool
off after your castle hikes (off-season 14:00-21:00, closed
Monday, 55 AS).

For a major thrill on a sunny day, drop by the tiny airport in Hofen across the river and fly. A small single-prop
plane (three people for 30 minutes, 1,200 AS; 60 minutes
for 1,900 AS) can buzz the Zugspitze and Ludwig's castles
and give you a bird's-eye peek at Reutte's Ehrenberg ruins
(that's about the cost of three lift tickets up the Zugspitze,
and a lot easier). Or for something more angelic, how
about Segelfliegen? For 240 AS, you get 30 minutes in a
glider for two (you and the pilot). Just watching the tow
rope launch the graceful glider like a giant slow motion
rubberband gun is thrilling. (May through October,
11:00-19:00, in good weather, tel. 05672/3207.)

Füssen
Important as the southern terminus of the trade route
that is today's tourist trade route called the Romantic
Road, Füssen is romantically situated under a renovated
castle on the lively Lech River.

Unfortunately, it's entirely overrun by tourists—the
worst kind. Traffic in the summer is exasperating, but by
bike or on foot, it's not bad. The train station (where the
Romantic Road bus tour leaves each morning at 8:15 and
arrives each evening at 19:35, June through September) is
a few minutes walk from the TI, good rooms, the hostel,
and the town center, a cobbled shopping mall.

Halfway between Füssen and the border (as you drive)
is the Lechfall, a thunderous look at the river with a
handy potty stop.

Sightseeing Highlights—Castle Day Circle
▲▲▲ Neuschwanstein and Hohenschwangau
Castles (Königsschlösser)—The fairy-tale castle,
Neuschwanstein, looks like the home of the knights of
the Round Table, but it's actually not much older than the
Eiffel Tower. It was built to suit the whims of Bavaria's
King Ludwig II and is a textbook example of the romanti-
cism that was popular in nineteenth-century Europe.

It's best to see Neuschwanstein, Germany's most popular castle, early in the morning before the hordes hit. The
castle is open every morning at 9:00; by 10:00, it's
packed. Rushed 25-minute English tours leave regularly
telling the sad story of Bavaria's "mad" king. (Men, check
out the views from the castle urinals.)

After the tour, climb up to Mary's Bridge to marvel at
Ludwig's castle, just as Ludwig did. This bridge was quite
an engineering accomplishment a hundred years ago.
From the bridge, the frisky enjoy hiking even higher to
the Beware—Danger of Death signs and an even more
glorious castle view. For the most interesting (but
15-minute longer and extremely slippery when wet)
descent, follow signs to the Pöllat Gorge.

The big, yellow Hohenschwangau Castle nearby was

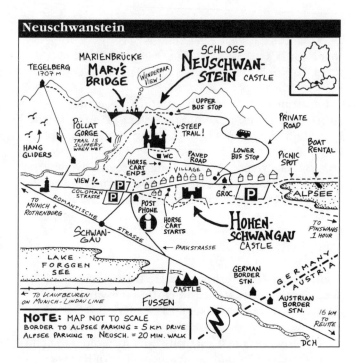

Neuschwanstein

Ludwig's boyhood home. It is more lived in and historic and actually gives a much better glimpse of Ludwig's life. (Both castles cost 8 DM and are open daily 9:00-17:30, November-March 10:00-16:00, tel. 08362/81035.)

The "village" at the foot of the castles was created for and lives off the hungry, shopping tourists who come in droves to Europe's "Disney" castle. The big yellow Bräu-stüberl restaurant by the lakeside parking lot is cheapest, with food that tastes that way. Next door is a little family-run, open-daily souvenir-grocery store with the makings for a skimpy picnic and a microwave fast-food machine. Picnic in the lakeside park or in one of the old-fashioned rent-by-the-hour rowboats. At the intersection is the bus stop, the post/telephone office, and a helpful TI.

Park, if possible, at the closest lot (the lakeside Schloss Parkplatz am Alpsee); they all cost 4 DM. As you'll notice, it's a steep hike to the castle. Horse carriages (slower than walking) and buses (5 DM round-trip) shuttle you most of the way up but still leave you with a fair hike. Your work continues inside the castle as your tour takes you up and down over 300 stairs. These castles are called *Königssch-lösser* in German.

To give your castle experience a romantic twist, hike or bike over from Hotel Schluxenhof in Austria. The mostly paved lane crosses a lonely German/Austrian border fence. It's an hour's hike with bus connections back to Füssen and Reutte or a great circular bike trip. Füssen–Hohenschwangau buses go twice an hour.

▲ **Tegelberg Gondola**—Just north of Neuschwanstein, you'll see hang gliders hovering like vultures. They jumped from the top of the Tegelberg gondola. For 22 DM, you can ride high above the castle to that peak's 5,500-foot summit and back down (last lift at 17:00). On a clear day, you get great views of the Alps and Bavaria and the vicarious thrill of watching hang gliders and parasailers leap into airborne ecstasy. From there, it's a pleasant two-hour hike down to Ludwig's castle.

▲▲ **Wies Church**—Germany's greatest rococo-style church, Wieskirche, is newly restored. Glorious no longer describes it. Flames of decoration, overripe but bright, bursting with beauty, this church is a droplet of heaven, a curly curlicue, the final flowering of the baroque movement. The ceiling depicts the Last Judgment. Walk down the side aisles to get close to the altar and the wooden statue of Christ that supposedly wept and still attracts countless pilgrims. Take a commune-with-nature-and-smell-the-farm detour back through the meadow, to the car park.

Wies is 30 minutes down the road from Neuschwanstein. Drive north, turn right at Steingaden, and follow the signs. The northbound Romantic Road bus tour stops here for 15 minutes. If you can't visit Wies, other churches that came out of a spray can from heaven are Oberammergau's church, Munich's Asam church, the Würzburg Residenz chapel, or the splendid (free and nearby) Ettal Monastery.

The Echelsbacher Bridge arches 250 feet over the Pöllat Gorge on the way from Wies to Oberammergau,
where you hit road 23. Drivers should let their passen-
gers walk across and meet them at the other side. Any
kayakers? Notice the painting of the traditional village
woodcarver (who used to walk from town to town with
his art on his back) on the first big house on the Oberammergau side, a shop called Almdorf Ammertal. It has a
huge selection of overpriced carvings and commission-
hungry tour guides.

▲ **Oberammergau**—The Shirley Temple of Bavarian
villages and exploited to the hilt by the tourist trade,
Oberammergau wears way too much makeup. It's worth a
wander only if you're passing through anyway. Browse
through the woodcarvers' shops—small art galleries
filled with very expensive whittled works, or the local
Heimat (folk art) Museum. (TI tel. 08822/1021, closed
Saturday afternoon and Sunday.)

Visit the church, a poor cousin of the one at Wies. This
church looks richer than it is. Tap on the "marble" columns. Wander through the graveyard. Ponder the deaths
that two wars dealt Germany. Behind the church are the
photos of three Schneller brothers, all killed within two
years in World War II.

Once a decade Oberammergau performs the Passion
Play (next show in the year 2000). Five thousand people a
day for 100 summer days attend the all-day dramatic
story of Christ's Crucifixion here. Until 2000, you'll have
to settle for reading the book and taking the theater's
45-minute tours (cheap, in English, regular departures
from 10:00-12:00 and 13:30-16:00) or seeing Nicodemus
tooling around town in his VW.

Gasthaus zum Stern (80-85 DM doubles, Dorfstr. 33,
8103 Oberammergau, tel. 08822/867) is friendly, serves
good food, and for this tourist town, is a fine value
(closed Wednesdays and November, will hold a room
with a phone call, English spoken). Oberammergau's
modern youth hostel (16 DM beds, open all year, tel.
08822/4114) is on the river a short walk from the center.

Driving into town, cross the bridge, take the second right, following Polizei signs, and park by the huge gray Passionsspielhaus. Leaving town, head out past the church and turn toward Ettal on road 23. You're 20 miles from Reutte.

▲▲ **Linderhof Castle**—This was Mad Ludwig's "home," his most intimate castle. It's small and comfortably exquisite, good enough for a minor god. Set in the woods, 15 minutes from Oberammergau, surrounded by fountains and sculpted, Italian-style gardens, it's the only palace I've toured that actually had me feeling envious. Don't miss the grotto (April-September, 10:00-17:00, off-season 10:00-16:00, July and August until 17:30, fountains often erupt at 17:00, English tours constantly, tel. 08822/512, 8 DM). Plan for lots of crowds, lots of walking, and a two-hour stop. There are several buses a day from Füssen and Oberammergau, included on Eurailpass.

▲ **Fallershein**—A special treat for those who may have been Kit Carson in a previous life, this extremely remote log cabin village is a 4,000-foot-high, flower-speckled world of serene slopes and cowbells. Thunderstorms roll down the valley like it's God's bowling alley, but the pint-sized church on the high ground, blissfully simple after so much baroque, seems to promise that this huddle of houses will survive and the river and breeze will just keep flowing. The couples sitting on benches are mostly Austrian vacationers who've rented cabins here. Many of them, appreciating the remoteness of Fallershein, are having affairs.

For a rugged chunk of local Alpine peace, spend a night in the local Matratzenlager Almwirtschaft Fallershein, run by friendly Kerle Erwin (80 AS per person with breakfast; open, weather permitting, May-November; 27 very cheap beds in a very simple loft dorm, meager plumbing, good inexpensive meals; 6671 Weissenbach 119a, b/Reutte; tel. 05678/5142, rarely answered, and then not in English). Crowded only on weekends. Fallershein is at the end of a miserable 2-kilometer fit-for-jeep-or-rental-car-only gravel road that looks more closed than it is, near Namlos on the Berwang road southwest of Reutte. To avoid cow damage, park 300 meters below the village at the tiny lot before the bridge.

Sleeping in Reutte (US$1 = about 10 AS)
In July, August, and September, Munich and Bavaria are packed with tourists. Austria's Tirol is easier and cheaper. The town of Reutte, just over the border, is my home base for the area. I choose it because it's not so crowded in peak season, because of the easygoing locals' contagious love of life, because I like Austria's ambience, and out of habit.

The Reutte tourist office (one block in front of the station, or Bahnhof, open weekdays 8:30-12:00 and 13:00-17:00 or 18:00, Saturday 8:00-12:00 and, from mid-July to mid-August on Saturday and Sunday afternoons from 16:00-18:00, tel. 05672/2336, or, direct from Germany, 0043-5672/2336) is very helpful. Go over your sightseeing plans, ask about a folk evening, pick up a city map, ask about discounts with the hotel guest cards. Reutte has no laundromat.

Youth Hostels: Reutte has plenty of reasonable hotels and Zimmer and two excellent little youth hostels. If you've never hosteled and are curious, try one of these. The downtown hostel is clean, rarely full, serves no meals but has a fine members' kitchen, and accepts nonmembers (70 AS per bed, a pleasant 10-minute walk from the town center, follow the Jugendherberge signs to the Kindergarten sign, 6600 Reutte, Prof. Dengelstr. 20, Tirol, open mid-June to late August, tel. 05672/3039).

The **Jugendgastehaus Graben** (120 AS beds with breakfast, A-6600 Reutte-Höfen, Postfach 3, Graben 1, from downtown Reutte, cross the bridge and follow the road left along the river, about a mile from the station, tel. 05672/2644) accepts nonmembers, has 2 to 12 beds per room and includes breakfast, shower, and sheets. Frau Reyman, who keeps the place traditional, homey, clean, and friendly, serves a great dinner. No curfew, open all year, bus connections to Neuschwanstein Castle.

Zimmer: The tourist office has a list of over 50 private homes that rent out generally elegant rooms with facilities down the hall, a pleasant communal living room, and breakfast. They charge about 160 AS per person a night, 20 AS cheaper for three-night stays, and will happily hold a room for you if you telephone. The TI can call and set you up just about any day of the year for free.

Edwin and Waltraud **Engl's Zimmer** (160 AS with breakfast, Mühler Strasse 23, tel. 05672/2326, summer only) is my favorite. They have only one room (for 2 or 3), plus an elegant TV/living/breakfast room, and speak only a little English but will hold a room if you phone. And they are just two blocks behind the Reutte train station.

Also near the station in a quiet residential street in the adjacent village of Breitenwang are the private rooms in the homes of **Maria Auer** (several very comfortable rooms at Kaiser Lothar Strasse 25, tel. 05672/29195) and **Walter Hosp** (Kaiser Lothar Strasse 29, tel. 05672/5377). Farther out, in the neighboring village of Ehenbichl, just behind the recommended Hotel Maximilian is the comfortable home of **Armella Brutscher** (Unterried 24, tel. 05672/4294).

Hotels: Reutte is very popular with Austrians and Germans who come here year after year for a one- or two-week vacation. The hotels are big, elegant, full of comfy carved furnishings and creative ways to spend so much time in one spot. They serve great food, and the owners send their children away to hotel management schools. Breakfast is included and showers are in the room. Your choices are right in Reutte, out of town in a nearby village, in a quiet meadow with the cows, or in the forest under the castle. (To call Reutte from Germany, dial 0043-5672 and the four-digit number.)

Hotel Goldener Hirsch (720 AS doubles, 6600 Reutte-Tirol, tel. 05672/2508 and ask for Helmut or Monika, fax 250 8100), a grand old hotel renovated with a mod Tirolean Jugendstil flair, has sliding doors, minibars, TV with cable in the room, and one lonely set of antlers. It's located right downtown (2 blocks from the station). They can help with cheaper rooms if they are full or too expensive. The Goldener Hirsch has a fine and reasonable restaurant (not serving on Monday). For those without a car, this is by far the most convenient hotel.

Hotel Maximilian, just down the river a mile or so in the village of Ehenbichl (800 AS doubles, A-6600 Ehenbichl-Reutte, tel. 05672/2585, fax 258554), is the best splurge. Its modern, 700 AS doubles include use of bicycles, sauna, Ping-Pong, a children's playroom, and the friendly service of the Koch family. Daughter Gabi speaks fine English. There always seems to be a special event here, and if you're lucky, you'll hear the Koch family make music, an Edelweiss experience. American guests are made to feel right at home. They can usually pick you up at the station.

Gasthof Schluxenhof gets the "remote old hotel in an idyllic setting" award (600-700 AS modern rustic doubles with the best breakfast in town, Family Gstir, A-6600 Pinswang-Reutte, follow the tiny road after the border just before the bridge, then the sign to Unterpinswang, tel. 05677/8452, fax 845223, no English spoken). This newly refurbished old lodge, filled with locals, just off the main road near the village of Pinswang north of Reutte, is a great place for kids—yours and the Gstir grandchildren. From Schluxen, it's a healthy hour's hike over the mountain to Neuschwanstein Castle. Consider parking here, having lunch (50-100 AS) on a sunny day with cowbells, and hiking (or biking, they rent bikes) to Ludwig's castle.

Gasthof-Pension Waldrast (550-650 AS per double, 6600 Ehenbichl, on Ehrenbergstr., a half-mile out of town toward Innsbruck, past the campground, just under the castle, tel. 05672/2443) separates a forest and a meadow and is warmly run by the Huter family. It has big rooms, like living rooms, many with a fine castle view, and it's a good coffee stop if you're hiking into town from the Ehrenberg ruins.

Eating in Reutte

Each of the hotels takes great pleasure in serving fine Austrian food at reasonable prices. Rather than go to a cheap restaurant, I'd order low on their menu. For cheap food, the **Prima** self-serve cafeteria near the station (Mühler Strasse 20, 9:00-19:00 Monday-Friday) and the **Metzgerei Storf Imbiss** (better but open only Monday-Friday 8:30-15:00) above the deli across from the Heimatmuseum on Untermarkt Street are the best in town.

Rooms in Füssen, Germany (1.5 DM = about $1)

Füssen, two miles from Ludwig's castles, is a cobbled, crenellated, riverside oompah treat, but it's very touristy. It has just about as many rooms as tourists though. Its tourist office with a free room-finding service is just two blocks past the train station (look for *Kurverwaltung*, open 8:00-12:00, 14:00-19:00, Saturday 10:00-12:00, 14:00-16:00, Sunday 10:00-12:00, closed off-season weekends, tel. 08362/7077). I prefer Reutte, but without your own car, this is a handier home base (unless you've got 35 DM for a taxi from the Füssen station to Reutte).

All places listed here are an easy walk from the train station and the town center. And they assured me they are used to travelers getting in about 20:00 off the Romantic Road bus and will hold rooms for a promise on the phone.

The excellent Germany run **Füssen youth hostel** (4- to 8-bed rooms, 17 DM for B&B, 7 DM for dinner, 3 DM for sheets, 27 is maximum age, laundry and kitchen facilities, Mariahilferstr. 5, tel. 08362/7754) is a 10-minute walk from town, backtracking from the station. You might rent a bike at the station to get there quick and easy.

Zimmer: Haus Peters (65 DM doubles with shower and breakfast, Augustenstr. 5½, 8958 Füssen, tel. 08362/7171) is Füssen's best value. This elegant home just a block from the station (toward town, second left) has 5 rooms, including a great 25 DM per person four-bed family loft room. The Peters are friendly, speak English, and know what travelers like; there is a peaceful garden, a self-serve kitchen, and a good price. The funky old **Pension Garni Elisabeth** (70 DM doubles plus 5 DM for showers, Augustenstr. 10, tel. 08362/6275) in a garden just across the street, exudes a chilling Addams family friendliness.

Hotels: Bräustüberl (76 DM doubles, Rupprechtstr. 5, just a block from the station, tel. 08362/7843) has clean and bright rooms in a rather musty old beer hall-type place filled with locals who know a good value meal.

Hotel Gasthaus zum Hechten is less colorful but friendly and right in the old town pedestrian zone (80-95 DM doubles, Ritterstr. 6, tel. 08362/7906).

Gasthof Krone is a rare bit of pre-glitz Füssen also in the pedestrian zone (bright, cheery, simple doubles 70 DM, shower down the hall, Schrannenplatz 17, tel. 08362/7824).

The biggest and most respected hotel in town is the **Hotel Hirsch** (175 DM doubles, Augsburger Tor Platz 2, tel. 08362/5080), which goes way beyond the call of hotel duty but charges for it. Still, those with money enjoy spending it here.

Inexpensive farmhouse Zimmer abound in the Bavarian countryside around Neuschwanstein and are a great value. Look for Zimmer Frei signs. The going rate is about 60 DM per double including breakfast; you'll see plenty of green vacancy signs. For a Zimmer in a classic Bavarian home within walking distance of Mad Ludwig's place, try **Haus Magdalena** (Brumme Family, Schwangauerstrasse, 8959 Schwangau, tel. 083/6281126).

REUTTE TO MUNICH

Today you'll drive past Germany's highest peak, possibly stopping for a little more Bavarian sightseeing and lunch at a monastery that serves the best beer in Deutschland, and then arrive in Munich in time to set up, orient, see the center of Bavaria's leading city, and enjoy some beer hall craziness tonight.

Munich, Germany's most livable city, is also one of its most historic, artistic, and entertaining. It's big and growing, with a population of over 1,500,000. Just a little more than a century ago, it was the capital of an independent Bavaria. Its imperial palaces, jewels, and grand boulevards constantly remind visitors that this was once a political as well as cultural powerhouse.

Suggested Schedule

8:00	Leave Reutte.
9:00	Ride to the summit of the Zugspitze if time, weather, and budget permit.
11:00	Drive to Andechs for lunch. Be very beerful.
14:00	Arrive in Munich, stop at TI, and check into hotel.
15:30	Explore the heart of town, subway to Odeonsplatz, tour Cuvillies Theater, see 17:00 Glockenspiel show at Marienplatz, shop, browse, stroll through center, drop into Hofbräuhaus.
20:00	Dinner and evening of oompah fun at Mathäser's beer hall.
Sleep	Munich.

Transportation: Reutte to Munich (90 miles)
Drivers leave Reutte following Innsbruck/Fernpass signs. Exit at Lermoos. Get to the Zugspitzebahn via Ehrwald and Obermoos. Signs direct you through Garmisch-Partenkirchen to the Munich autobahn. If you're stopping in Andechs, catch road #2 after Garmisch for Murnau, Weilheim, and Starnberg. From Andechs, a small road takes you into Munich. Otherwise, you'll autobahn in fol-

lowing signs to Zentrum and then Hauptbahnhof (main train station). Munich is a terrible city to drive in, so ideally pick up a city map from the TI or rest stop before entering and follow it straight to the station, find your room within a few blocks of there, and leave your car until it's time to go to Salzburg, following the Salzburg autobahn signs.

By train, it's 2 to 3 hours from Füssen to Munich with one connection. From Reutte, it's a 3-hour train ride to Munich with a change in Garmisch (10 trains a day).

Sightseeing Highlights—South of Munich

▲▲ **Zugspitze**—Germany's tallest mountain, 10,000 feet, is on the Austrian border. Lifts from both sides take you to the summit, where you can straddle the two countries while enjoying an incredible view. There are restaurants, shops, and telescopes at the summit.

The hour-long trip from Garmisch on the German side costs 55 DM (by direct lift or a combo cogwheel train/ cable car ride). From the less crowded Talstation Obermoos, above the Austrian village of Erwald, the new tram zips you to the top in only ten minutes and costs about 5 DM less (315 AS). The Austrian trip is tricky without your own car, but buses do connect Erwald village and the lift twice an hour.

▲▲ **Andechs**—A fine baroque church in a Bavarian setting at a monastery that serves hearty food and the best beer in Germany in a carnival atmosphere full of partying locals? That's the Andechs Monastery hiding happily between two lakes just south of Munich. Come ready to eat chunks of tender pork chain-sawed especially for you, huge and soft pretzels (best I've had), spiraled white radishes, savory sauerkraut, and Andecher monk-made beer that would almost make celibacy tolerable. Everything is served in medieval proportions; two people can split a meal. Great picnic center, too. Open daily 9:00 to 21:00, first-class view, second-class prices (tel. 08807/1048).

To reach Andechs from Munich without a car, take the S-5 train to Herrsching and walk two miles or catch the bus from there.

Munich

See tomorrow.

MUNICH

Spend all day immersed in the art and history of this cultural hub of Germany. With less than two days to see the exciting capital of Bavaria, you'll need to be selective and plan carefully. Today will include a mountain of baroque razzle-dazzle, crown jewels, great art, and *Biergarten* fun.

Suggested Schedule	
8:00	Breakfast. Consider renting a bike for the day.
9:00	Münchner Stadtmuseum, Viktualien Market (buy picnic here or at Alois Dallmayr).
11:00	Tour Residenz and Schatzkammer.
12:30	Picnic in Hofgarten. Walk to Alte Pinakothek.
13:30	Alte Pinakothek.
15:30	Haus der Kunst or free time.
17:30	Stroll through Englischer Garten, early dinner or a drink at the Chinese Pagoda.

Munich is big—Germany's third-largest city, after Berlin and Hamburg—and growing fast, but all hotels and sights (except hostel and Olympic grounds) are within about a 25-minute walk of Marienplatz and its excellent tourist information office and sleek subway system make life easy for the five million visitors who come to town each year.

Take full advantage of the TI office in the train station (open 8:00-22:00 daily, off-season Sundays 11:00-19:00, tel. 089/2391-256 or 257, opposite track 11). Have a list of questions ready, confirm your sightseeing plans, and pick up brochures (free city map, public transit info, consider buying the 2 DM "Monatsprogram" list of sights and calendar of events and the young people's guide, regardless of your age). They have a room-finding service (5 DM). If the line is dreadful, you can pick up the free map just inside the door. For recorded museum information,

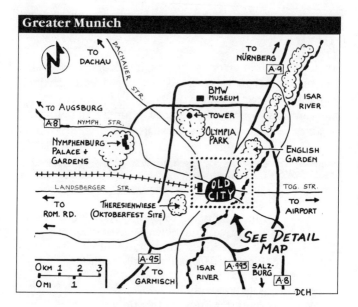

Greater Munich

call 089/239162; for parks and palaces, 089/239172; for train, 089/19419. Renate Suerbaum, (tel. 089/283374, 100 DM tours)is a good local guide.

The industrious and hardworking Eurail Aid office (halfway to the Bahnhof Mission, down track 11, open daily May through early October, 7:30-11:30 and 13:00-18:00, closes at 16:30 in May) is an American whirlpool of travel information designed for Eurailers and budget travelers. They know your train travel and accommodations questions and have answers in clear American English. The German rail company pays them to help you design your best train travels and you pay them 6 DM to find the cheapest available rooms in and around Munich. They also do Dachau and King Ludwig tours, both a bit frustrating for those without cars. Pick up their free newsletter.

At the other end of the station, near track 30, is Radius Touristik (open daily, 8:30-18:30, May through mid-October, tel. 089/596113, run by an Englishman, Patrick Holder), which rents three-speed bikes (4 DM/hour, 20 DM/day) and organizes introduction walks of old Munich (almost daily, starting at the station at 10:00, finishing at

Marienplatz for the noon Glockenspiel performance, 12.30 DM) and faster-moving bike tours of the city (three hours, 28 DM). Patrick gives out free copies of *Munich Found* (a good English "What's Happening" for Munich, on sale in newspaper stands). After a day on one of his bikes, I learned that Munich—level, compact, with plenty of bike paths—is a biker's city.

For a quick orientation in the station, use the big wall maps of the train station, Munich, and Bavaria (through the center doorway as you leave the tracks on the left). For a quick rest stop, the Burger King upstairs has toilets as pleasant and accessible as its hamburgers.

The great Munich tram, bus, and subway system is a sight in itself. Subways are called U- or S-bahns. Eurail passes are good on the S-bahn. The fares are complicated, and four rides will cost you the same as an "all-day after 9:00" pass, so spend 8 DM, sign it, validate it in a machine, and you have Munich by the tail for a day (for sale at tourist offices, subway booths, and in machines at most stops). The entire system works on the same tickets. Taxis are expensive and needless.

The center of Munich is the Marienplatz. From here, a pedestrian-only street runs west toward the train station. Orient yourself with the west-east axis that runs: the main train station (Hauptbahnhof)–Karlstor–Kaufinger-strasse–Marienplatz–Isartor. Most sights are within a few blocks of this entertaining walk.

You'll find Munich's architecture a bit sterile, as most of its historic center has been rebuilt since the World War II bombings. Its hotels are expensive, but after that, food, fun, and transportation are cheap. Most Munich sights are closed on Monday. Telephone code: 089.

Sightseeing Highlights—Munich

▲▲ **Marienplatz and the Pedestrian Zone**—The essence of Munich is best experienced as the escalator takes you out of the underground system and into the sunlit Marienplatz (Mary's Place). Surrounding you is the glory of Munich: great buildings bombed flat and rebuilt, the ornate facades of the new and old City Halls (the

Neues Rathaus, built in neo-Gothic style in 1867, and the
Altes Rathaus), outdoor cafés, and people bustling and
lingering like the birds and breeze they share this square
with. From here the pedestrian mall (Kaufingerstrasse
and Neuhauserstrasse) leads you through a great shopping area past plenty of entertaining street singers, the
twin-towering Frauenkirche (with its 350-foot-high
viewpoint, built in 1470, rebuilt after World War II,
closed through 1994 for more work), and several fountains, to Karlstor and the train station. The old Glockenspiel "jousts," as it has for generations, on Marienplatz
daily through the tourist season at 11:00, 12:00, 17:00,
and a shorty at 21:00. (If you liked the Rothenburg
Meistertrunk show, you'll love this one!) A 3 DM elevator
takes those in search of a view high above the Glockenspiel. For a totally unobstructed view, but with no elevator, I prefer the St. Peter's church tower just a block away.
It's a long 2 DM climb, much of it with two-way traffic on
a one-way staircase, but the view is dynamite. Try to be
two flights from the top when the bells ring at the top of
the hour (or when your friends ask you about your trip,
you'll say, "What?").

▲▲ **Residenz**—For a good dose of imperial Bavarian
grandeur, tour the palace of the Wittelsbach family.
Different wings are open in the morning and afternoon,
but either tour is ample. For 600 years, the Wittelsbachs
ruled Bavaria from here. Don't miss the Schatzkammer
(treasury), a thousand years of Wittelsbach knickknacks,
which, like the palace, is open Tuesday through Saturday
10:00 to 16:30, Sunday 10:00 to 13:00, 4 DM. Take U-3, or
U-6, to Odeonsplatz or walk from Marienplatz.

▲ **The Cuvillies Theater**—Attached to the Residenz,
this National Theater, designed by Cuvillies, is dazzling
enough to send you back to the days of the divine
monarchs (open Monday-Saturday 14:00-17:00, Sunday
10:00-17:00, 3 DM).

▲▲ **Münchner Stadtmuseum**—The underrated
Munich city museum just a few blocks off Marienplatz is a
pleasant surprise—great old photography exhibit, life in
Munich through the centuries, historic puppets, the story

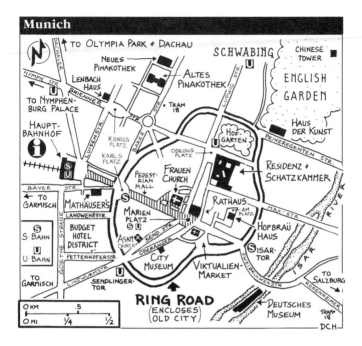

of beer, a huge collection of musical instruments from around the world, and a changing collection of living rooms from 1700 to 1930, often with some fine Jugendstil art. No crowds, bored and playful guards (open Tuesday-Saturday 10:00-17:00, Wednesday until 20:30, Sunday 10:00-18:00, closed Monday, 5 DM, free on Sunday, St. Jakob's Platz 1).

▲▲▲ **Alte Pinakothek**—Bavaria's best collection of art is stored in a pleasing, easy-to-handle museum, strong on Italian and North European artists, such as Rubens and Dürer. Here, and at Vienna's Kunsthistorisches Museum, is your best chance to see great European masterpieces on this tour. It took the Wittelsbach family 400 years to amass this collection (open 9:15-16:30, 19:00-21:00 on Tuesday and Thursday, closed Monday, 4 DM, free on Sunday). Take U-2 to Königsplatz or tram 18.

▲ **Haus der Kunst**—Built by Hitler as a temple of Nazi art, this bold and fascist building now houses modern art, much of which the Führer censored. It's a fun collection —Kandinsky, Picasso, Dali, and much more from this century (open 9:00-16:30, Thursday evenings 19:00-21:00, closed Monday, 3.50 DM). Take U-3, U-5, or U-6 to Odeonplatz, then a peaceful walk through the Hofgarten and past the Kriegerdenkmal, a bombed building left as a war memorial. Or, take bus 53 or 55, or tram 20.

Bayerisches Nationalmuseum—An interesting collection of Riemenschneider carvings, manger scenes, traditional living rooms, and old Bavarian houses (open 9:30-17:00, closed Monday, 3.50 DM, free on Sunday). Take tram 20 or bus 53 or 55 to Prinzregentenstrasse 3.

▲▲ Deutsches Museum—The German answer to our Smithsonian Institution has everything of scientific and technical interest from astronomy to zymurgy but can be disappointing because of its overwhelming size and lack of English descriptions. Pick up the 4 DM guide through the collections, skip the German-only planetarium, and focus on the lower floors where you'll find more English information. With 10 miles of exhibits, even those with roller skates will need to be selective. There is lots of hands-on gadgetry, but the collections seem to have been left in the dust by the computer age. Despite its reputation, unless you are (or wish you were) an engineer, 2 hours is enough time here. Self-serve cafeteria. Open 9:00 to 17:00, 8 DM admission. S-Bahn to Isartorplatz or tram 18.

Schwabing—Munich's artsy, bohemian university district or "Greenwich Village" has been called "not a place but a state of mind." All I experienced was a mental lapse. The bohemians run the boutiques. I think the most colorful thing about Schwabing is the road leading back downtown. U-3 or U-6 will take you to the München-Freiheit Center if you want to wander. Most of the jazz and disco joints are near Occamstrasse.

Englischer Garten—One of Europe's great parks, Munich's "Central Park" is the Continent's largest, laid out in 1789 by an American. Bike rentals are at the south entrance, and there's a huge beer garden near the Chinese Pagoda. Caution: nude sunbathers (although a new law requires them to wear clothes. . .on the tram). A rewarding respite from the city, especially fun on a bike.

Asam Church—Near the Stadtmuseum, this private church of the Asam brothers shows off their very popular baroque-concentrate style. If you missed (or loved) the Wies Church, visit the gooey drippy masterpiece by these two rococonuts.

▲ **Olympic Grounds**—Munich's great 1972 Olympic stadium and sports complex is now a fine park offering a tower (commanding but rather boring view from 820 feet, 8:00-24:00, 5 DM), an excellent swimming pool (open to the public 7:00-22:30, Monday from 10:00, Thursday closed at 18:00, 5 DM), a good look at its striking "cobweb" style of architecture, and plenty of sun, grass, and picnic potential. Easy access on the U-3 or U-2 to Olympiazentrum.

BMW Museum—The BMW headquarters, located in a striking building across the street from the Olympic Grounds, offers free factory tours (normally one a day in English) and a 5 DM museum. Call 389-53307 for the tour plans. The museum gets mixed reviews from car buffs.

Organized bus tours of the city and nearby countryside—Panorama Tours (at the station, tel. 591504) offers all-day tours of Neuschwanstein and Linderhof (65 DM) and one-hour city orientation tours (at 10:00, 11:30, and 14:30, 13 DM).

Shopping—Felzmann's, across from St. Peter's tower entrance, has the best Birkenstock selection in Germany with prices 40 percent below those in the U.S.A.

▲▲ **Nymphenburg Palace**—This royal summer palace is great, but if you've already seen the Residenz, it's only mediocre. If you do tour it, don't miss King Ludwig's "Gallery of Beauties"—a room stacked with portraits of Bavaria's loveliest women (according to Ludwig; notice his taste for big noses). The palace park, good for a royal stroll, contains the tiny Amalienburg Palace, a rococo jewel of a hunting lodge by Cuvillies. The sleigh and coach collection (Marstallmuseum) is especially interesting for Mad Ludwig fans. The palace cafeteria is reasonably priced. (Open 10:00-12:30 and 13:30-16:00, closed Monday, shorter hours October-March, admission 5 DM, use the little English guidebook, tel. 179080.) Take the

U-1 to Rotkreuzplatz and then tram 12 toward Amalienburgstrasse, to Schloss Nymphenburg.

▲▲ **Dachau**—Since you'll visit the even more powerful
Mauthausen concentration camp, I haven't worked
Dachau into the schedule. But if you won't be going to
Mauthausen on your way to Vienna, visit Dachau. Dachau
was the first Nazi concentration camp (1933). Today it's
the most accessible camp to travelers and a very effective
voice from our recent but grisly past, warning and plead-
ing "Never Again," the memorial's theme. This is a valuable experience and when approached thoughtfully, well
worth the drive. In fact, it may change your life. See it.
Feel it. Read and think about it. After this most powerful
sightseeing experience, many people gain more respect
for history and the dangers of not keeping tabs on their
government.

On arrival, pick up the miniguide and notice when the
next documentary film in English will be shown (20
minutes, normally at 11:30 and 15:30). The museum and
the 25-minute movie are exceptional. Notice the Expres-
sionist fascist-inspired art near the theater, where you'll
also find English books, slides, and a good W.C. Outside,
be sure to see the reconstructed barracks and the
memorial shrines at the far end. (The camp is open
9:00-17:00, closed on Monday.)

Take the S-bahn 2, direction Petershausen, to Dachau
and catch bus 722 (Dachau-Ost) from the station to
Gedenkstätte. If you're driving, Dachauerstrasse leads
from downtown Munich to Dachau. If lost, signs to Augs-
burg will lead to signs to Dachau. Then follow the KZ-
Gedenkstätte signs. (Note: train travelers should see
Dachau rather than Mauthausen. Transportation instruction sheet at the Munich TI.) The town of Dachau (TI tel.
08131/84566) is much more pleasant than its image.

Oktoberfest

When King Ludwig I had a marriage party in 1810 it was
such a success that they made it an annual bash. These
days the Oktoberfest starts on the third Saturday in Sep-

tember with an opening parade of over 6,000 partici-
pants and fills six or eight huge beer tents with about
6,000 people each. Sixteen days and a million gallons of
beer later, they roast the last ox.

While you can always find a festival in Munich's beer
halls, the entire city celebrates each fall with this mother
of all keggers. It's crowded, but if you arrive in the morning (except Friday or Saturday), the TI will be able to find
you a room.

The fairgrounds known as the Wies'n (a few blocks
from the station) erupts in a frenzy of rides, dancing,
strangers strolling arm-in-arm down rows of picnic
tables, and tons of beer, pretzels, and wurst in a bubbling
caldron of fun. The "three loops" roller coaster must be
the wildest on earth (do it before the beer drinking). During the fair, the city functions even better than normal,
and it's a good time to sightsee even if beer hall rowdiness
isn't your cup of tea. The Fasching carnival time (early
January to mid-February) is nearly as crazy.

Sleeping in Munich (1.5 DM = about US$1)

Rooms in Munich are costly—you can't avoid it. Youth
hostels strictly enforce their 26-year-old age limit, and
side-tripping in is a bad value. But there are plenty of
good rooms, most located within a few blocks of the
Hauptbahnhof (central train station). August, September,
and early October are most crowded, but conventions
can clog the city on any day. Ideally, call ahead and
reserve one of the places I've listed below. Receptionists
usually speak English, know what's available by 9:00, and
will hold a room for your arrival later that day. Otherwise,
use the TI.

The area immediately south of the station is full of
budget hotels (that's 80 DM doubles in Munich with
breakfast but without a private shower) but has gotten
quite seedy. My listings are in more polite neighbor-
hoods, nearly all within a 5- or 10-minute walk of the station and handy to the center. Those farthest from the station are most pleasant. There are some very bad values to
be had if you just choose one out of the blue. I've listed

places in order of closeness to the station.

Jugendhotel Marienherberge (32 DM singles, 26 DM in 2- to 6-bed rooms, very close to the station at Goethestr. 9, tel. 089/555891) is a very pleasant, friendly convent accepting young women only (loosely enforced 18- to 25-year age limit). If you qualify, sleep here.

Hotel Gebhardt (90 DM doubles, Goethestr. 38, 8000 Munich 2, just 3 minutes from the station, tel. 089/539446) offers a decent combination of neighborhood, comfort, and price surrounded by cold institutional plastic and plaster. They have some less-expensive 3- and 4-bed rooms.

Hotel Erbprinz (90-125 DM doubles, Sonnenstr. 2, 8000 Munich 2, tel. 089/594521) has "French doubles" for couples wanting to sleep cheap and together.

YMCA (CVJM), open to people of all ages and most sexes (90 DM doubles, less if under 27 years old, very central, just two blocks south of the station at Landwehrstr. 13, tel. 089/5521410, fax 525818), has modern and simple rooms. Reservations are necessary. Cheap dinners served 18:00 to 21:00, Tuesday through Saturday.

Hotel Pension Erika (75-95 DM doubles, Landwehrstr. 8, 8 Munich 2, tel. 089/554327) is as bright as dingy yellow can be. Its cheap doubles are a great value.

Hotel Pension Luna (90-105 DM doubles, next to the YMCA at 5 Landwehrstr., 8000 Munich 2, tel. 597833, fax 523 2561) is in a dumpy building, with bright and cheery rooms and a safe street.

Hotel Pension Zöllner (85-130 DM doubles, Sonnenstr. 10, 8000 Munich 2, tel. 089/554035) is plain, clean, and concrete on the big ring road between the station and the old center. Avoid their noisy street-front rooms.

Hotel Pension Utzelmann (95-135 DM doubles, 48 DM singles, 150 DM for 4, Pettenkoferstr. 6, 8000 Munich 2, tel. 089/594889 or 596228) is the best value of all. Most of the rooms are huge, especially the curiously cheap room 6. Each room is richly furnished with homey lace tablecloth finishing touches. It's in an extremely decent neighborhood a 10-minute walk from the station, a block off Sendlinger Tor. Easy parking.

Hotel Uhland (150-230 DM doubles, with a huge breakfast, 1 Uhlandstr., near the Theresienwiese Oktoberfest grounds, a 10-minute walk from the station, tel. 089/539277, fax 531114), a mansion with sliding glass doors and a garden, is a worthwhile splurge. Easy parking.

Pension Mariandl (90-105 DM doubles, 42 DM per person in larger rooms, Goethestr. 51, tel. 089/534108) is an old formerly elegant mansion with peeling vinyl floors, weak lights, and yellow corridors. The rooms are basic but fine, the neighborhood is peaceful and residential, and the classy dining hall plays free classical music Monday through Friday with dinner.

Pension Diana (90 DM doubles, Altheimer Eck 15, 8000 Munich 2, tel. 089/2603107) on the third floor with no elevator, has 15 bright and airy doubles, an environment perfect for retired and married nuns. In the old center, a block off the pedestrian mall.

Pension Linder (90-115 DM doubles, Dultstr. 1-Sendlinger Strasse, Munich 2, tel. 089/263413) is clean, quiet, modern, and very concrete. The most central of my listings, it's across the street from the city museum, a few blocks from Marienplatz.

Hostels: Munich's youth hostels charge 15 to 25 DM and strictly limit admission to YH members who are under 27. The **Burg Schwaneck hostel** (30 minutes from the center, S-bahn to Pullach, then walk 8 minutes, tel. 089/7930643) is a renovated castle.

Internationales Haus (40 DM per bed, Elisabethstr. 87, tel. 089/120060) offers 480 beds in simple 2- to 5-bed rooms. They'll hold a room with a phone call and normally have beds available. Easy to find (far from station, subway U-2 to Hohenzollernplatz, then 20-minute walk or bus 33 or tram 12 to second stop, Barbarastr.), easy parking.

"The Tent," Munich's **International Youth Camp Kapuzinerhölzl**, offers up to 400 places on the wooden floor of a huge circus tent with a mattress, blankets, good showers, and free tea in the morning for 6 DM to anyone under 25. It's a fun experience—kind of a cross between

Woodstock (if anyone under 24 knows what that was)
and a slumber party. Call 1414300 before heading out to
it. No curfew. Take U-bahn 1 to Rotkreuzplatz, catch tram
12 to Botanischer Garten (direction Amalienburgstrasse),
and follow the youthful crowd down Franz-Schrank-
strasse to the big tent. This is near the Nymphenburg Palace. Open late June through August. There is a theft problem, so sleep on your bag or leave it at the station.

Eating in Munich
Munich's most memorable budget food is in the beer
halls. There are many to choose from, but I'm stuck on
the **Mathäser Bierstadt** (tel. 089/592896) at Bayerstrasse 5, halfway between the Hauptbahnhof (train station) and Karlstor. The music-every-night atmosphere is
thick; the fat and shiny-leather band has church mice
standing up and conducting 3/4 time with a breadstick.
Meals are inexpensive (for a light 8.50 DM meal, I like #94
on the menu, Schweinswurst and Kraut), huge, liter beers
called *ein Mass* (or "ein pitcher" in English) are 8.50 DM,
white radishes are salted and cut in delicate spirals, and
huge surly beer maids pull mustard packets from their
cavernous cleavages. Notice the vomitoriums in the W.C.

The most famous beer hall, the **Hofbräuhaus** (Platzl
9, near Marienplatz, tel. 089/221676, menu #165 is a good
hearty 10 DM meal), is much more touristy. But do check
it out; it's fun to see 200 Japanese people drinking beer in
a German beer hall. Also memorable, tasty, and rowdy is
the **Weisses Bräuhaus** at Tal 10, between Marienplatz
and Isartor. Hitler met with fellow fascists here in 1920
when his Nazi party was in an embryonic state. The
Lowenbrauhaus, next to the Hofbräuhaus, is a calmer,
classier alternative. Another good and untouristy alternative beer hall is **Jodlerwirt** (4 Altenhofstrasse, between
the Hofbräuhaus and Marienplatz).

For outdoor atmosphere and a cheap meal, spend an
evening at the **Englischer Garten's Chinese Pagoda**
(Chinesischer Turm) **Biergarten**. You're welcome to
BYO food and grab a table or buy from the picnic stall

(*Brotzeit*) right there. Don't bother to phone ahead: there are six thousand seats!

For university atmosphere, cheap food, beer, and crowded basements of conversation, head out to the **Studentenstadt** (university dorm) **Bierstuben**. The fastest cheap and central meal is found at **Mathäser's** stand-up self-serve bar (facing Bayerstrasse), or gather a picnic at the lively open-air Viktualien Market, just behind Marienplatz.

The classiest picnic of the tour can be purchased in the historic, elegant, and expensive **Alois Dallmayr** delicatessen at 14 Dienerstrasse just behind the Rathaus (9:00-18:30, Saturday 9:00-14:00, closed Sunday). Wander through this dieter's purgatory, put together a royal picnic, and eat it in the nearby, adequately royal Hofgarten. To save money, browse at Dallmayr's, but buy in the basement of the Kaufhof across Marienplatz.

MUNICH TO SALZBURG

After some last sightseeing or exploring in Munich, you'll take the autobahn two hours south back into Austria, setting up in Salzburg by midafternoon. Today's sightseeing plan is flexible. There are four major sights. You can pick two—the Nymphenburg Palace and the Deutsches Museum in Munich (see Sightseeing, Day 6) or the Berchtesgaden Salt Mines and the Hellbrunn Castle near Salzburg. Speedsters with a car and enough coffee could do three, but I'd rather do two and get comfortably set up to take a rest before a hopefully music-filled Salzburg evening.

Suggested Schedule	
9:00	Check out of hotel. Tour Nymphenburg Palace or the Deutsches Museum.
11:30	Drive south, picnicking en route.
14:00	Tour the Berchtesgaden Salt Mines or the Hellbrunn Castle.
17:00	Arrive in Salzburg, visit TI, check into hotel.
21:30	Stroll through gardens to Augustiner Keller for dinner, with a floodlit city-from-the-bridge view for dessert.
22:00	Wander the streets of old Salzburg.

Transportation: Munich to Salzburg (100 miles)
By car, leave Munich the way you came in, heading away from town on Bayerstrasse and following the autobahn signs to Salzburg, just 90 minutes to the southeast. You'll pass Chiemsee on your left. (Ludwig's third castle, Schloss Herrenchiemsee, is on the island in the lake. Boats go from Prien.)

After crossing the border, stay on the autobahn, taking the Süd Salzburg exit in the direction of Anif. This road leads you north into town, passing first the Schloss Hellbrunn and then the TI. Ask the TI for advice on locating your hotel and parking. Mozart never drove in the old town, and neither should you. Park your car and walk or use Salzburg's fine bus system. The easiest, cheapest, and most central parking lot is the giant 1,500-car Altstadt lot in the tunnel under the Mönchsberg (150 AS per day).

By train, it's an easy 90-minute shot to Salzburg. Use the Salzburg station TI and catch a city bus from there to Hellbrunn if you like (bus 55, two an hour, buy the 24-hour pass, 15-minute ride). Berchtesgaden is a direct train ride from Munich with an easy, scenic, and more-direct-than-train bus connection into Salzburg.

Sightseeing Highlights on the Road to Salzburg

▲ **Hitler's First Autobahn Rest Stop**—At Chiemsee, the very first autobahn rest stop built during Hitler's rule and frescoed with *Deutschland über alles* themes, is now an American armed forces recreation center and hotel. Drop in for a glimpse at how the other half lives.

Take the Feldon exit off the Munich–Salzburg autobahn and follow the small road between the freeway and the lake. Continue toward Salzburg for half a mile, past the campground into U.S. military land, to a large lakeside hotel. Enter near the pillars where the sign says "AFRC Chiemsee hotel check-in." A plaque outside the door tells the Nazi history, and a friendly receptionist inside will direct you past the cafeteria to the large dining hall with its 1938 murals depicting good hardworking Nazis from every walk of life.

Homesick travelers are welcome to use the cafeteria (three meals, every day, cheap, dollars or marks) and U.S. mail service there. Pick up a Salzburg tourist map and stamps at the postcard shop. Any old civilian is welcome to eat and hang around, but you've got to be military to sleep there.

▲▲ **Berchtesgaden**—This Alpine resort just across the German border flaunts its attractions very effectively, and you may find yourself in a traffic jam of desperate tourists looking for ways to turn their money into fun. From the station and the helpful TI (tel. 08652/5011), buses go to the idyllic Königsee (2-hour scenic cruises, four per hour,

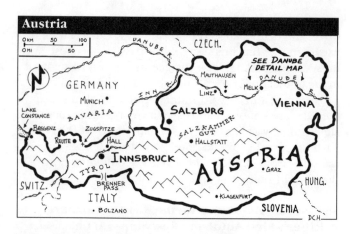

stopovers anywhere, 16 DM, tel. 08652/4026) and the salt
mines (a 30-minute walk otherwise).

The salt mines are open daily 8:30 to 17:00 (winter,
Monday-Saturday, 12:30-15:30, tel. 08652/60020). For 14
DM, you put on the traditional miners' outfits, get on
funny little trains, and zip deep into the mountain. For 90
minutes, you'll cruise subterranean lakes, slide speedily
down long slick wooden banisters, and learn how they
mined salt so long ago. Call for crowd avoidance advice.
You can buy a ticket early and browse through the town
until your tour time.

Hitler's famous (but overrated) "Eagle's Nest" towered
high above Berchtesgaden. Now Kehlstein and Obersalz-
berg are open to visitors, but little of Hitler's Alpine
retreat, which he visited only five times, remains. The
bus ride up the private road and the lift to the top cost
about 22 DM. If the weather's cloudy, as it often is in the
morning, you'll Nazi a thing. In that case, tour the salt
mine first.

Berchtesgaden caters to long-term German guests. Its
hardworking tourist center arranges lots of activities (rafting, rowing, shooting, cycling, folk evenings, concerts)
and is full of advice for walks and hikes in the neighborhood.

Hellbrunn Castle and Other Salzburg Sights
See tomorrow.

Austria (Österreich, the Kingdom of the East)
- 32,000 square miles (the size of South Carolina, or two Switzerlands).
- 7.6 million people (235 per square mile and holding, 85% Catholic).
- 1 AS = about US$.10; about 10 AS = US$1.

During the grand old Habsburg days, Austria was Europe's most powerful empire. Its royalty built a giant kingdom of more than 50 million people by making love, not war (having lots of children and marrying them into the other royal houses of Europe).

Today this small landlocked country does more to cling to its elegant past than any other in Europe (the waltz is still the rage). Austrians are very sociable; more so than anywhere else, it's important to greet people you pass on the streets or meet in shops. The Austrian's version of "Hi" is a cheerful *Grüss Gott* (may God greet you). You'll get the correct pronunciation after the first volley—listen and copy.

The Austrian schilling (S or AS) is divided into 100 groschen (g). Divide prices by ten and to get approximate costs in dollars (e.g., 420 AS is $42). About 6.9 AS = 1 DM (merchants and waiters near the border accept DM and usually give you a reasonable 6.8).

While they speak German, accept German currency (at least in Salzburg, Innsbruck, and Reutte), and talked about unity with Germany long before Hitler ever said "*Anschluss*," the Austrians cherish their distinct cultural and historical traditions. They are not Germans. Austria is mellow and relaxed compared to Deutschland. Gemütlichkeit is the local word for this special Austrian cozy-and-easy approach to life. It's good living—whether engulfed in mountain beauty or bathed in lavish high culture. The people stroll as if every day were Sunday, topping things off with a visit to a coffee or pastry shop.

It must be nice to be past your prime—no longer troubled by being powerful, able to kick back and be as happy as St. Francis's birds in the clean, untroubled mountain air. While the Austrians make less money than their neighbors, they enjoy a short work week and a long life span. Austria was a neutral country throughout the cold war. It is now free to get closer to Europe's economic community.

Austrians eat on about the same schedule we do. Treats include *Wiener Schnitzel* (breaded veal cutlet), *Knödel* (dumplings), *Apfelstrudel*, and fancy desserts. Don't miss the *Sachertorte*, a great chocolate cake from Vienna. White wines, *Heurigen* (new wine), and coffee are delicious and popular. Service is included in restaurant bills.

Shops are open from 8:00 to 17:00 or 18:00. Banks keep roughly the same hours but usually close for lunch.

Salzburg Orientation

With a well-preserved old town, gardens, churches, and lush surroundings, set under Europe's biggest intact medieval castle, and forever smiling to the tunes of Mozart and *The Sound of Music*, Salzburg knows how to be popular.

This city of 140,000 (Austria's fourth largest) is divided into old and new. The very touristy old town, sitting between the Salzach River and the 1,600-foot-high hill called Mönchsberg, holds all the charm. It's served by a fine bus system (18 AS single-ride tickets sold on the bus; 24-hour "Ticket 1" pass includes the lifts up to the castle and the Mönchsberg elevator and is sold at local Tabak shops).

The helpful tourist office (at the train station, on Mozartplatz in the old center, and on the freeway entrance to the city, tel. 847568 or 88987) is your essential first stop. When you arrive at the TI, get a room, confirm your plans, and have your questions answered. Ask for the "hotel plan" map, a list of sights, the "Youth in Salzburg" booklet, and a schedule of events. Try to book a concert or folk evening.

The American Express office (Mozartplatz 5, open Monday-Friday 9:00-17:30, Saturday 9:00-12:00, tel. 842501) will hold mail for their check or card users.

Salzburg's old town postal code is A-5020. Many phone numbers are changing. Usually the new number is the same as the old with an "8" at the beginning. Telephone code: 0662.

Salzburg

Sightseeing Highlights—Salzburg and Beyond

▲ **Hohensalzburg Fortress**—This castle, one of Europe's mightiest, dominates Salzburg's skyline. The interior is so-so unless you catch a tour. Unfortunately, the disorganized castle crew doesn't really know when or if there will be one in English. The basic entry fee (20 AS) gives you only the view and the courtyard. Buy the full castle, museum, and tour ticket (45 AS) and check at the castle tour office to see when an English tour may go. The museum has the noisiest floorboards in Europe. Even so the prince had a chastity belt. You can see it next to other gruesome torture devices that need no explanation.

Upstairs is a mediocre military museum offering a chance to see photos of nice looking young Nazi officers whose government convinced them that their operation was a just cause.

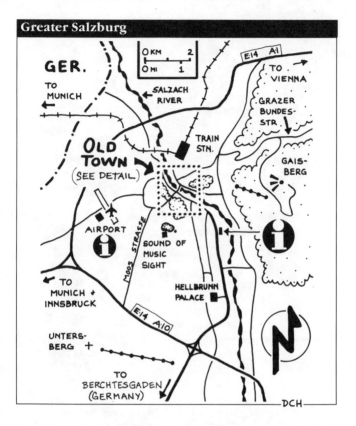

The funicular zips you effortlessly to the castle (27 AS round-trip, free with transit pass, rides leave constantly). The castle is open daily, 9:30 to 18:30, fewer hours in off-season.

▲ **City Walking Tour**—A great one-hour, 60 AS, guided walking tour of the old town leaves from the TI at Mozart-platz Monday through Saturday at 12:15 (May-October, tel. 847568).

For some walking on your own, be sure to browse through St. Peter's Cemetery (from the base of the castle lift, tours of early Christian catacombs) and through the open-air market on Universitätsplatz.

And for a most enjoyable approach to the castle, consider riding the elevator to the Café Winkler and walking 20 minutes through the woods high above the city to

Festung Hohensalzburg (stay on the high trails or you'll have a needless climb back up to the castle).

▲ **Sound of Music Tour**—I took this tour skeptically (as part of my research chores) and was very impressed. It includes a quick but good general city tour, hits all the S.O.M. spots (including the stately home and the wedding church), and shows you a lovely stretch of the Salzkammergut.

The Salzburg Panorama Tours Company charges 250 AS for the 4-hour, English-only tour, which leaves from Mirabellplatz daily at 9:00 and 14:00. Telephone 874029 for a reservation and a free hotel pickup if you like. (They give travelers with this book who buy their ticket at the Mirabellplatz ticket booth a 10% discount.) This is worthwhile for S.O.M. fans without a car or who won't otherwise be going into the Salzkammergut. Warning: You'll be rolling through the Austrian country with 30 Americans singing "Do, a Deer."

Panorama Tours' City and Country tour (#5, daily at 13:00, 5 hours, 480 AS, less 10% with this book) is also worth considering and often stops for the Sommerrodlebahn (luge) ride.

▲ **Salzburg Cathedral** (daily 8:00-17:00, free) is one of the great Renaissance and baroque buildings in northern Europe. Check out its 10,000-pipe organ. For a fee you can tour the excavation site under the church and the Dom Museum in the church.

▲ **Getreidegasse**—Old Salzburg's main drag, this very lively and colorful street, famous for its many old wrought iron signs, still looks much as it did in Mozart's day.

▲ **Mozart's Birthplace (Geburtshaus, 1756)**—Maybe it's just me, but I find the birthplaces of famous people are usually as dead as they are. But this is almost a pilgrimage, and if you're a fan, you'll have to check it out. It's right in the old town on colorful Getreidegasse, #9 (open daily 9:00-19:00, shorter hours off-season, 50 AS). His residence is next door. A combined ticket will save you a little money.

▲ **Carillon**—The bell tower on Mozartplatz chimes throughout the day. The man behind the bells gives fascinating 20-minute tours daily at 10:45 and 17:45 except

in bad weather. You'll actually be up on top among 35 bells
as the big barrel turns, the music flies, and you learn what
a "dingbat" is. Buy your 20 AS ticket 10 minutes early.

Mirabell Gardens and Palace (*Schloss*)—The bubbly
gardens are always open and free, but to really enjoy the
lavish palace, try to get a ticket to a *Schlosskonzerte* in the
Mirabell Palace. Baroque music contained in a baroque
hall is a happy bird in the right cage. Tickets are around
250 AS (students, half price) and rarely sold out (tel.
872788).

▲ **Hellbrunn Castle**—The real attraction here is a garden full of clever trick fountains and the sadistic joy the
tour guide gets by soaking the tourists in his group. The
archbishop's seventeenth-century palace is hardly worth
a look. His garden, one of the oldest baroque ones in
Europe, is pretty enough, but bring a raincoat and dive
into the bubbly fountain tour (open 9:00-18:00 daily,
fewer hours off-season, tel. 841696, 50 AS for the
40-minute tour and admission, 3 miles south of Salzburg
just off the road as you enter, or bus 55 from downtown).
The restored "I Am 16, Going on 17" gazebo is now sta-
tioned at Hellbrunn.

▲▲ **Salzburg Festival**—Each summer from late July to
the end of August, Salzburg hosts its famous Salzburger
Festspiele, founded in 1920 by composer Richard Strauss.
This fun and festive time is very crowded, but except for
a few days, there are plenty of beds and some tickets
available the day of the concert. Salzburg is busy with
concerts in its palaces and churches year-round. If you
want music, this is the place to come. Regardless of when
you visit, you'll be able to get tickets to one of the 1,600
cultural performances Salzburg hosts every year (ticket
office on Mozartplatz; contact the Austrian National Tourist Office in the U.S.A. for specifics on this year's festival
schedule and tickets).

▲▲ **Tiroler Folk Evenings** are literally a kick in the
pants. Salzburg usually offers three a week (for about 160
AS, usually at the Steiglkeller and up in the Fortress).
Check the schedule upon arrival.

Sleeping in Salzburg

Finding a room in Salzburg, even during the Music Festival, when several college dorms open for visitors, is usually easy. The tourist offices have a pamphlet listing all the pensions, hostels, and private rooms in town. Or, for a couple of dollars, they'll find you an inexpensive bed in a private home in the area of your choice. If you want dorm-style budget alternatives, ask for their extensive list. There are about 10 youth hostels and student dorms. English is spoken at all my listings.

Your big decision in Salzburg is, pay more and deal with parking problems in the atmospheric old town, or trade character for simplicity and bus in from a room on the edge of town.

Rooms on Linzergasse: The first three listings are on Linzergasse, directly across the bridge from Mozart-ville and an easy 10-minute walk from the station. Its bustling crowds of shoppers overwhelm the few shy cars that venture on to it. Parking is a problem, but there are free streets a 10-minute walk away from the river or expensive garages.

Institute St. Sebastian (130 AS dorm beds and 360 AS doubles, breakfast is extra if served, guests with sheets save 20 AS, Linzergasse 41, enter through arch at #37, tel. 0662/871386 or 882606) is a friendly, clean, historic convent. Mozart's mom is buried in the courtyard, and they usually have rooms available.

Hotel zum Jungen Fuchs (350 AS doubles, across from Institute St. Sebastian at Linzergasse 54, tel. 0662/875496) is wonderfully located in a funky, dumpy old building, very plain but clean, with an elderly management, serves no breakfast, and charges extra for showers.

Gasthaus Ganslhof (700-800 AS doubles, Vogelweiderstr. 6, a 10-minute walk up Linzergasse from the old town, tel. 0662/873853) is clean, reasonable, central, and comfortable, with Motel 6 ambience and a parking lot.

Gasthof Jahn (550-700 AS doubles, Elisabethstr. 31, tel. 0662/871405) is a plain and decent place on the third floor, no elevator, about a 5-minute walk from the station.

Gasthaus "Zur Goldenen Ente" (1,200 AS doubles, Goldgasse 10 in the old center, tel. 0662/845622) is a great splurge if you like to sleep in a 600-year-old building above a fine restaurant as central as you can be on a pedestrian street in old Salzburg. Somehow the modern and comfortable rooms fit into this building's medieval-style stone arches and narrow stairs. The breakfast is huge, they give a parking permit for the old town (*Steifgasse*), and hold a room if you leave your credit card number. For dinner, try their roast *Ente* (duck).

Hotel-Restaurant Elefant (1100-1500 AS, Sigmund-Haffner-Gasse 4, tel. 0662/843397, fax 632725) has been an inn for 400 years but only recently added the sliding glass doors, hair dryers, and minibars. Like the Goldenen Ente, it is on a central pedestrian street in the old town and has a fine restaurant.

Naturfreundehaus (100 AS per person in four-bed dorm, 45 AS breakfast, 70 AS dinner with city view, Mönchsberg 19, two minutes from the top of the 20 AS round-trip Mönchsberg elevator, tel. 0662/841729, 23:00 curfew, open May-October) is a local version of a mountaineer's hut. It's a great budget alternative guarded by the chirping birds and snuggled in the remains of a fifteenth-century castle wall overlooking Salzburg with a magnificent old town and mountain view. From the town, it's the stone house to the left of the glass Cafe Winkler.

Salzburg has about 60 homes renting out rooms for around 200 AS per person. These are generally roomy, modern, very comfortable, and come with a good breakfast. Many charge extra for those only staying one or two nights. Most are a bus ride from town, but with the cheap 24-hour pass and the frequent service, this shouldn't keep you away. Many places will pick you up at the station. Moosstrasse, south of Mönchsberg, is lined with Zimmer. Those farther out are farmhouses. From the station, catch bus 1 and change after you cross the river to bus 60. From the old town, it's bus 60.

Helga Bankhammer (400 AS doubles, Moosstr. 77, tel. 0662/830067) rents five rooms, two in her house and three in the old barn (quite elegant for a barn), where you'll get very fresh milk in the rustic breakfast room. Many of its guests are American students attending the school across the street, or their relatives.

Maria Gassner (400-500 AS doubles, Moosstr. 126-B, tel. 0662/824990) rents five clean, comfortable rooms in her modern house. She can often pick you up at the station.

Gästehaus Blobergerhof (400-500 AS doubles, Hammerauerstr. 4, Querstrasse zur Moosstrasse, 5020 Salzburg, tel. 0662/830227) is a large and pleasant farmhouse run by Inge Keuschnigg.

Frau Kernstock (500 AS doubles, Karolingerstr. 29, 5020 Salzburg-Maxglan, buses 27 and 77, tel. 0662/827469) works hard to keep her many American guests happily singing "The Lonely Goatherd." She's listed in all the guidebooks. The neighboring Gasthof Kuglhof serves up reasonable, delicious Austrian specialties.

Eating in Salzburg
Salzburg boasts many fun and atmospheric places to eat. My favorites are the big cellars with their smoky Old World atmosphere, heavy old arches, time-darkened paintings, many antlers, and hearty inexpensive meals. The town is touristy, and these places are famous with visitors but also enjoyed by the locals.

Gasthaus "Zum Wilder Mann" (enter from Getreidegasse 20 or Griesgasse 17, tel. 0662/841787, food served 11:00-21:00) is the place if you're in the mood for Hofbräu atmosphere in one small well-antlered room and a hearty cheap meal 2 minutes from Mozart's place. For a quick 100 AS lunch, get the Bauernschmaus, a mountain of dumpling, kraut, and peasant's meats. Share a table, and wish your neighbors *Guten Appetit*.

Sternbräu (Griesegasse 23, also two minutes from Mozart's place, serving until midnight) is a huge, atmospheric institution of a restaurant with several rustic rooms and outdoor garden seating offering another fine, inexpensive way to get really schnitzeled.

Krimplestätter (Müllner Hauptstr. 31, 10 minutes north of the old town near the river) employs 500 years of experience serving authentic old Austrian food in its authentic old Austrian interior or in its cheery garden. For fine food with a wild finale, eat here and drink at the nearby Augustiner Bräustübl.

Augustiner Bräustübl (Augustinergasse 4, walk through the Mirabellgarten, over the Müllnersteg bridge and ask for "Müllnerbräu," its local nickname, 1,000 seats, open daily 15:00-23:00). This monk-run brewery is so rustic and crude that I hesitate to show my true colors by recommending it, but I must. It's like a Munich beer hall with no music but the volume turned up, a historic setting with beer-sloshed smoke-stained halls, and a pleasant outdoor beer garden serving another fine monastic brew. Local students mix with tourists eating hearty slabs of schnitzel with their fingers or cold meals from the picnic counter. It'll bring out the barbarian in you. For dessert, enjoy the incomparable floodlit view of old Salzburg from the nearby pedestrian bridge.

Stiftskeller St. Peter (next to St. Peter's church at the foot of Mönchsberg) is classier, more central and expensive, and your best splurge for traditional Austrian cuisine in medieval sauce.

Café Haydn Stube (1 Mirabellplatz at the entry to the Aicherpassage, Monday-Friday 9:30-20:00), run by the local music school, is cheap and very popular with students. The **Mensa Aicherpassage**, in the basement, serves even cheaper meals Monday through Friday 11:30 to 14:00.

Classy Salzburg delis, especially on Linzergasse, serve great, cheap sit-down lunches on weekdays. Have them make you a sandwich or something hot, sneak in a carrot, a piece of fruit and yogurt, and sit at a small table with the local lunch crowd. Try **Frauenberger** across from 16 Linzergasse.

SALZBURG AND THE SALZKAMMERGUT

You can wonder what the town would be like today if Wolfgang Mozart and Julie Andrews worked elsewhere as you sift through the crowds and enjoy the sights of Salzburg. Spend the afternoon in *Sound of Music* country—the Salzkammergut Lake District—settling down in the postcard-pretty fjord-cuddling town of Hallstatt.

Suggested Schedule

8:30	Good morning Salzburg hike from Cafe Winkler to castle, tour Hohensalzburg.
10:45	Visit the Glockenspiel as it performs or tour the festival houses.
14:00	Drive into the Lake District.
Afternoon and evening	Free in Hallstatt (Eurailers will stay in Salzburg and take 14:00 Sound of Music Tour for a look at the lakes).
Sleep	Hallstatt.

Transportation: Salzburg to Hallstatt (50 miles)
Everything in Salzburg today can be done on foot. When you're ready to depart, leave Salzburg on the Grazer Bundesstrasse (up Linzer Bundesstrasse, over the tracks, right on Minnesheimstrasse, and wind out of town following signs to Gaisberg, Fuschlsee, St. Gilgen, Salzkammergut, and Graz). A detour up the Gaisberg takes you to a 3,800-foot summit and a good view. Soon the "hills are alive," and you're surrounded by the loveliness that has turned on everyone from Emperor Franz Josef to Julie Andrews. To us English-speakers, this is the *Sound of Music* country (alias the Salzkammergut Lake District).

The road to Hallstatt leads first past Fuschlsee (mediocre Sommerrodlebahn summer luge ride, 28 AS, open when dry 10:00-17:00, at Fuschl an See), to St. Gilgen (pleasant but touristy), to Bad Ischl (the center of the Salzkammergut with a spa, salt mine tour, casino, the emperor's villa if you need a Habsburg history fix, and a

good tourist office, tel. 06132/3520), and along Hallstat-
tersee to Hallstatt.

   Hallstatt is basically traffic-free. Park in the middle of
the tunnel; you'll see a P-1 sign and a waterfall. If this is
full, the lakeside lot (P-2) just after the tunnel should have
a place. If you're traveling off-season and staying downtown, you can drive in and park by the boat dock (your
"guest card" makes you a temporary resident, giving you
permission). The town is a pleasant 5-minute lakeside
walk from the end of the tunnel.

   While the Salzkammergut is well served by trains and
buses, Eurailers in a hurry can see it from the window of
the Sound of Music bus tour (described in Day 7), spend
the night in Salzburg again, and take the early train
toward Vienna. If you do take the train into the Salzkammergut, the ride to Hallstatt is gorgeous. *Stefanie* (a boat)
meets you at the station and glides across the lake into
town (15 AS, with each train). From Hallstatt, the Vienna-
bound trains get you to Melk on the Danube in 4 hours
with one change.

Sightseeing Highlights in Salzburg area (see Day 7)
▲ Bad Dürrnberg Salzbergwerke—This salt mine
above the town of Hallein, 8 miles from Salzburg, gives
the best tours in the region, but as in the other salt mines,
90-minute tours are in German only. English-speakers get
information sheets or headphones but none of the jokes.
Still, it's a fun experience—wearing white overalls, sliding down the sleek wooden chutes, and crossing underground from Austria into Germany (daily 9:00-17:00, bus
and train connections from Salzburg).
▲▲ Salzkammergut—This is Austria's "commune with
nature" country. Idyllic, majestic, but not rugged, it's a
gentle land of lakes, forested mountains, storybook villages, endless hiking opportunities, and plenty of inexpensive rooms in private homes and cheap youth hostels.
While you could easily stay in a Zimmer here and make
this area the focus of your trip, you are just sneaking it in
quickly, content to get in a representative taste and a very
pleasant and restful evening.

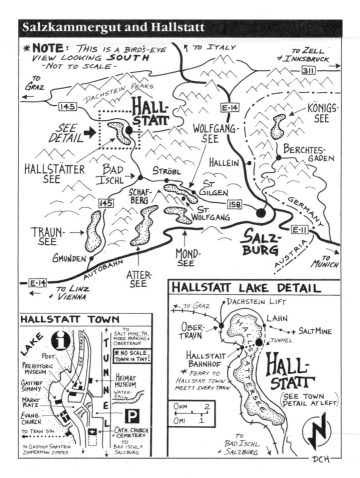

Salzkammergut and Hallstatt

NOTE: THIS IS A BIRD'S-EYE VIEW LOOKING **SOUTH** –NOT TO SCALE–

TO ITALY · TO ZELL & INNSBRUCK · 311 · TO GRAZ · DACHSTEIN PEAKS · HALL-STATT · E·14 · KÖNIGS-SEE · WOLFGANG-SEE · SEE DETAIL · HALLSTÄTTER SEE · BAD ISCHL · STRÖBL · HALLEIN · BERCHTES-GADEN · SCHAFBERG · ST. GILGEN · 158 · GERMANY · 145 · ST. WOLFGANG · TRAUN-SEE · E·11 · SALZ-BURG · AUSTRIA · GMUNDEN · AUTOBAHN · MOND-SEE · TO MUNICH · E·14 · TO LINZ & VIENNA · ATTER-SEE

HALLSTATT TOWN

LAKE · SEE STRASSE · POST · PREHISTORIC MUSEUM · GASTHOF SIMONY · MARKT PLATZ · EVANG. CHURCH · TO TRAIN STN. · TO GASTHOF SARSTEIN ZIMMERMAN ZIMMER · TUNNEL · TO SALT MINE, YH, MORE PARKING, OBERTRAUN · *NO SCALE* TOWN IS TINY! · HEIMAT MUSEUM · WATER-FALL · P · CATH. CHURCH + CEMETERY · TO BAD ISCHL + SALZBURG

HALLSTATT LAKE DETAIL

TO GRAZ · DACHSTEIN LIFT · OBER-TRAUN · LAHN · SALT MINE · TUNNEL · HALLSTATT BAHNHOF · *FERRY TO HALLSTATT TOWN MEETS EVERY TRAIN* · HALLSTÄTTERSEE · HALL-STATT (SEE TOWN DETAIL AT LEFT) · 0 KM 2 · 0 MI 1 · TO BAD ISCHL & SALZBURG

DCH

▲▲▲ **Hallstatt**—Your target is Hallstatt, a town whose photograph always draws desirous gasps when I show it to my travel classes. You'll love Hallstatt, a tiny town bullied onto a ledge between a selfish mountain and a sleepy lake with a waterfall ripping furiously through its middle. It can be toured on foot in about 10 minutes. The TI (tel. 06134/208, open daily) can find you a room.

The town is one of Europe's oldest, going back centuries before Christ. The humble Prehistory Museum adjacent to the TI is interesting since little Hallstatt was the Vienna of this part of prehistoric Europe. Three thousand years ago, Celtic tribes dug for precious salt, and there have been many interesting finds from what archaeologists all over the world call the Hallstatt Period. Your Prehistory Museum ticket gets you into the Heimat (Folk Culture) Museum around the corner (30 AS), cute and barely worth the trouble.

From the boat dock, hike up the covered old stairway to the church cemetery. The town is so old that bones get only 12 peaceful buried years before making way for the freshly dead. The result is a fascinating chapel of bones. Each skull is lovingly named, dated, and often decorated.

The Hallstatt salt mine tour is fun but time consuming, and the lift is about 200 AS. You'll ride a frighteningly steep funicular high above the town, take a short hike, do the same old miners' clothes and underground train routine as at Hallein and Berchtesgaden, and listen to an English tape-recorded tour while your guide speaks German. The well-publicized ancient Celtic graveyard excavation sites are really dead.

The charm of Hallstatt is the village and lakeside setting. Go there to relax, eat, walk, and paddle. Note: In August, tourist crowds trample much of Hallstatt's charm.

Mountain lovers, hikers, and spelunkers can keep busy for days using Hallstatt as their home base. Get information from the TI on the various caves with their ice formations, the thunderous rivers, mountain lifts, and nearby walks. For a tough but rewarding all-day hike, ask the TI about taking trail 613 to Hintergausausee and then a bus back to Hallstatt. Telephone code: 06134.

Sleeping in Hallstatt

The TI can almost always find you a room. Only August—especially the first two weeks—is bad. There are plenty of 150 AS per night Zimmer. Some charge much more for stays less than three nights.

Gasthof Simony (450-700 AS doubles, 4830 Hallstatt, tel. 06134/231) is my stocking-feet-tidy favorite, right on the square with a lake view, balconies, creaky wood floors, slip-slidey rag rugs, antique furniture, and a huge breakfast. Call Susan Scheutz for a reservation.

Pension Sarstein (200 AS per person with breakfast,

Gosaumühlstr. 83, tel. 06134/217) is a modern building, a few minutes walk along the lake from the center, with a view, run by friendly Frau Fisher. Her sister, Frau Zimmermann (170 AS per person B&B, Gosaumühlstr. 69, tel. 06134/309), runs a small Zimmer in a 500-year-old house with low beams, time-polished wood, and fine lake views just down the street. These elderly ladies speak almost no English, but you'll find yourself caught up in their charm and laughing together like old friends.

Gasthaus Zauner (700-800 AS doubles, Marktplatz 51, tel. 06134/246) is a business machine offering more normal hotel rooms on the main square with a good restaurant specializing in grilled food.

The **Gasthaus Mühle Naturfreunde-Herberge** (155 AS per bed in small rooms or 115 AS in 20-bed coed dorm with breakfast, cheaper if you BYO hostel sheet, run by Ferdinand, Kirchenweg 36 just below the tunnel car park, tel. 06134/318) is a good value with 3- to 6-bed rooms and hearty food. Ferdinand also runs a pizzeria in the Gasthaus providing the cheapest dinners in town. Closed in November. ("Nature's friends houses" are found throughout the Alps. Like mountaineers' huts, they're a good, fun, and basic bargain.)

The **youth hostel** (very cheap, Salzbergstr. just below the salt mine lift, five minutes past the tunnel, tel. 06134/279) is clean, without character, and open mid-May through mid-September.

The nearby village of Obertraun is a peaceful alternative to Hallstatt in August. You'll find plenty of Zimmer and a luxurious youth hostel (tel. 06131/360).

Itinerary Options
Eurailers should consider two nights in a row in Salzburg, taking the Sound of Music bus tour for a look at the Lake District. But if you're feeling good and energetic, try to spend the night in Hallstatt. If you prefer rivers to lakes and have had enough of Salzburg by noon, hit the road for the Danube River valley and spend the night in Melk in an entirely different, more Eastern-feeling world on a river that could float you all the way to Russia.

DAY 9
HALLSTATT TO VIENNA

Today, assuming you don't decide to junk the itinerary and stay in Hallstatt, you'll head to this tour's easternmost point. Travel as quickly as possible to the Danube River, where you'll tour the powerful Mauthausen concentration camp and explore the romantically ruined castles, vineyards, glorious abbeys, and scenery of the Danube River valley. By dinner time, you'll be checked into your hotel and ready to experience Paris's eastern rival, the Habsburg capital—Vienna.

Suggested Schedule

8:00	Hallstatt (or Salzburg) early departure.
10:00	Tour Mauthausen concentration camp.
12:00	Danube Valley on autobahn to Melk. Picnic and tour at the abbey, drive, bike, or cruise to Krems and into Wien.
17:00	Arrive in Wien, visit tourist information office.
18:00	Check into your hotel.
19:00	Stroll through center with *A to Z* book. Dinner near Am Hof (maybe at Esterhazy Keller), late wine at Brezel-Gwölb.

Transportation: Hallstatt to Vienna (210 miles)
Forget easygoing Austria—today is very demanding (unless you can splice in an extra day, which Hallstatt and the Wachau Valley could easily gobble up). Drivers will want the earliest start from Hallstatt. Follow scenic route 145 through Gmunden to the autobahn and head east. Just after Linz, take the St. Valentine exit and follow the Mauthausen signs (8 km) to the concentration camp. Cross the Donau (Danube, hum "dut duh da da, dee dee, doo doo"), go through Mauthausen town, and follow signs to Ehemaliges KZ-lager. From Mauthausen, the speedy route is the autobahn to Melk, but the curvy, scenic route 3 along the river is worth the nausea.

This region, from Persenbeug to Melk, is Nibelungen-

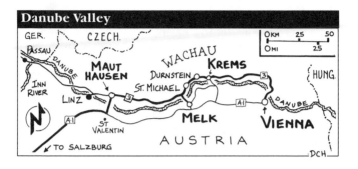

Danube Valley

gau, the fourth- and fifth-century home of the legendary
Nibelung tribe, dramatized in Wagner's opera. Next stop:
Melk's great abbey. Cross the bridge and follow the signs
not into town but to the *Benediktinerstift* (Benedictine
abbey).

The most scenic stretch of the Donau is the Wachau
Valley lying between Melk and Krems. From Melk (the TI
can give you a Vienna map if you don't already have one),
cross the river again and stay on route 3. After Krems, it
hits the autobahn (A22), and you'll speed right into
Vienna's traffic.

Navigating in Vienna, as in any big European city, is a
mess. Study the map and see the series of *Ringstrasse*
looping out from the Donau. As you approach the city,
you'll cross the North Bridge and land right on the *Gürtel*, or outer ring. Circle around on this thoroughfare until
you reach the "spoke" street you need. Treat the inner
Ringstrasse the same way.

Train travelers should skip Mauthausen (Dachau, outside of Munich, has much easier public access) and take
the train straight to Melk where you can tour the abbey
and picnic on the scenic Melk-to-Krems Danube River
cruise. Boats (free with Eurailpass) leave Melk at 10:00,
14:00, 14:30, and 15:30 (May-September). Call the DDSG
boat company's office, 0732/771090 in Linz or 0222/
21750-0 in Vienna, or the Melk TI at 02752/2307-0 to
confirm these times. It's a 2-hour ride (220 AS) to the
attractive town of Krems where you can connect with an
hourly 60-minute train ride into Vienna (it's a 15-minute

walk from the Krems boat dock to the train station). The
14:30 boat goes all the way to Vienna, arriving at 20:00.

If you take the train directly into Vienna (3 hours from
Salzburg), you can easily do the Wachau train/boat excursion as a day trip later on. Remember, the 6-knot flow of
the Donau makes downstream (eastbound) trips about a
third faster.

Sightseeing Highlights—Danube Valley
▲▲▲ Mauthausen Concentration Camp—More
powerful and less American-oriented than Dachau, this
slave labor and death camp functioned from 1938 to 1945
"for the exploitation and extermination of Hitler's oppo-
nents." Over half of its 206,000 quarry-working
prisoners were killed here. Set in a strangely beautiful setting next to the Danube and a now still and overgrown
quarry, Mauthausen is open daily from 8:00 to 18:00 (last
entry at 17:00, closes from mid-December through January and at 16:00 off-season). The camp barracks house a
museum (some English labels, but it helps to pick up the
English guidebook for a complete translation) and a
graphic 45-minute movie (top of each hour, ask for an
English showing—assemble a group if you need to). Go
downstairs for the most emotionally moving rooms and
the gas chamber. The ghosts of the victims of these hor-
rors can still be felt. Outside the camp each victim's country has erected a gripping memorial. Many yellowed
photos sport fresh flowers. Walk to the barbed wire
memorial overlooking the quarry. By visiting a concentration camp and putting ourselves through this emo-
tional wringer, we are heeding and respecting the fervent
wish of the victims of this fascism—that we "never forget." Too many people forget by choosing not to know.
▲ Melk—Sleepy and elegant under its huge abbey that
seems to police the Danube, the town of Melk offers a
pleasant stop before the bustle of Vienna. The helpful TI
on the traffic-free main square has lots of ideas for sightseeing in the area (nearby castle, bike rides along the
river, etc.). Melk is on the main Salzburg to Vienna train

line, on the same autobahn, and is the starting point for the Wachau (Danube) Valley bike or boat trip. Melk TI tel. 02752/2307.

Melk makes a fine overnight stop. **Hotel Fürst** (500 AS doubles with breakfast and shower, Rathausplatz 3-5, A-3390 Melk, tel. 02752/2343) is a fluffy, creaky old place with 15 rooms, run by the Madar family, right on the traffic-free main square with a fountain out your door and the abbey hovering overhead. **Gasthof Goldener Stern** (400 AS doubles with breakfast and showers down the hall, Sterngasse 17, A-3390, Melk, tel. 02752/2214) is traditional and also very quiet on a pedestrian street in the center. . . but less cozy and almost too clean. **Gasthof Baumgartner** (300 AS, across from the station, tel. 02752/2419) is pretty dumpy but cheap. The modern **youth hostel** (tel. 02752/2681) is a few minutes walk from the station.

▲▲ **Melk Abbey (Benediktinerstift)**—The newly restored abbey beaming proudly over the Danube Valley is one of Europe's great sights. Freshly painted and gilded throughout, it's a baroque dream, a lily alone. To see its lavish library, church, palace rooms, and the great Danube view from the abbey balcony, you must take a tour. German ones are available constantly, English tours only with groups of 20 or more (open daily 9:00-18:00; call 02752/2312 to find out when the next English group is scheduled—normally at 11:30, other times haphazardly). The abbey garden, café, and cute village below make waiting for a tour pleasant.

▲▲ **Wachau (Danube) Valley**—By car, bike, or boat, the 30-kilometer stretch of the Danube between Melk and Krems is as pretty as they come. Drive or pedal along the north bank following the TI's "Cycle Track" brochure. You can rent bikes cheaply at the boat dock. It's about a 2-hour pedal to Krems where you can drop the bike. The boat (free with Eurail, 220 AS otherwise) goes 4 times daily in season (see Transportation, above). You can go half and half by trading in the boat for a bike at the Spitz stop.

Art buffs will recognize the town of Willendorf where the oldest piece of European art was found. A few blocks off the river (follow the signs to Venus) you can see the monument where the well-endowed, 30,000-year-old fertility symbol, the Venus of Willendorf, was discovered.

There are good wine gardens, with tasting, all along the river. St. Michael has a small wine garden and an old tower you can climb for a view.

Durnstein is a touristic flypaper luring hordes of visitors with its traffic-free quaintness and its one claim to fame (and fortune): Richard the Lion-Hearted was imprisoned here in 1193. You can probably sleep in his bedroom.

Krems is a great little gem of a town. From the boat dock walk a few blocks to the TI (pick up a town map and a Vienna map if you don't have one). Then walk into the traffic-free, shopper's wonderland old town. If nothing else, it's a very pleasant stroll to the station, where there are hourly one-hour trains into Vienna (to the Franz Josef Bahnhof). The local TI (open daily 9:00-18:00, tel. 02732/82676) can find you a cheap bed in a private home (180 AS B&B) if you decide to side-trip into the big city from this very small town alternative.

Vienna
See tomorrow.

DAY 10
VIENNA

Vienna is a head without a body. Built to rule the once-grand Habsburg Empire—Europe's largest—she started and lost World War I, and with it, her far-flung holdings. Today, you'll find a grand capital of 1.7 million people (20% of Austria's population) ruling a relatively small and insignificant country. Culturally, historically, and from a sightseeing point of view, this city is the sum of its illustrious past. The city of Freud, Maria Theresa, Kafka, Brahms, a gaggle of Strausses, and a dynasty of Holy Roman emperors is right up there with Paris, London, and Rome. Last night you got oriented. Today, attack.

Suggested Schedule

9:00	Ride tram #1 or #2 360 degrees around the Ringstrasse, get off at City Hall and walk through Hofburg Gardens to the Opera (check Opera House tour schedule).
10:30	Catch the "Getting Acquainted" city orientation tour.
12:00	Naschmarkt, stroll, buy picnic, eat in Burggarten with Mozart.
13:30	Neuburg museums and Hofburg.
15:00	Kunsthistorisches Museum.
17:00	Tram to the Kursalon in the Stadtpark. Concert behind Kursalon until 18:00.
19:00	Classical music or evening at the Prater amusement park or in old town.

Vienna Orientation

Vienna (Wien), one of Europe's great capitals, is so big, busy, and culturally complex that a little chaos would be understandable. Even though administrative districts of the city are called *Bezirke*, the place is very orderly and has gone to great lengths to make life easy—if not cheap—for its visitors.

The city map is like a target. The bull's-eye is the cathe-

Greater Vienna

dral, the first circle is the *Ring* and the second is the *Gürtel*. The old town snuggles around towering St. Stephan's cathedral south of the Donau, bound tightly by the Ringstrasse. The Ring marks what was the city wall and this circles the first Bezirk. The Gürtel is a broader ring road containing the rest of downtown, Bezirke 2 through 9. Addresses start with the Bezirk followed by street and street number. Any address higher than the 9th Bezirk is far from the center. The middle two digits of Vienna postal codes show the district, or Bezirk. The address "7, Lindengasse 4" means in the seventh district, #4 on Linden Street. Its postal code would be 1070. Nearly all your sightseeing will be done in the core first district or along the inner Ringstrasse. As a tourist, concern yourself only with this small old center and the city suddenly becomes manageable.

Vienna's tourist offices, located in each train station, at the freeway entrances, and behind the Opera House at

Kärntnerstrasse 38 (open daily 9:00-19:00, or later in the stations, tel. 0222/513 8892 or 211140) are often crowded but are excellent. They find rooms (35 AS per reservation) and provide visitors with pamphlets on whatever they need. Stop by here first with a list of needs and questions, to confirm your sightseeing plans, and to pick up the free city map (with a small guidebook's worth of local infor-mation including transit deals and emergency numbers); the museum brochure (listing hours, prices, telephone numbers, and handicap accessibility); walking tour schedule; the monthly program of concerts, walks, and other events; the very helpful *Youth Scene* magazine; and the essential *Vienna from A to Z* book (30 AS). This book is all you need to see the town. Every important building has a flag banner with a number on it that keys into this guidebook. Every city should spoil its visitors like this. Use *A to Z* in conjunction with the city map since the key numbers are used in both. If you're lost in the city, find one of the "famous building flags" and match the num-ber to your map. If you're at a "famous building" check the map to see if any other key numbers are nearby, then check the *A to Z* book to see if you want to drop by.

Special budget tip: Those with a MasterCard credit card get free entry to most of Vienna's museums and sights (saving 15-45 AS per stop) at least through September 1992. The tourist office has a special flyer with specifics.

Vienna has a fine transit system of buses, trams, and sleek easy subways. To simplify the complicated fare sys-tem (even though it may not pay for itself), buy the 24-hour (45 AS) or 72-hour (115 AS) subway/bus/tram pass at any Tabak shop. I use it mostly to zip along the Ring (tram 1 or 2). A transit map (15 AS) is available at tran-sit ticket windows. Without a pass, blocks of four tickets for 60 AS are cheaper than 20 AS individual tickets. Eight-day, 235 AS transit passes can be shared (for instance, four people for two days each). Vienna's comfortable, honest, and easy to flag down taxis start at 22 AS and mount quickly; you'll pay about 60 AS for a 5-minute ride.

Don't drive in Vienna. Ask at your hotel where to park your car and leave it there. Blue lines mean limited parking. Many streets allow unlimited parking. Several people told me that out-of-country cars can ignore parking tickets. Parking garages abound (around 200 AS per day).

Vienna has two main train stations: Westbahnhof serving most of Europe; and Südbahnhof serving Italy, Yugoslavia, and Greece. Tram 58 connects the Westbahnhof with the center, tram D takes you from the Südbahnhof downtown, and tram 18 connects the two stations. Trains to Krems and the Wachau Valley leave from a third station, the Franz Josef Bahnhof. For train information, call 1717.

Vienna is slowly expanding its telephone system. A digit will be inserted in the second place. If a number is wrong, dial 16 for assistance. Also, Vienna's phones let you dial right through to the extension; numbers with a dash should be dialed straight through. Tel. code: 0222 (from inside Austria) and 1 (from outside Austria).

Sightseeing Highlights—Vienna

▲ **Ringstrasse**—In the 1860s, Emperor Franz Josef had the city's ingrown medieval wall torn down and replaced with a grand boulevard 190 feet wide arcing nearly 3 miles around the city's core. One of Europe's great streets, it's lined with diverse, interesting, and often tasteless architecture. Trams 1 and 2 circle the whole route and so should you.

▲ **St. Stephan's Cathedral**—Stephansdom is the Gothic needle that the whole city spins around. With hundreds of years of history carved in its walls and buried in its crypt (open 10:00-11:30, 14:00-16:30, tel. 515 52 563), this is a fascinating starting point for a city walk. Tours of the church are in German only, the 50-minute daily mass is impressive (times listed near the entry), and the crowded lift to the north tower (daily 9:00-17:30) shows you a big bell but a bad view. A great view is only 343 tightly wound steps away, up the spiral staircase to the watchman's lookout (south tower, open daily 9:00-17:00), 246 feet above the postcard stand. From the top, orient yourself in the town, using your *Vienna from A to Z* to locate the famous sights. The church is nearly always open.

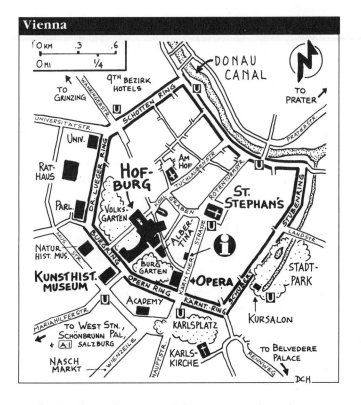

The Stephansplatz around the square and nearby
Graben (ditch) Street are colorful and lively with top-
notch street entertainment and an exotic plague monument. Lazy ones can ride the elevator to the top floor of
the glitzy Haas Haus shopping tower across from the
cathedral for a cafe with a capital view.

The cathedral museum (Dom und Diözesan Museum,
open 10:00-16:00, Thursday until 18:00, Sunday until
13:00, closed Monday) is at Stephansplatz 6.

Visiting the remains of the Habsburgs—This is not
as easy as you might imagine. These original organ
donors left their bodies in the Kaisergruft (Capuchin
Crypt, Neuer Markt), their hearts in St. George Chapel in
the church of the Augustinian friars (in the Hofburg,
Augustinerstr. 3, Monday, Tuesday, and Thursday
8:00-9:30, Wednesday 8:00-8:45, Friday 8:00-8:45,

10:00-12:00), and their entrails in the crypt below the cathedral. Don't chase down all these body parts; the magnificence of this city is the real remains of the Habsburgs. Pan up, watch the clouds glide by the ornate gables of Vienna.

▲▲ **Hofburg**—The complex, confusing, imposing Imperial Palace demands your attention. It was the home of the Habsburg rulers until 1918 and is still the home of the Spanish Riding School, the Vienna Boys' Choir, the Austrian president's office, and several important museums. Your *A to Z* sorts out this time-blackened, jewel-stained mess nicely. While you could lose yourself in its myriad halls and courtyards, I suggest that you focus on three things, after a strolling overview:

▲▲ **The Imperial Apartments**—These lavish Versailles-type rooms are the ultimate in "wish I were God" royal interiors (open Monday-Saturday 8:30-16:00, Sunday 8:30-12:30, entrance from courtyard under the dome of St. Michael's Gate, Michaelerplatz, tel. 587 555 4515). Tours are required and technically in German only. Be sure that every eager wide-eyed English-speaker in your group politely lets your guide know you're dying to hear some English. This is a small downtown version of the even grander Schönbrunn Palace. If you're rushed, skip one or the other.

▲▲ **Treasury**—The Weltliche and Geistliche Schatz-kammer (secular and religious treasure room) is one of the world's great collections of historical jewels. Don't miss the 1,000-year-old crown of the Holy Roman Emperor. (10:00-16:00, closed Tuesday.)

▲ **The Neuburg**, or new palace, is the last (from this century) and most impressive addition to the palace, newly opened to visitors. Its grand facade arches around Heldenplatz. Check it out quickly, not only to see its fine collection of weapons, musical instruments, and classical statuary from ancient Ephesus but also to just wander among those royal Habsburg halls, stairways, and painted ceilings. (10:00-16:00, closed Tuesday.)

▲▲ **Opera**—The Staatsoper facing the Ring, just up from Stephansdom and next to the TI, is a central point for any visitor. While the critical reception of the building 120 years ago led the architect to commit suicide, and it's been rebuilt since the World War II bombings, it's a dazzling place. Even though you probably saw it in the film *Amadeus*, it deserves a firsthand look. (Tours only, daily in English, July and August at 10:00, 11:00, 13:00, 14:00, and 15:00; other months, afternoons only; 30 AS. Tours are often canceled for rehearsals and shows, so check the posted schedule or call 51444 2613.)

The Vienna State Opera, with the Vienna Philharmonic Orchestra in the pit, is one of the world's top opera houses. There are performances almost nightly, except in July and August, with shows normally sold out. If you really want to see a performance and it's sold out, try for one of 500 *Stehplatz* (standing room spots). Join the Stehplatz line-up at the Abendkasse side door where the number of places available is posted. The ticket window opens an hour before each performance. Buy your place at the padded leaning rail. If your spot isn't numbered, tie your belt or scarf to it and you can slip out for a snack and return to enjoy the show.

▲▲▲ **The Kunsthistorisches Museum**—This museum has the most exciting and varied collection of paintings on this tour. You'll see the great Habsburg collection of masterpieces by the likes of Dürer, Rubens, Titian, Raphael, and especially Brueghel. There's also a fine collection of Egyptian and classical art and applied arts including a divine golden salt shaker by Cellini. There are often English tours at 11:00 and 15:00 (if you forgot to pack the chapter from *Mona Winks*). The paintings are hung on one easy floor, and clear charts are posted to keep you on course. (Open Tuesday-Sunday, 10:00-18:00, closed Monday. Parts of the picture gallery are open on Tuesday and Friday from 19:00-21:00, tel. 934541.) Picnic in the lovely park outside.

▲ **Academy of Fine Arts**—Just three minutes from the Opera, their small but exciting collection includes works by Bosch, Botticelli, and Rubens, a Venice series by Guardi, and a self-portrait by 15-year-old Van Dyck. (Schillerplatz 3, Tuesday, Thursday, and Friday 10:00-

14:00, Wednesday 10:00-13:00 and 15:00-18:00, Saturday
and Sunday 9:00-13:00, 15 AS, tel. 588160.)

▲ **Albertina Collection of Graphic Arts**—Two
minutes from the Opera is a lovely collection of etchings
by many of the masters, offering a behind-the-scenes
appreciation of artists like Raphael, Dürer, and Rubens.
Unfortunately, only copies are displayed. (Augustinerstr.
1, open Monday, Tuesday, and Thursday 10:00-16:00,
Wednesday 10:00-18:00, Friday 10:00-14:00, Saturday
and Sunday 10:00-13:00, closed Sunday in July and
August; rustic, fast, cheap cellar restaurant downstairs.)

▲ **Belvedere Palace**—The elegant palace of Prince
Eugene of Savoy (conqueror of the Turks) houses the Austrian Gallery of nineteenth- and twentieth-century art.
Skip the lower palace and focus on the fine garden and
the top floor of the upper palace (*Oberes Belvedere*) for a
winning view of the city and a fine collection of Jugendstil art, Klimt, and Kokoschka. (Tuesday-Sunday 10:00-
17:00, entrance at Prince Eugen Strasse 27.)

▲▲ **Schönbrunn Palace**—The Schloss Schönbrunn,
Vienna's finest palace, is second only to Versailles in all of
Europe. Located far from the center, it was the Habsburgs' summer residence. It is big—1,441 rooms—but
don't worry, only 40 rooms are shown to the public.
(Open 8:30-17:00, 9:00-16:00 off-season. English tours
leave between 9:30 and 16:30; check the schedule near
the ticket kiosk. Saturday and Sunday are most crowded;
12:00 to 14:00, and after 16:00 are least crowded.) Entry,
including the required tour, is 50 AS, half-price with student card. The 30 AS guidebook gives an unnecessary
room-by-room description but is a nice souvenir. Pass
any waiting time around the corner in the four light,
happy Bergl rooms—painted gaily for Maria Theresa by
Bergl (including an interesting palace history exhibit).
The sculpted gardens and Gloriette Park are open until
dusk, free; long walk to Gloriette for nothing but a fine
city view (tel. 81113).

▲ **Jugendstil**—Vienna gave birth to its own wonderful
brand of Art Nouveau around the turn of the century.
Jugendstil art and architecture is popular around Europe

these days, and many come to Vienna solely in search of it. The TI has a brochure laying out Vienna's twentieth-century architecture. The best of Vienna's scattered Jugendstil sights are in the Belvedere collection, the Karlsplatz "Golden Cabbage" subway stop, and the clock on Höher Markt. The Museum of Applied Arts is disappointing.

City Park—Vienna's Stadtpark is a wonderful world of gardens, memorials to local musicians, ponds, peacocks, music in bandstands, and local people escaping the city. Notice the Jugendstil entry at the Stadtpark subway station. The Kursalon orchestra plays Strauss waltzes daily in summer from 16:00 to 18:00 and from 20:00 to 23:00. You can buy an expensive cup of coffee for a front row seat or join the local senior citizens and ants on the grass for a free fringe view.

Prater—Vienna's sprawling amusement park tempts any visitor with its huge (220-foot-high), famous ferris wheel called the Riesenrad, endless food places, and rides like the roller coaster, bumper cars, and Lilliputian Railroad. This is a fun, goofy place to share the evening with thousands of Viennese. For a family local-style dinner, eat at Schweizerhaus or Wieselburger Bierinsel.

Naschmarkt—A typical old Vienna produce market bustles daily, near the Opera along Wienzeile Street. It's likably seedy, surrounded by sausage stands, cafés, and theaters, and each Saturday it's infested by a huge flea market (Monday-Friday 6:00-18:30, Saturday 6:00-13:00).

City Tours—Of Vienna's many tours, I'd recommend its guided walks (90 minutes, many to choose from daily, 100 AS, tel. 51450, brochure at TI) and the "Getting Acquainted" bus tour that leaves daily from the Opera at 10:30, 11:45, 15:00, and, in summer, 16:30. This 75-minute introduction to the city covers a surprising amount of ground for 180 AS. No reservations necessary, tel. 712 46 830. Cut out of the tour at the Upper Belvedere if you'd like to see its collection of Klimt and Art Nouveau.

Eva Prochaska (tel. 0222/513 5294, 1, Weihburggasse 13-15) is an excellent private guide who charges 1,000 AS for a half-day.

Sunbathing—The Austrians, like most Europeans, worship the sun. Their lavish swimming centers are as much for tanning as for swimming. The Krapfenwaldbad, in the high-class nineteenth district, is renowned as the gathering point for the best-looking topless locals. For the best man-made island beach scene, take the underground to Donauinsel.

▲▲ **Music**—Vienna is Europe's music capital, but, sadly, in July and August, the Boys' Choir, the Opera, and many more music companies are on vacation like you. The music season thrives from October through June, reaching a symphonic climax during the Vienna Festival each May and June. Normally, the bigger halls attract the best talent. The "Summer of Music" festival (special brochure at TI, tel. 4000-8400 for information, tickets at Rathaus office) assures that even in the summer you'll find lots of top-notch classical music.

Try to take in a concert somewhere such as the summer concerts on two evenings weekly in front of the Rathaus. For classy street music, don't miss the action along the Graben on summer evenings.

For a trip back into Vienna's glory days of music, spend a Wednesday, Friday, or Saturday evening (early May until mid-October) at the Wiener Mozart Konzerte. The orchestra, clad in historic costumes, looks better than it sounds, performing Mozart's greatest hits including his famous opera arias. This makes for a fun evening.

Remember, there are plenty of ticket agencies, but you'll save their 22 percent commission by booking tickets directly from theater and concert hall box offices. Vienna takes care of its starving artists (and tourists) by offering lots of standing room places to top-notch music and opera nearly free.

The Vienna Boys' Choir—The boys sing at mass in the Imperial Chapel of the Hofburg (entrance at Schweizerhof) at 9:15 each Sunday except from July through mid-September. Seats (50-180 AS) must be reserved at least two months in advance but standing room is free and open to whoever lines up first. Concerts are also given Fridays at 15:30 in May, June, September, and October (300-500 AS).

Spanish Riding School—Performances are normally sold out in advance, but training sessions (only a little less boring) are open to the public (mid-February through June and September through October, Tuesday-Saturday from 10:00-12:00, 60 AS at the door, Josefsplatz in the Hofburg, long line).

▲ **Wine Gardens**—The Heurigen is a uniquely Viennese institution celebrating (and drinking) the *Heuriger*, or new wine. When the Habsburgs let the vintners sell their own new wine, 300 families opened up Heurigen wine garden/restaurants clustering around the edge of Vienna, and a tradition was born. Today they do their best to maintain their old village atmosphere, serving the homemade new wine with light meals and strolling musicians (which can be delicious). There are many Heurigen suburbs. Grinzing is the most famous and touristy, but the Perchtoldsdorf and Gumpoldskirchen districts are more popular with locals. Neustift am Walde (bus 35A) is a local favorite with much of its original charm intact. Haus Zimmermann at Mitterwurzgasse 20, tel. 441207, is a local favorite, remote and without music. For more crowds and music with your meal, visit Beethoven's home in Heiligenstadt (tel. 371287, tram 37 to last stop and walk to Pfarrplatz). You can bring in your own picnic, but Heurigen have fun cold-cut buffets. Many locals say it takes several years of practice to distinguish between Heuriger and vinegar.

▲ **The Viennese Coffeehouse**—In Vienna, the living room is down the street in a cozy coffeehouse. This tradition is just another example of the Viennese expertise in good living. Each of Vienna's many long-established (and sometimes even legendary) coffeehouses has its individual character. They offer newspapers, great pastries, sofas, elegance, and a "take all the time you want brother" charm for the price of a cup of very good and very strong coffee. You may want to order *brauner* (with a little milk) rather than *schwarzer* (black).

Some of my favorites are: **Cafe Hawelka** (1, Dorotheergasse 6, closed Tuesday, just off the Graben) with a rumpled "brooding Trotsky" atmosphere, paintings on the

walls by struggling artists who couldn't pay, a saloon
wood flavor, chalkboard menu, smoked velvet couches,
international selection of newspapers, and a phone that
rings for regulars; the **Central** (1, Herrengasse 14, Jugendstil decor, great topfen strudel); the **Jugendstil Café
Sperl** (6, Gumpendorfer 11, just off Naschmarkt); and
Café Ritter (6, Mariahilferstr. 73, near the corner of
Mariahilferstr. and Amerlingstr. and many of my recommended hotels), a true, basic, and stylish café with an
interesting local crowd, no tourists, and the best-smelling
urinals in Europe.

Honorable Mention—There's much, much more. The
city museum brochure lists them all. If you're into Espe-
ranto, Undertakers, Tobacco, Clowns, Firefighting, or the
homes of dead composers, you'll find them all in Vienna.
Several museums that try very hard but are submerged in
the greatness of Vienna are Historical Museum of the City
of Vienna (Karlsplatz, Tuesday-Sunday 9:00-16:30); Folk-
loric Museum of Austria (8, Laudongasse 15, tel. 43 89
05); and the Museum of Military History (Heeresgeschicht-
liches museum, at 3, Arsenal, Objekt 18, 10:00-16:00,
closed Friday), one of Europe's best if you like swords
and shields. The Jesuit Church (9 on your city map, on
Dr. Ignaz Seipel Platz) has a fascinating false dome
painted on its ceiling. Mariahilferstrasse is the best-value
shopping street. Waluliso is a famous peacenik you'll
probably see floating around the tourist centers in a
white angel-of-peace toga, ringing a tinkly bell and calling for peace. His name stands for water, air, light, and
sun. He seems a bit crazy, but when you read the newspapers, so do we all, so do we all.

Dishonorable Mention—Considering the very tough
competition and your limited sightseeing time, you need
to be selective. Be sure to miss these overrated sights:
Spanish Riding School Practice Session (in summer, it's
the closest you'll get to the famous Royal Lippizaner stal-
lions, crowded and boring); the homes of Freud, Haydn,
Mozart, and all 47 of Beethoven's residences (many
famous people chose to live in Vienna—unless you're a
devotee, their houses are as dead as their former resi-

dents); City Hall tours (the exterior is lovely, the interior blah); Museum of Applied Arts (disappointing garage sale of Jugendstil furniture); and Demels Café (with a slow and steady flow of gawking Americans who only miss TV's *Lifestyles of the Rich and Famous* when they're out of the country). Sorry, I'm paid to have opinions.

Nightlife

If old music or new wine isn't your thing, Vienna has plenty of alternatives. An area known as the Bermuda *Dreieck* (Triangle), north of the cathedral between Rotenturmstrasse and Judengasse, is the hot local night spot with lots of classy pubs or *Beisles* (such as Krah Krah, Frosch, Stamperl, and Kitsch & Bitter) and popular music spots (such as the disco P1 at Rotgasse 3, tel. 535 9995, and Jazzland at Franz Josefs-Kai 29, tel. 533 2575). Tunnel is popular with local students, with live music and cheap meals (open daily 11:00-2:00, behind the Rathaus at 8, Florianigasse 39, tel. 423465). For a complete and up-to-date rundown on fun after dark, get the TI's free *Youth Scene* magazine.

A Side Trip East?

Prague and Budapest are about three hours and no visa away. Train tickets are purchased easily at any travel agency (Budapest 550 AS round-trip, Prague 750 AS round-trip). Intropa, next to the TI on Kärntnerstrasse is an efficient place to get train tickets, as well as tours, and concert tickets (with 22% fee).

Sleeping in Vienna (about 10 AS = US$1)

Vienna's TI room-finding service will set you up for a 35 AS charge. Plan to spend 160 AS for a hostel bed or 500 AS for a small pension or hotel double with breakfast. Beds in a central private home are cozier but no cheaper than simple pensions. In the summer, call a few days in advance. All places listed speak English and most will hold a room without a deposit if you promise to arrive before 17:00. Be wary of people hustling tourists at the train stations. Vienna's busiest months are May, June,

August, and September. I've chosen three handy and central locations. The places are listed within each area roughly in order of value, not cost. (Postal code is 1XX0 with XX being the district.)

Southwest of Ring, Mariahilferstrasse Area

These are a 10-minute walk to the Hofburg and Opera in a fun, comfortable, and vibrant area filled with local shops, cafés, and Viennese being very Viennese. It's a 15-minute walk or two stops on the U-3 subway from the Westbahnhof.

Privatzimmer F. Kaled (500-600 AS doubles, 150 AS for extra bed, optional 50 AS breakfast in bed, 7, Lindengasse 42, tel. 939013), a unique find, is lovingly run by Tina and Fred Kaled. It's bright, airy, homey, quiet, and has TVs (with CNN) in each room. Hardworking Tina is Hungarian and is a mini tourist information service. (She has a good contact for people visiting Budapest.) If you leave your credit card number, she'll hold a room for late arrivals.

Pension Lindenhof (560-800 AS doubles, 7, Lindengasse 4, tel. 930498) is well worn but clean, filled with plants, and well (strictly) run.

Pension Reimer (560-760 AS doubles, 7, Kirchengasse 18, tel. 936162) has locks everywhere and a pay elevator, and, except for a few small rooms, most are large and comfortable.

Pension Esterhazy (460 AS doubles, 6, Nelkengasse 3, tel. 58 75 159) is run with a man's touch, wacky colors, rumpled carpets, claustrophobic hallway, clean basic rooms, no breakfast, shower down the hall, great location, and a classic example of not judging a place by its exterior (or interior).

Privatzimmer Hilde Wolf (470 AS doubles, 4, Schleifmühlgasse 7, tel. 574 9094) just off Naschmarkt and Karlsplatz, is a very homey place, with a fine breakfast and huge rooms like old libraries.

Jugendherberg Myrthengasse/Neustiftgasse (IYHF hostel, 140 AS including breakfast in 2-, 4-, or 6-bed rooms, plus 30 AS if you don't have a hostel card, 7,

Myrthengasse 7, tel. 939429) is actually two hostels side by side. Both are new, cheery, very well run, have a 1:00 curfew, will hold a room with a phone call until 16:00, and offer cheap meals. The second hostel, on Neustift-gasse (tel. 937462) has a few more first-come first-served doubles.

Across the street is **Believe It Or Not** (160 AS per bed, 110 AS from November through April, 7, Myrthengasse 10, apt #14, tel. 526 4658), which is a wonderfully friendly and basic place with one big dorm for ten travelers. Run by an entrepreneurial and charming Pole named Gosha, it's packed with Frommer and *Let's Go* readers in summer but cheaper and normally wide open in the off-season. Locked up from 10:30 to 12:30, no curfew.

Turmherberge "Don Bosco" (60 AS dorm beds, 25 AS for sheets, 30 AS extra for those without IYHF cards, 3, Lechnerstr. 12, tel. 713 1494) is far away but I stayed there in 1973 and it's still the cheapest place in Vienna. Catholic-run, closed 12:00-17:00, open to people of any sex from March through November, take tram 18 from either train station to Stadionbrücke.

Northwest of the Ring in the 9th Bezirk

This area is quieter and more elegant. No one is quite sure why Freud lived here. Each place listed is about 3 minutes from the Ring near the Schottentor subway stop (U-2).

Pension Samwald (460-560 AS doubles, 330 AS sin-gles, cheaper off-season, 10% extra for one-nighters, 9, Hörlgasse 4, tel. 347407) is well worn, well run, in a great locale with tatty chandeliers, hardwood floors, high ceil-ings, low prices, and a young-at-heart European clientele. This place is great for groups (230 AS per person).

Pension Columbia (630 AS doubles, 8, Kochgasse 9, Wien, tram 5 from Westbahnhof, bus 13A from Südbahn-hof, tel. 426757) offers huge rooms and classy (if dog-eared) Old World elegance rare in this price range.

Pension Franz (1200 AS doubles, 9, Währingerstr. 12, tel. 343637, fax 343637-23) is a lush dark palace of a place run by Sir Johnny (Sirdjani is his Iranian name) offering spacious richly decorated rooms and a first-class breakfast.

Pension Falstaff (500-700 AS doubles, 9, Müllner-gasse 5, tel. 349127, fax 3491864) is clean, basic, and professional.

Hotel Goldener Bär (550 AS doubles, showers down the hall, 9, Türkenstr. 27, tel. 345111) is well run, well located, basic, and newly refurbished.

Porzellaneum der Wiener Universität (160 AS per bed in singles, doubles, and quads, open July through September, at 9, Porzellangasse 30, between the Ring and Franz Josefs Bahnhof, tram D to Fürstengasse, tel. 347282). This is one of many student dorms that are rented as *Saisonhotel* to travelers from July through September, usually for around 420 AS per double. The TI has a brochure listing them all.

Within the Ring, in the Old City Center

These places are better, and more expensive, than most of my other listings. They are listed in other guidebooks and tend to fill up. The first three are in the shadow of St. Stephan's cathedral, on or near the Graben where the elegance of old Vienna strums happily over the cobbles. Of course, things cost a bit more in this historic core of the city, but it's worth the splurge. The subway zips you directly from the Westbahnhof to Stephansplatz. The last two listings are near the Opera (Subway line 1, 2, or 4 to Karlsplatz) on the famous Kärntner Strasse near the tourist office and three minutes from the cathedral.

Pension Nossek (750-1100 AS doubles, 1, Graben 17, tel. 533 7041, fax 535 3646) is understandably popular, so call in advance. Its elevator takes you high above any street noise into a family-run world where the dog and children seem to be placed among the lace and flowers by an interior designer. Their two doubles without a shower are a budget find. Street musicians, a pedestrian mall filled with cafés, and the plague monument are just outside your door.

Pension Aclon (700-960 AS doubles, 1, Dorotheer-gasse 6-8, tel. 512 79 400, fax 513 8751) is quiet, elegant, a block off the Graben, and above my favorite Vienna café.

Pension Pertschy (1200-1300 AS doubles, 1, Habsburgergasse 5, tel. 5344949) is more hotelesque than the others with more mini bar-type extras mixed into its Old World flavor.

Pension Suzanne (900-1050 AS doubles, 1, Walfisch-gasse 4, tel. 513 2507) is as baroque and doily as you'll find in this price range, wonderfully located a few yards from the Opera. It's professional, quiet, and friendly with pink elegance bouncing on every bed.

Hotel zur Wiener Staatsoper (1100-1200 AS, 1, Krugerstr. 11, tel. 513 1274, fax 513 1274-15) is rich and hotelesque, ideal for people whose hotel taste is a cut above this book's.

Eating in Vienna

The Viennese appreciate the fine points of life, and right up there with the waltz is eating. The city has many atmospheric restaurants. As you ponder the menus, remember Vienna's diverse empire may be gone, but its flavor lingers. You'll find Slavic and Eastern European specialties here along with wonderful desserts and local wine. Most of my listings are the well-discovered *typisch* places, fun but a bit clichetic.

You can find a colorful *Beisl* (Viennese tavern) filled with poetry teachers and their students, couples loving without touching, housewives on their way home from cello lessons, and waiters who thoroughly enjoy serving hearty food and good drink at an affordable price on nearly every corner. I hesitate to send you hiking to a particular place, but I've listed a few good bets according to neighborhood that will make filling your tank a bit more fun and less expensive.

These Wine Cellars are fun, central, touristic but typical, in the old center of town with painless prices and lots of smoke. **Esterhazykeller** is an inexpensive, rowdy, smoky self-service cellar (open 16:00-21:00, at Haarhof near Am Hof, just off Naglergasse). **Augustinerkeller** is fun, inexpensive, and, like the Esterhazykeller, a bit touristy (open 10:00-24:00, two minutes from the Opera under the Albertina Museum on Augustinerstrasse). **Rathauskeller**, under the city hall, serves moderately

priced meals to lots of tour groups but still offers a good
time and a good value. The wine decanters make the
place look like a party for people plugged into IVs (live
music after 19:00 in the Grinzingerkeller, closed Sunday,
tel. 421219). **Zu den Drei Hacken** has great inexpensive
goulash and atmosphere, at 1, Singerstrasse 28. Also
check out the **Purstner** restaurant spilling onto the side-
walk one block away at Riemergasse 10.

Other atmospheric or otherwise memorable eateries
within a 5-minute walk of the cathedral are the following.
Brezel-Gwölb is a wonderful wine cellar with outdoor
dining on a quiet square. Delicious, moderately priced
light meals, fine Krautsuppe, and local dishes. Ideal for a
romantic late glass of wine (open 11:30-1:00 daily, at
Ledererhof 9, off Am Hof). Around the corner, **Zum
Scherer Sitz u. Stehbeisl** (Judenplatz 7, near Am Hof,
Monday-Saturday 11:00-1:00, Sunday 17:00-24:00) is just
as untouristy, with indoor or outdoor seating, a soothing
woody atmosphere, intriguing decor, local specialties.

Figlmüller is a popular Beisl serving giant schnitzels
(one can easily feed two) near St. Stephan's cathedral (just
down the 6 Stephansplatz alley at Wollzeile 5). **Buffet
Trzesniewski** is justly famous for its elegant and cheap
finger sandwiches (8 AS) and small beers (8 AS). Three
sandwiches and a *kleines Bier* make a fun, light lunch
(just off the Graben, across from the brooding Cafe
Hawelka, on Dorotheergasse, Monday-Friday, 9:00-19:30,
Saturday 9:00-13:00).

The **city cafeteria** (about a block to the right of the
cathedral as you face it) serves tasty meals at subsidized
prices.

Naschmarkt, a couple of minutes from the Opera, is
Vienna's best Old World market (open 6:30-18:00, Saturday until 13:00, closed Sunday) with very fresh produce,
plenty of cheap eateries, cafes, and sausage stands. For
about the cheapest hot meal in town, lunch at the nearby
Technical University's Mensa or cafeteria in the huge,
modern, light green building just past Karlsplatz at Wied-
ner Hauptstrasse 8-19, second floor (open Monday-
Friday, 12:00-14:00). Anyone is welcome to eat here with

a world of students. The snack bar is less crowded but the bigger mensa on the same floor has a more interesting selection.

For cheap, fast meals, you'll find **Billa grocery stores** all over. **Würstelstands** are the popular local hot dog stands.

Three interesting drinks to try are *Grüner Veltliner* (green wine), *Storm* (very very new wine, autumn only), and *Traubenmost* (a heavenly grape juice on the verge of wine, autumn only, sometimes just called *Most*). Since the Austrian wine is often very sweet, remember the word *Trocken* (German for dry). See the special sightseeing sections on wine gardens and coffeehouses, above.

DAY 11
VIENNA TO THE TIROL

After some last-minute sightseeing and scurry time in Vienna and a tour of the Opera, spend the early afternoon visiting the magnificent Schönbrunn Palace, then hit the autobahn for a nonstop long drive westward to the Tirol. Spend the night in a small town just outside Innsbruck before carrying on into Switzerland tomorrow.

Suggested Schedule	
9:00	Morning free, check out of hotel, visit another museum or browse downtown.
11:00	Opera tour.
12:00	Lunch at Augustiner Keller or picnic at Schönbrunn.
13:00	Drive to Schönbrunn, tour.
15:00	Hit the autobahn, five-hour drive to near Innsbruck.
20:00	Arrive at Hall in Tirol.
Sleep	Hall.

(handwritten note: 280 miles)

Transportation: Vienna to Hall in Tirol (280 miles)
To leave Vienna, skirt the Gürtel to the Westbahnhof, turn right, and follow the signs to Schloss Schönbrunn, which is directly on the way to the West A-1 autobahn to Linz. The king had plenty of parking. Leave by 15:00, beating rush hour, following the autobahn signs to West A-1, passing Linz and Salzburg, nipping through Germany, turning right onto route 93 in the direction of Kufstein, Innsbruck, and Austria at the *Dreieck* Inntal (autobahn intersection). Crossing back into Austria, you'll follow the scenic Inn River valley, stopping a few miles east of Innsbruck at Hall in Tirol. There is an autobahn tourist information station just before Hall (open 10:00-22:00 daily in season, working for the town's hotels but still helpful). This 5-hour ride is nonstop autobahn all the way. (Notice all the little CS and H cars from Czechoslovakia and Hungary.)

Eurailers should enjoy the rest of today in Vienna and catch the overnight train straight to Switzerland. There is a nightly 21:00 departure from the Westbahnhof (train information, tel. 7200), getting into Zürich at 8:30. Reserve a bed (*Liege-platz*) at the station when you arrive in Vienna.

HALL

Hall in Tirol

Hall was a rich salt-mining center when Innsbruck was just a humble bridge (*Brücke*) town on the Inn River. Hall actually has a larger old town than sprawling Innsbruck, 5 miles away.

Take a lovely "gee, it's great to be alive" walk through easygoing Hall. From Gasthof Badl (just off the autobahn one stop before Innsbruck in Hall), walk over the old pedestrian bridge into town. The first old building you'll see is Hasegg Castle (pick up a map and a list of town sights). Hall has a very colorful morning scene before the daily tour buses arrive. The Hall-Innsbruck bus leaves four times an hour (15 minutes, 26 AS). Sleepy Hall closes down tight on Sunday and for its daily siesta.

Back when salt was money, Hall was loaded. If the salt mines of the Salzburg area were too crowded, expensive, or time-consuming, try catching a tour (call first) of Hall's Bergbaumuseum, where the town has reconstructed one of its original salt mines, complete with pits, shafts, drills, tools, and the climax of any salt mine tour—the slippery wooden slide (open by tour only, April through October, 9:00-12:00, 14:00-17:00, closed Sunday, tel. 05223/6269).

To give your trip a special splash check out Hall's magnificent *Freischwimmbad*, a huge outdoor pool with four diving boards, a giant lap pool, and a kiddies' pool, all surrounded by a lush garden, a sauna, minigolf, and lounging locals (47 AS).

Sleeping and Eating in Hall

The problem with today's plan is that you'll arrive late in a popular little town. Ideally, call in a reservation. Hall's TI (open 9:00-12:00 and 14:00-18:00, Saturday until 12:00, closed Sunday, tel. 05223/6269) can find you a

room from their list of Zimmer, Pension, and Gasthäuser.
Zimmer charge about 140 AS per person but generally
don't accept one-night stays. Gasthof Badl has Hall and
Innsbruck maps and information in English.

Gasthof Badl (500-600 AS doubles, Innsbruck 4,
A-6060, Hall in Tirol, tel. 05223/6784, fax 67843) is a big,
comfortable, friendly place run by sunny Frau Steiner and
her family. It's easy to find, immediately off the Hall in
Tirol freeway exit (3 miles before Innsbruck) with an
orange-lit Bed sign. It's not cheap, but take it for the con-
venience, the big breakfast, and the fact that they'll hold a
room for a phone call. Freeway noise is no problem. For a
cheaper room in a private home, call **Frieda Tollinger**
(150 AS per person with breakfast, Schopperweg 8, across
the river from Badl, tel. 41366), who rents out three
rooms and accepts one-nighters.

Since autobahn rest stop food isn't great and you'll
probably be short on time, consider a rolling picnic dinner for tonight. Hall's kitchens close early but Gasthof
Badl's restaurant serves excellent and reasonably priced
dinners until 22:00.

For your Tirolean folk fun, Hall has weekly Folk
Abends, and Innsbruck has an entertaining evening of
slap dancing and yodeling nearly every summer night.

FROM THE TIROL TO SWITZERLAND'S APPENZELL

After an easy morning in the town of Hall, a Tirolean mountain joyride, or a look at Innsbruck, you'll picnic at Innsbruck's Olympic ski jump. Then it's three Alpine hours on the autobahn to Switzerland's moo-mellow, storybook-friendly Appenzell, the warm, intimate side of the land of staggering icy Alps.

Suggested Schedule	
8:00	Walk through Hall.
9:00	Visit Innsbruck, see center, tour museum, or skip Innsbruck and joyride with a picnic at the Olympic ski jump.
12:00	Drive to Switzerland.
15:00	Cross the border, stop at the Stoss viewpoint.
16:00	Set up in or near Appenzell, consider a quick visit to Urnäsch museum.
20:00	Appenzeller folk evening?

Transportation—Hall to Appenzell (130 miles)

This morning, after a walk through Hall, you have two choices: a Tirolean joyride or a look at Innsbruck. If it's sunny, I'd joyride. Backtrack on the freeway to Rattenberg (exit: Kramsach) and take the small riverside road 171 along the Inns River through the cute towns of Rattenberg, Schwaz, and Volders. If you'd prefer mountain villages rather than a river valley, cross under the freeway from Hall and climb the scenic road through Tulfes, Rinn, Sistrans, and Igls—great scenery, great names.

For the faster, rainy day city option, autobahn from Hall to the Innsbruck Ost exit, and follow the signs to Zentrum, then Kongresshaus, and park as close to the old center on the river (Hofgarden) as you can. City buses (4 and 5) go regularly from Hall to Innsbruck in 15 stress-free minutes.

Just south of Innsbruck is the Olympic ski jump (from
the autobahn take the Innsbruck Süd exit and follow
signs to "Bergisel"). Park at the end of the road near the
Andreas Hofer Memorial (an Austrian patriot, killed fighting Napoleon) and climb to the empty grassy stands for a
panoramic picnic.

Leaving Innsbruck (from ski jump, go down into town
along huge cemetery, thoughtfully placed just beyond the
jump landing, and follow blue A12, Garmisch, Arlberg
signs), head west on the autobahn to Bregenz and Arlberg. The 8-mile-long Arlberg tunnel saves you 30
minutes but costs 150 AS and lots of scenery. For a joyride
and to save a few bucks, skip the tunnel, exiting at St.
Anton, and go via Stuben.

After the speedy Arlberg tunnel, you're 30 minutes
from Switzerland. Pass Feldkirch (and another long tunnel) and exit the autobahn at Rankweil/Feldkirch Nord,
following signs for Altstätten. Crossing the baby Rhine
River, you leave Austria. From there it's an easy scenic
drive through Altstätten and Gais to Appenzell. At the
Swiss border you must buy an annual road-use permit for
300 AS (get 3 SF back) or 30 SF if you want to use the
Swiss autobahns (you do). It's easy to slip across the border without buying one. But anyone driving on a Swiss
autobahn without this tax sticker is likely to be cop-
stopped and fined.

By train, I'd streamline things by overnighting it from
Vienna to Zürich, taking the 3-hour train ride to Brienz,
spending the afternoon in Ballenberg, and getting into
the Interlaken region for dinner. Swiss trains are great,
and you'll have plenty of English-speaking help at each
station.

Sightseeing Highlights—Western Austria
Alpine Side Trip by Car to Hinterhornalm—In
Gnadenwald, a village sandwiched between Hall and its
Alps, pay a small toll, pick up a brochure, then corkscrew
your way up the mountain. Marveling at the crazy
amount of energy put into such a remote road project,
you'll finally end up at the rustic Hinterhornalm Berg res-

taurant (serving hearty food and offering three simple double rooms and a precarious dorm hut or *Lager* with cheaper beds and a cliff-hanger of a view, tel. 05223/ 2170, crowded on summer weekends, closed through winter).

From there it's a level 20-minute walk to the Walderalm farm, where you can wander around a working dairy farm that shares its meadow with the clouds. The cows ramble along ridgetop lanes surrounded by cut glass peaks. The lady of the farm serves snacks and drinks (very fresh milk in the afternoon) on rough plank tables. Below you spreads the Inn River Valley and, in the distance, Innsbruck.

Karwendel Valley— This pristine, remote valley just north of Innsbruck offers a fine hike. Park at Scharnitz and walk among glaciers and cows. For soup, strudel, or schnapps, lunch at Larchet Ulm Inn.

Innsbruck— After Salzburg and Vienna, Innsbruck (population 150,000) is stale strudel. If you do stop, the Golden Roof (Goldenes Dachl, 2,657 gilded copper tiles, built by Emperor Maximilian in 1496 as an impressive viewing spot for his medieval spectacles) is the historic center of town. From this square you'll see a tourist information booth with maps and lists of sights, the newly restored baroque-style Helblinghaus, the city tower (climb it for a great view, 18 AS), and the new Olympics museum with exciting action videos for winter sports lovers (24 AS, 9:30-17:30 daily). There is a 32 AS combo tower/Olympics ticket.

Nearby are the palace (Hofburg), the church (Hof-kirche), and the very important Tiroler Volkskunst Museum. This museum (20 AS, open in season 9:00-17:00 daily, closed Sunday afternoon) is the best look anywhere at traditional Tirolean lifestyles, with fascinating exhibits ranging from wedding dresses and babies' cribs to nativity scenes. The upper floors have Tirolean homes through the ages. Use the helpful English guidebook.

A very popular mountain sports center and home of the 1964 and 1976 Winter Olympics, Innsbruck is surrounded by 150 mountain lifts, 1,250 miles of trails, and 250 hikers' huts. If it's sunny, consider taking the lift right

out of the city to the mountaintops above (300 AS less
15% if ticket purchased at TI).

Innsbruck's Alpenzoo is one of its most popular attractions (understandable when the competition is the
Golden Roof). You can ride the funicular up to the zoo
(free if you buy your zoo ticket before boarding) and get a
look at all the animals that hide out in the Alps—wildcats,
owls, elk, vultures, and more (60 AS, daily 9:00-18:00).

Innsbruck hotels host nightly folk evenings (200 AS,
21:00) throughout the summer. (TI open daily 8:00-19:00,
tel. 0512/5356.)

Side Trip over Brennerpass into Italy?—A short
swing into Italy is fast and easy and would give your trip
an exciting new twist (45-minute drive, easy border
crossing, no problem with car, Austrian shillings accepted
in the border region). To get there take the great Europa
Bridge over Brennerpass. It's expensive (about $15), but
in 30 minutes you'll be at the border. (Note: traffic can be
very heavy on summer weekends.) In Italy, drive to the
colorful market town of Vipiteno/Sterzing. Just south of
town, down a small road next to the autobahn, is the
Reifenstein Castle. The lady who lives there gives tours at
9:30, 10:30, 14:00, and 15:00. She speaks German, Italian,
and a little English. It's a unique and wonderfully preserved
medieval castle (tel. from Austria 00-39-472/765879).

Venice—Imagine parking your car in Innsbruck and
catching the night train ($60) to Venice for a day or two.
Parking is easy near the station, and a day in Venice (with
two nights in a row on the train) gives a fun twist to any
half-timbered schnitzel tour.

Tobadill—This peaceful village near Landeck is good for
a quiet break, especially if you sleep and eat at Alpengasthof
Rifflerblick. Adolf and Elfriede Greisser and their gourmet
son Harry offer good beds with a memorable candlelit
dinner and view (640 AS doubles with breakfast, 140 AS
dinners, 6551 Tobadill 42, Post Pains, tel. 05442-62030).

Vorarlberg—The westernmost corner of Austria has a
special style and charm. Both Feldkirch and Bregenz have
well-preserved old quarters. For a good one-hour walk,
drive 4 miles out of Dornbirn past Gutle to the Rappen-

lochschlücht Gorge and hike from the car park up to a peaceful lake through the impressive river gorge.

Side Trip through Liechtenstein?—If you must see the tiny and touristy country of Liechtenstein, take this 30-minute detour: from Feldkirch south on E77, drive through Schaan to Vaduz, the capital. Park near the city hall, post office, and tourist office. Passports can be stamped (for a small fee) in the tourist office. Stamp collectors make a beeline for the post office across the street while the prince looks down on his four-by-twelve-mile country from his castle a 20-minute hike above Vaduz (it's closed but offers a fine view; catch the trail from Café Berg). Liechtenstein's banks (open until 16:30) sell Swiss francs at uniform and good rates. To leave, cross the Rhine at Rotenboden, immediately get on the autobahn heading north from Sevelen to the Oberriet exit, and check another country off your list.

Switzerland (Schweiz, Suisse, Svizzera)

- 16,000 square miles (half the size of Ireland, or 13 Rhode Islands).
- About 6 million people (400 per square mile, declining slightly).
- One Swiss Franc = about US$.73, 1.4 SF = about US$1

Switzerland, Europe's richest, best-organized, and most mountainous country, is an easy oasis and a breath of fresh Alpine air, particularly refreshing after intense Italy. Like Boy Scouts, the Swiss count cleanliness, neatness, punctuality, tolerance, independence, thrift, and hard work as virtues, and they love pocket knives. They appreciate the awesome nature that surrounds them and are proud of their little country's many achievements.

The average Swiss income (among the highest in the world), a great social security system, and their super-strong currency, not to mention the Alps, give them plenty to be thankful for.

Switzerland, 40 percent of which is uninhabitable rocks, lakes, and rugged Alps, has distinct cultural regions and customs. Two-thirds of the people speak German, 20 percent French, 10 percent Italian, and a small group of

Switzerland

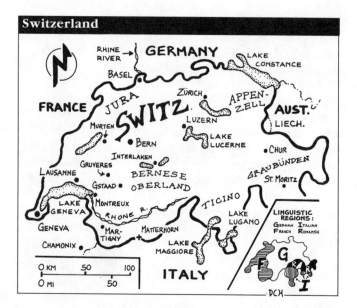

people in the southeast speak Romansh, a direct descendant of ancient Latin. Within these four language groups, there are many dialects. The sing-songy Swiss German, the spoken dialect, is quite a bit different from High German, which is Switzerland's written German. An interest in these regional distinctions will win the hearts of locals you meet. As you travel from one valley to the next, notice changes in architecture and customs.

Historically, Switzerland is one of the oldest democracies. Born when three states, or cantons, united in 1291, the Confederation Helvetica as it was called in Roman times (the "CH" decal on cars doesn't stand for chocolate), grew, as our original 13 colonies did, to the 23 of today. The government is decentralized and cantonal loyalty is very strong.

Switzerland loves its neutrality and stayed out of both world wars, but it is far from lax defensively. Every fit man serves in the army and stays in the reserve. Each house has a gun and a bomb shelter. There are 600,000 rifles in homes and 12,000 heavy guns in place. Swiss vacuum-packed emergency army bread, which lasts two years, is said to also function as a weapon. Airstrips hide inside mountains behind Batmobile doors. With the push of a button, all road, rail, and bridge entries to the country can be destroyed, changing Switzerland into a formidable mountain fortress. Notice the explosive patches checkerboarding the roads at key points like mountain summits (and hope no one invades until you get past). Sentiments are changing, and in 1989, Switzerland came close to voting away its entire military. August 1 is the very festive Swiss national holiday.

Switzerland has a low inflation rate and a strong franc. Gas is less than $3 a gallon, cheap for Europe. Dormitory accommodations are plentiful and cheap, groceries are reasonable, and hiking is free, but Alpine lifts and souvenirs are expensive. Shops throughout the land thrill tourists with carved, woven, and clanging mountain knickknacks, clocks, watches, and Swiss army knives (Victorinox is the best brand).

The Swiss eat when we do and enjoy a straightforward, no-nonsense cuisine. Specialties include delicious fondue, rich chocolates, a melted cheese dish called *raclette*, fresh dairy products (try Muesli yogurt), 100 varieties of cheese, and Fendant, a good crisp local white wine, too expensive to sell well abroad but worth a taste here. The Co-op and Migros grocery stores are the hungry hiker's best budget bet.

You can get anywhere quickly on Switzerland's fine road system (the world's most expensive to build per mile) or on its scenic and efficient trains. Families should take advantage of the super-saver Family Pass, available for free at Swiss stations for train and Alpine lift discounts.

Tourist information offices abound. While Switzerland's booming big cities are cosmopolitan, the traditional culture lives on in the Alpine villages. Spend most of your time getting high in the Alps. On Sundays, you're most likely to enjoy traditional sports, music, clothing, and culture.

Appenzell

Appenzell is Switzerland's most traditional region—and the butt of much local humor because of it. This is

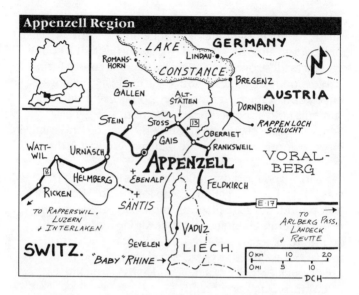

Appenzell Region

Landsgemeinde country, where entire villages would
meet in town squares to vote. Until 1991, the women of
Appenzell couldn't vote on local issues. A gentle beauty
blankets the region overlooked by the 8,200-foot peak,
Säntis. As you drive, you'll enjoy an ever-changing parade
of finely carved chalets, traditional villages, and photo-
genic cows. While farmer's daughters make hay in bikinis,
old ladies walk the steep roads with scythes, looking as if
they just pushed the messenger of death down the hill.

If you're here in late August or early September there's
a good chance you'll get in on—or at least have your road
blocked by—the ceremonial procession of flower-
bedecked cows and whistling herders in traditional, for-
mal outfits. The festive march down from the high
pastures is a spontaneous move by the herding families,
and when they finally do burst into town (a slow motion
Swiss Pamplona), everyone becomes a child, dropping
everything and running into the streets. When locals are
asked about their cheese, they clench their fists as they
say, "It's the best."

From picturesque Altstätten, you'll wind up a steep
mountain pass and your world becomes H.O.-gauge. Park
at the summit at the tiny Stoss railroad station. Cross to

the chapel, walk through the meadow and past munching cows to the monument that celebrates a local Appenzeller victory over Habsburg Austria. From this spectacular spot you can see the Rhine Valley, Liechtenstein, and the mountains of Vorarlberg back in Austria. This is an appropriate first stop in fiercely independent Switzerland. Enjoy the sun and the wind; stretch out on the stone for a snooze or a picnic. Back by the chapel, the 300-year-old Wirtschaftz Stoss Inn is a rustic place for a drink, snack, or rest stop (W.C. in the hallway).

Now carry on through Gais and into Appenzell town. This is the most "typical" town around where the kids play barn not house while mom and dad watch yodeling on TV. It's the best headquarters for the night. The TI is very good (9:00-12:00 and 14:00-17:00, Saturday 9:00-12:00, tel. 071/874111, on the main street, Hauptgasse 19). Ask about an Appenzeller folk evening (every night but Tuesday somewhere in town, July-September, about 10 SF without dinner, dinner usually optional). Do your best to see one of these shows tonight. The little folk museum across the street is good—unless you're going to its Urnäsch equivalent (see Day 13). The Appenzeller bier is famous, good, and cheap.

Lodging in Appenzell

Switzerland is more expensive than Austria, and any time you get a double for less than $40 you're doing great. But it is also wonderfully organized—easy phone system, helpful TIs, English widely spoken, and plenty of excellent youth hostels and dorm-type alternatives to expensive hotels. If your budget is tight, be sure to chase down youth hostels (many with "family rooms") and keep your eyes peeled for *Matratzenlagers* (*Lager* means dorm; *Matrat* doesn't mean check under your mattress before bedding down).

Appenzell town is small but quite touristy. Hotels are expensive, the Zimmer are a 10-minute walk from the center. Fierce competition drives some places to offer special "bed and fondue" deals. Ask at the TI.

The **Gasthaus Hof** offers by far the best cheap beds in town in its brand new Matratzenlager (19 SF per bed in 6-

to 8-bed rooms with breakfast, sheets 4 SF more, cen-
trally located just off the Landsgemeindeplatz, tel.
071/872210). Outside of peak times, you'll be sleeping
alone in a warehouse of bunkbeds. Gasthaus Hof serves
good 20 SF Rösti, the cheesy potato specialty of the area.

Hotel Säntis is very hotelesque with romantic Old
World elegance, on the main square (150-200 SF, Landsgemeindeplatz, tel. 071/878722). **Hotel Taube** is also
good (80-110 SF, near Postplatz, tel. 071/871149) but can
be smoky and noisy. The only reasonable hotel in town,
Pension Union (65 SF doubles, a block behind the TI,
tel. 071/871420) is a peaceful, grandfatherly old place that
doesn't accept one-nighters.

Haus Lydia (70 SF doubles with breakfast, Eggerstan-
denstr. 53, CH 9050 Appenzell, east of the center over the
bridge and over the Esso station, tel. 071/874233) is an
Appenzell-style home filled with tourist information and
a woodsy folk atmosphere, on the edge of town with a
garden and a powerful mountain view. This wonderful
6-room Zimmer is run by Frau Mock-Inauen.

Johann Ebneter speaks English and runs a friendly
and modern Zimmer in the same area (70 SF doubles
with breakfast, Mooshaldenstr. 14, tel. 071/873487).

Ebenalp (a thin air alternative to Appenzell town)
While the Appenzell region's forte is the folk culture
rather than staggering peaks, it is presided over by
7,800-foot-high Säntis Peak. It is accessible by lift but a
more backdoor experience is riding the lift from Wasserauen, 5 miles south of Appenzell town, to Ebenalp (5,000
feet, with a sneak preview of the cave church and guest
house on the way up, God's view of the entire region all
the way to Lake Constance (Bodensee) from the top, and
an interesting 90-minute hike down through a prehistoric
cave home (tiny museum always open), Wildkirchli, a
400-year-old cave church (hermits lived there from
1658-1853), and a 100-year-old guesthouse built precari-
ously into the cliffside (Berggasthaus Ascher, see below).
These are perched together on a sunny ledge about 12
minutes down "twisted ankle lane" below the top of the

lift. From this perch you can almost hear the cows munching on the far side of the valley. The hike down is steep but a joy. In the distance, below Säntis, is your destination, the Seealpsee (lake). Only the parasailers, like neon jellyfish, tag your world twentieth century. The Ebenalp lift runs twice an hour until 19:00 in July and August, 18:00 in June and September, otherwise the last lift is at 17:00 (19 SF round-trip, 12 SF one-way).

There's no real reason to sleep in Appenzell town. The Ebenalp lift in Wasserauen is a few minutes' drive south. For a more memorable experience, stay in the **Berggasthaus Ascher** (12 SF for a dorm bed, blankets but no sheets required or provided, 10 SF for breakfast, Family Knechtle-Wyss, 9057 Weissbad, 12 minutes by steep trail below top of lift, tel. 071/881142, open daily May-October). Their 100-year-old house is built onto the rock, has only rain water and no shower, is often festive, and often very quiet, can sleep 40 people (four hikers to three mattresses) and often does on Saturdays, but you'll normally get a small woody dorm to yourself. The hut is actually built on to the cliff side; its back wall is the rock. From the toilet you can study this alpine architecture. Sip your coffee on the deck, behind drips from the gnarly overhang a hundred yards above. The goats have their cliff hut adjacent.

Less atmospheric and more normal is the **Berg Gasthaus Ebenalp**, just above the lift (22 SF dorm bed with breakfast, 68 SF doubles with breakfast, family Sutter, tel. 071/881194). From Wasserauen at the base of the lift, you can walk 30 minutes uphill to **Berggasthaus Seealpsee**, situated on an idyllic alpine lake by the same name (Dörig family, 9057 Weissbad, tel. 071/881140, 70 SF doubles with breakfast, or 9 SF in the loft dorm, plus 9 SF for breakfast).

3 Hours

APPENZELL TO THE BERNER OBERLAND

After a few short stops in cowbell country, drive three scenic hours to the Interlaken area, spending the afternoon at Switzerland's greatest open-air folk museum, Ballenberg. Climb through traditional houses from every corner of this diverse country and sample the handicrafts and baking in action. Then stop for a look at Interlaken before driving deep into the heart of the Alps. Leave your car in Stechelberg and ride the gondola to the stop just this side of heaven—Gimmelwald.

Suggested Schedule

8:00	Joyride through Appenzell, cheese tour in Stein.
10:00	Drive direct to Ballenberg, picnic en route or late at Ballenberg. Telephone Walter to see if he's cooking dinner tonight.
14:00	Ballenberg Museum. (If it's sunny, consider hiking today and returning for the museum.)
17:00	Drive to Interlaken, quick "travel chores stop" in Interlaken. Drive to Stechelberg for 18:55 lift.
19:00	Check into Walter's Hotel Mittaghorn in Gimmelwald.
19:30	Dinnertime at Walter's.

Transportation: Appenzell to Interlaken (120 miles)
It's a 3-hour drive from Appenzell to Ballenberg and another hour from there to the Gimmelwald lift. Head west out of Appenzell town on the Urnäsch road, taking the first right (after about two miles, it's easy to miss, sign to Herisau/Wattwil) to Stein. In Stein, look for a big modern building and the Schaukäserei sign. From there, wind scenically south to Urnäsch and down the small road (signs to Hemberg) to Wattwil. Somewhere along the Urnäsch-Hemberg road stop to ask an old local if this is the way to Wattwil, just to hear the local dialect and to see

the healthy outdoor twinkle in his or her eyes up close. Drive through Ricken, into the town of Rapperswil, following blue signs to Luzern and Zurich over the long lake bridge, and southward following blue signs to Gotthard. You'll go through the town of Schwyz, the historic core of Switzerland that gave its name to the country. From Brunnen, one of the busiest, most expensive to build, most impressive roads in Switzerland wings you along the Urnersee. It's dangerously scenic, so stop at the parking place after the first tunnel (on right, opposite Stoos turnoff) where you can enjoy the view and a rare Turkish toilet. At Flüelen get on the autobahn for Luzern, vanishing into a long tunnel that should make you feel a little better about your 30 SF autobahn sticker. Be careful to exit at the Stans-Nord exit (follow the signs to Interlaken) where a small road takes you along the Alpnachersee south toward Sarnen. Take the small chunk of autobahn, and continue past Sarnensee to Brienzwiller before Brienz. A sign at Brienzwiller will direct you to the Ballenberg Frei Luft (Swiss Open-Air) Museum/Ballenberg Ost. You can park here, but I prefer the west entrance, a few minutes down the road near Brienz.

From Brienzwiller, drive along the congested but scenic north side of Lake Brienz (or save 20 minutes by taking the new autobahn to Interlaken on the other side). From the north shore road, follow the blue, not green, exit sign into Interlaken. Turn right after the bridge and cruise through the old resort town down its main street past the cow field with a great Eiger-Jungfrau view on your left and grand old hotels, the TI, post office, and banks on your right. At the end of town you'll hit the West Bahnhof. Park around there.

To get to Gimmelwald (from downtown Interlaken or from the autobahn), follow signs south to Lauterbrunnen, pass through Lauterbrunnen town, noticing the train station on your left and the funicular across the street on your right, and drive to the head of the Stechelberg valley, a glacier-cut cradle of Swissness, where you'll see the base of the Schilthornbahn (a big gray gondola station). This parking lot is safe and free. Allow 30 minutes to drive from Interlaken to the Stechelberg gondola parking lot. Ride the 18:55 lift (walk into town, hard right at PTT, signs direct you up the path, 5 minutes, 6.20 SF, two trips an hour at :25 and :55) to Gimmelwald. A steep 200-yard climb brings you to the chalet marked simply "Hotel." This is Walter Mittler's Hotel Mittaghorn. You have arrived.

Eurailers, take the Zürich–Luzern–Brünig–Brienzwiller train. At the Brienzwiller station, check your bag, note when later trains depart for Interlaken, buy your Ballenberg ticket, and follow the footpath into the museum. Carry on later by train to Interlaken-Ost (East).

While most major trains leave from Interlaken-West station, private trains (not covered by Eurailpass) go from the Interlaken-East station into the Jungfrau region. Ask at the station about discount passes and special fares. Spend some time in Interlaken before buying your ticket to Lauterbrunnen. It's a pleasant walk between the East and West stations.

Take the train to Lauterbrunnen, cross the street to catch the funicular to Mürren. You'll ride up to Grütschalp where a special scenic train (*panorama fahrt* in German) rolls you along the cliff into Mürren. From there, walk an easy, paved 40 minutes downhill or walk 10 minutes across town to catch the gondola (7 SF and a 5-minute steep uphill backtrack) to Hotel Mittaghorn. If you walk, turn left out of the station and walk through the town keeping eyes open for left turn (yellow sign) down to Gimmelwald. Your hotel will greet you at the edge of Gimmelwald. A good bad-weather option is to ride the post bus from Lauterbrunnen (leaves at 5 minutes past the hour) to the base of the Stechelberg-Schilthorn gondola and ride up to Gimmelwald from there. The hike from Stechelberg to Gimmelwald is well marked and as enjoyable as a steep 2-hour hike can be. (Note that for a week or so from late April to early May and from late November to early December, the Schilthornbahn is closed for servicing. During this time, Gimmelwald is a serious headache to get to and Hotel Mittaghorn is closed. Schilthornbahn tel. 036/231444.)

Sightseeing Highlights—On the Road to Gimmelwald

▲▲ **Stein**—The Appenzell Showcase Cheese Dairy (Schaukäserei) is open daily from 8:00 to 19:00. Cheese is actually being made, normally from 9:00 to 11:00 and from 13:00 to 15:00. It's fast, free, and well explained in the free English brochure (with cheese recipes). The lady at the cheese counter loves to cut the cheese so you can enjoy small samples. They also have yogurt and cheap boxes of cold iced tea for sale. The TI and a great folk (*Volkskunde*) museum are right next door (10:00-18:00, closed Monday, 7 SF). This is the ultimate cow culture museum with old-fashioned cheese-making demonstrations, peasant houses, fascinating and complex weaving machinery, lots of cow art, and folk craft demonstrations daily in the summer. If you missed the cows on parade, this moo-seum is the next best thing.

▲ **Urnäsch**—An appealing one-street town, which has my nomination for Europe's cutest museum. The Appenzeller Museum (on the town square, open only from 13:30-17:00 daily, July-October; Wednesday, Saturday, and Sunday April-June; closed in winter; 4 SF, good English description brochure, will open for groups of five or more if you call the director at 581487 or 582322) brings this region's folk customs to life. Warm and homey, it's a happy little honeycomb of Appenzeller culture. The Gasthaus Ochsen, three doors down from the museum, is a fine traditional hotel (80 SF doubles with breakfast, tel. 071/581117) with good food and wonderful atmosphere. Peek into its old restaurant.

Einsiedeln—Just a few minutes off the road south of Rapperswil is Switzerland's most important pilgrimage church. It's worth a look if the spirit moves you—sort of an Alpine Lourdes.

▲▲▲ **Ballenberg**—The Swiss Open-Air Museum Ballenberg is a rich collection of traditional and historic farmhouses from every region of the country. Each house is carefully furnished, and many feature a traditional craftsperson at work. The sprawling 50-acre park, laid out roughly as a huge Swiss map, is a natural preserve providing a wonderful setting for this culture-on-a-lazy-Susan look at Switzerland.

The Thurgau house (#621) has an interesting wattle and daub (half-timbered construction) display and a fun bread museum upstairs. Use the 2 SF map/guide. The more expensive picture book is a better souvenir than guide. (Open daily 10:00-17:00, mid-April through late October, 10 SF entry, 2-hour private tours are 50 SF by prior arrangement, tel. 036/511123.) There is a reasonable outdoor cafeteria inside the west entrance, and fresh baked bread, sausage, and mountain cheese or other cooked goodies are available at several houses. Picnic tables and grills with free firewood are scattered throughout the park.

Before leaving, drive through the little wooden village of Brienzwiller (near the east entrance). It's a museum itself with a lovely little church. (Trains go regularly from Interlaken to Brienz where buses connect you with Ballenberg.)

▲ **Interlaken**—When the nineteenth-century romantics redefined mountains as something more than cold and troublesome obstacles, Interlaken became the original Alpine resort. Ever since then, tourists have flocked to the Alps "because they're there." Interlaken's glory days are long gone, its elegant old hotels eclipsed by the new, more jet-setty Alpine resorts. Today, its shops are filled with chocolate bars, Swiss army knives, and sunburned backpackers.

But it's a good administrative center. You'll find a handy post office with boxes (7:30-12:00, 13:45-18:30), long-distance phone booth (next to the post office, easy 1.5 SF/minute calls to the U.S., even cheaper on Saturday, Sunday, and after 21:00), plenty of banks (the West train station exchange desk has fair rates and is open daily until 18:00), and major trains to all corners of Europe.

Interlaken is a handy place to wash your filthy clothes. Helen Schmocker's Wascherei Laundry (from the post office, follow Marktgasse over two bridges to Beatenbergstr., open 7:00-22:00 daily for self-service, 8 SF to wash and dry 10 pounds; Monday-Friday 8:00-12:00 and

Interlaken

13:30-18:00 for full service, drop off 10 pounds and 12 SF in the morning and pick it up clean that afternoon, tel. 221566) has a change machine, soap, English instructions, and a pleasant riverside place to hang out.

Interlaken is your best Swiss shopping town. I'd take care of business, give the town a quick look, and head for the hills. The big Migros supermarket across from the West station is handy.

The tourist office (at the West station, 7:30-12:00, 13:30-18:00 daily, until 19:00 in summer, tel. 036/222121) has good information for the whole region and advice on Alpine lift discounts. Pick up a Bern map, a Jungfrau region map, and a Jungfrau region timetable. There is another good TI on Innsbruck's main street. For mountain train information, call 264233.

Luzern—Train travelers may pass through Luzern. Near the station is the tourist office and the pleasant lakeside old center with its charming covered bridges—worth a walk. The sightseeing highlight, apart from ogling the 50,000 SF watches in the shop windows near the lakefront (only the cheaper 10,000 SF ones are left out at night), is Luzern's huge Museum of Transportation (Verkehrshaus der Schweiz) outside of town on the lake (boats and cable cars go there from the center). Europe's best transport museum, it's open daily from 9:00 to 18:00 (November-February, 10:00-16:00), 12 SF.

Sleeping and Eating in Gimmelwald (4,500 feet; 1 SF = about US$.73)

To inhale the Alps and really hold it in, sleep high in Gimmelwald. Poor, stuck happily in the past, avalanche-zone Gimmelwald has a youth hostel, a pension, and a hotel. The only bad news is that the lift costs about 7 SF each way.

The **Mountain Hostel** (7 SF per bed in 2- to 15-bed rooms, 2 SF for sheets, closed mid-December through mid-March, tel. 036/551704) is simple, less than clean, rowdy, cheap, and very friendly. Its 45 beds are often taken in July and August, so call ahead to Lena, the elderly woman who runs the place. The hostel has low ceilings, a self-serve kitchen, enough hot water for ten (1 SF, 5-minute) hot showers a day (or you can drop by the Mürren Sports Center with a towel and 2 SF), and coed washrooms. It's 50 yards from the lift station.

This relaxed hostel is struggling to survive. Please read the signs, respect its rules, leave it cleaner than you found it, and treat it and Lena with loving care. Without Lena, I'm afraid there's no hostel in Gimmelwald. The place, because of the spirit of its rugged but sensitive visitors and Brian (a local Texan), almost runs itself.

The **Pension Gimmelwald** (with a cheap dorm on its top floor and decent 70 SF doubles, 2-night minimum, tel. 551730) next door serves meals.

Hotel Mittaghorn (60 SF doubles with breakfast, cheaper triples, quads, and quints, loft beds with breakfast are 20 SF, CH-3826 Gimmelwald [Bern], tel. 036/551658, phone reservations are a good idea, call a few days ahead), the treasure of Gimmelwald, is run by Walter Mittler, a perfect Swiss gentleman (and former chef for Swissair).

It's a classic, creaky, Alpine-style place with memorable

beds, ancient (short) down comforters, and a million-dollar view of the Jungfrau Alps. The hotel has two rooms with a private shower and a single communal 1 SF shower. Walter is careful not to get too hectic or big and enjoys sensitive, backdoor travelers. He runs the hotel with the help of Don von Gimmelwald (actually "von" Winnipeg) keeping it simple but with class. This is a good place to receive mail from home.

To some, Hotel Mittaghorn is a fire just waiting to happen, with a kitchen that would never pass code, terrible beds, nowhere near enough plumbing, run by an eccentric man. These people enjoy Interlaken, Wengen, or Mürren, and that's where they should sleep. Be warned, you'll meet maybe more of my readers than you hoped for, but it's a fun crowd, an extended family. Walter closes his place for a week or so around early May and again in late November when the local lift is closed for servicing. He's also closed from mid-December through March.

Gimmelwald feeds its goats better than its people. The hostel has a decent members' kitchen but serves no food, and the village grocery is open only every other morning. The wise and frugal buy and pack in food from the Co-ops in Mürren and Lauterbrunnen. Walter, at Hotel Mittaghorn, is Gimmelwald's best cook (not saying much, but he is good). Dinners must be preordered and prepaid by 16:00; there's no menu, his salad is best eaten one leaf at a time with your fingers, and it's served at 19:30 sharp. When Walter's in the mood, his place is the best bar in town; cheap and good beer, strong *Kaffee fertig* (coffee with schnapps). Otherwise, you can eat at the pension in the center of the village.

Sleeping and Eating in Mürren (5,500 feet)
Mürren is as pleasant as an Alpine resort can be. It's traffic-free, filled with bakeries, cafes, souvenirs, old-timers with walking sticks and Japanese making movies of each other with a snowy backdrop. Its chalets are prefab-rustic, it sits on a ledge 2,000 feet above the Lauterbrunnen Valley, and it's surrounded by a brilliant chorus of mountains. It has all the comforts of home and

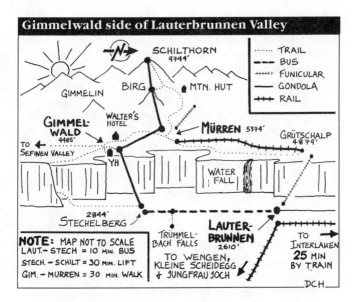

Gimmelwald side of Lauterbrunnen Valley

then some, with very high prices. Mürren's Tourist Office
is very helpful, can find you a room, and has a late-hours
bank (in the Sporthaus, 9:00-12:00, 14:00-18:00, tel.
551616).

Hotel Belmont (50-65 SF, some rooms with great
views, across from the train station, tel. 513535, fax
553531) offers Mürren's best budget rooms. **Hotel
Alpenblick** (tel. 551327, fax 551391) is clean, efficient,
very Swiss, and another good value.

Hotel Alpina (110 SF doubles with shower, breakfast,
and the great view, baths more expensive, no view
cheaper, CH-3825 Mürren, tel. 036/551361) is clean,
friendly, modern, like something you'd expect in Port-
land but hanging literally on the cliff. If you don't mikd
the hike, **Pension Sonnenberg** (tel. 551127) and **Flora
Suppenalp** (tel. 551726) are two small restaurants that
offer cheap dorm beds high above Mürren. Mürren's
laundromat (9:00-12:00, 14:00-17:00, tel. 553700) is next
to the Edelweis Hotel. For a rare bit of ruggedness and the
best budget food in the center of Mürren, eat at the

Stägerstübli, right in downtown. Jet-setters drink at the Palace Hotel's **Inferno Bar.**

Sleeping in Wengen (4,200 feet)

On the slick scale: if Gimmelwald is granola, Mürren is a Denver omelet, and Wengen is eggs Benedict. (Wengen's tourist office, tel. 036/551414). Wengen is a fancy "Mürren" on the other side of the valley. Both are traffic-free and an easy lift above Lauterbrunnen. Wengen is halfway up to Kleine-Scheidegg and Männlichen. It has more tennis courts than budget beds.

Hotel Bernerhof (85 SF doubles with breakfast, tel. 036/552721) has 18 SF dorm beds. The **Hotel Jungfraublick** has dorm beds (30 SF with breakfast, tel. 036/552755). The **Chalet Schweizerheim Garni** (100 SF doubles, tel. 036/551581) is another choice.

Sleeping Below Gimmelwald near the Stechelberg Lift (2,800 feet)

Chalet Alpenglühn (50 SF per room for two or three, kitchenette but no breakfast, 3824 Stechelberg across from the Breithorn Campground, tel. 036/551821), a tiny drive before the Schilthornbahn, on the valley floor surrounded by the meadow, waterfalls, and birds, with low ceilings and simple Alpine elegance, is the home of Theo Van Allmen who makes art with leather and budget travelers happy.

The local **Naturfreundehaus Alpenhof** (cheap dorm, Stechelberg, tel. 036/551202) is a rugged Alpine lodge for local hikers at the far end of Lauterbrunnen Valley which I've never felt very welcome in.

Sleeping in Lauterbrunnen town (2,600 feet)

Masenlager Stocki (8 SF a night in an easygoing little coed dorm, with a kitchen, tel. 551754) is a great value; across the river, take the first left. **Gasthaus Bären** (60 SF doubles, tel. 551723) is at the far end near the waterfall. Two campgrounds just south of town work very hard to provide 15 to 25 SF beds. They each have dorms, 2-, 4-, and 6-bed bungalows, no sheets, kitchen facilities, and big English-speaking tour groups. **Camping Jungfrau** (tel. 552010) is romantically situated just beyond the stones hurled by Staubbach Falls, huge and well organized, with clocks showing the time in Sydney and Vancouver, and even a "Heidi Shop." They also have fancier cabins and trailers for the classier camper. **Schützenbach Campground** (tel. 551268), on the left just past Lauterbrunnen toward Stechelberg, is simpler.

Sleeping in Interlaken, Brienz, or Halfway to the Jungfrau

Balmer's Herberge, an Interlaken institution (16 SF dorm beds, 25 SF per person in simple doubles with breakfast, and even cheaper in overflow on-the-floor accommodations, Haupstr. 23, in Matten, a 15-minute walk from either Interlaken station, tel. 036/221961), is run by a creative tornado of entrepreneurial energy named Eric Balmer. With movies, Ping-Pong, laundromat, a secondhand book-swapping English library, rafting excursions, plenty of tips on budget eating and hiking, and a friendly hardworking, mostly American staff, the place is home for those who miss their fraternity, while making sure travelers of all ages feel welcome.

For 30 SF dorm beds *mit Frühstück* high in the mountains, you can sleep at Kleine Scheidegg (**Bahnhof Buffet**, tel. 036/551151) or at Männlichen (**Berg Restaurant Männlichen**, dorm and double rooms, tel. 036/551068).

If you get sidetracked in Brienz, its lakeside **hostel** (cheap, Strandweg, tel. 036/511152) is great. And for something really different—almost weird—drive or bus up the frighteningly narrow and winding Rosenlaui Valley road south from Meiringen (near Brienz) to the mountain climbers' Hilton. At 4,000 feet, in the middle of nowhere, is the Old World, tattered but elegant **Berg-Gasthaus Rosenlaui** (60 SF doubles, open June-early October, tel. 036/712912). At the head of that valley, you can hike from there (or catch the mountain goat bus) over Grosse Scheidegg and down to Grindelwald.

FREE DAY IN THE ALPS—HIKE!

Today is your vacation from this go-go vacation. And a great place to recharge your touristic batteries is up here high in the Alps where distant avalanches, cowbells, the fluff of a down comforter, and the crunchy footsteps of happy hikers are the dominant sounds.

If the weather's good, ride the lift from Gimmelwald to a classy breakfast at the 10,000-foot Schilthorn's revolving restaurant. Linger among Alpine whitecaps before riding or hiking down (5,000 feet) to Mürren and home to Gimmelwald.

Suggested Schedule

8:00	Ride the Gimmelwald-Schilthorn lift.
8:30	Breakfast on the Schilthorn, ride or walk down to Mürren, browse, buy a picnic lunch. Hike to Gimmelwald via Gimmelen.

Gimmelwald—So undeveloped because of its "avalanche zone" classification, Gimmelwald is one of the poorest places in Switzerland. Its economy is stuck in the hay, and many of the farmers, unable to make it in their disadvantaged trade, are subsidized by the kinder and gentler Swiss government. For some, there's little to see in the village. Others spend a fascinating day sitting on a bench. Be sure to take a walk and pay attention to the traditional log cabin architecture. The numbers on the buildings are not addresses but fire insurance numbers. The cute little hut near the station is for storing and aging cheese, not youth hostelers (the stone plates under it work to keep bugs out). Be careful not to confuse obscure Gimmelwald with very touristy and commercialized Grindelwald just over the Kleine Scheidegg ridge.

Evening fun in Gimmelwald is found at the hostel (lots of young Alp-aholics and a good chance to share information on the surrounding mountains) and up at Walter's. Walter's bar is a local farmers' hangout. When they've made their hay, they come here to play. They look like what we'd call "hicks" (former city slicker Walter still isn't fully accepted by the gang), but they speak some English and are fun to get to know. Walter knows how many beers they've had according to if they're talking, singing, fighting, or snoring. For less smoke and some powerful solitude, sit outside (benches just below the rails 100 yards down the road from Walter's) and watch the sun tuck the mountaintops into bed as the moon rises over the Jungfrau.

▲▲▲ **Hike 1: The Schilthorn, Hikes, Lifts, and a 10,000-Foot Breakfast**—Walter serves a great breakfast, but if the weather's good, skip his and eat atop the Schilthorn, in the slowly revolving mountain-capping restaurant (of James Bond movie fame). The early-bird special gondola tickets (rides before 9:00) take you from Gimmelwald to the Schilthorn and back, with a great continental breakfast on top for 52 SF. (Get discount gondola tickets from Walter.) Bear with the slow service and ask for more hot drinks if necessary. For a lighter meal, try the Birchermuesli-yogurt treat.

The Gimmelwald-Schilthorn hike is free, if you don't mind a 5,000-foot altitude gain. I ride up and hike down or, for a less scary hike, go halfway down by cable car and walk down from the Birg station. Lifts go twice an hour and the ride takes 30 minutes. Watch the altitude meter in the gondola. (The round-trip excursion early-bird fare is cheaper than the Gimmelwald-Schilthorn-Birg ticket. If you buy that ticket, you can decide at Birg if you want to hike or ride down.)

Linger on top. There's a souvenir shop, the rocks of the region on the restaurant wall, a chart showing the engineering of this rugged mountain perch, the best toilet view in all of Europe, telescopes, and very thin air. Watch hang gliders set up, psych up, and take off, flying 30 minutes with the birds to distant Interlaken. Walk along the ridge out back to the No High Heels signpost. You can even convince yourself you climbed to that perch and feel pretty rugged (and take a picture to prove it). For another cheap thrill, ask the gondola attendant to crank

Alpine Lifts in the Jungfrau

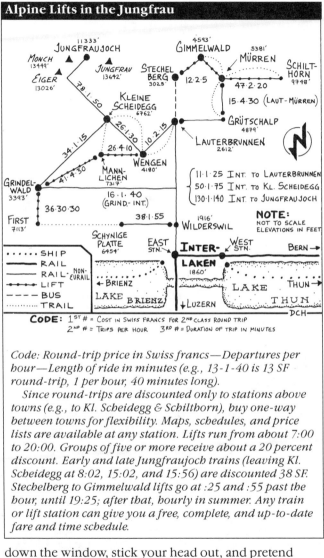

Code: *Round-trip price in Swiss francs—Departures per hour—Length of ride in minutes (e.g., 13-1-40 is 13 SF round-trip, 1 per hour, 40 minutes long).*

Since round-trips are discounted only to stations above towns (e.g., to Kl. Scheidegg & Schilthorn), buy one-way between towns for flexibility. Maps, schedules, and price lists are available at any station. Lifts run from about 7:00 to 20:00. Groups of five or more receive about a 20 percent discount. Early and late Jungfraujoch trains (leaving Kl. Scheidegg at 8:02, 15:02, and 15:56) are discounted 38 SF. Stechelberg to Gimmelwald lifts go at :25 and :55 past the hour, until 19:25; after that, hourly in summer. Any train or lift station can give you a free, complete, and up-to-date fare and time schedule.

down the window, stick your head out, and pretend you're hang gliding (ideally, over the bump going down from Gimmelwald).

Think twice before hiking down from the Schilthorn (weather can change, have good shoes). Most people have

more fun hiking (steeply) down from Birg. Just below
Birg is a mountain hut. Drop in for soup, cocoa, or a coffee schnapps. You can spend the night in the loft (40 mattresses, open July-September, tel. 036/552640). Youth
hostelers scream down the ice fields on plastic-bag sleds
from the Schilthorn. (English-speaking doctor in Mürren.)

The most interesting trail from Birg (or Mürren) to Gimmelwald is the high one via Suppenalp, Schiltalp, Gim-
meln, and the Sprütz waterfall. Mürren has plenty of
shops, bakeries, tourist information, and banks, and a
modern sports complex for rainy days. Ask at the Schilthorn station in Mürren for a souvenir pin or sticker.

▲▲▲ **Hike 2: The Männlichen-Kleine Scheidegg
Hike**— This is my favorite easy Alpine hike, entertaining
you all the way with glorious Eiger, Mönch, and Jungfrau views.

If the weather's good, descend from Gimmelwald
bright and early. Drive (or catch the post bus) to the Lauterbrunnen train station, parking at the large multistoried
pay lot behind the station. Buy a ticket to Männlichen,
and catch the train. Ride past great valley views to Wengen, where you'll walk across town (don't waste time
here if it's sunny), buy a picnic if you like, and catch the
Männlichen lift (departing every 15 minutes) to the top of
the ridge high above you.

From the tip of the Männlichen lift, hike 20 minutes
north to the little peak for that king of the mountain feeling. Then walk (very easy) about an hour around to
Kleine Scheidegg for a picnic or restaurant lunch. If
you've got an extra 80 SF and the weather's perfect, ride
the train through the Eiger to the towering Jungfraujoch
and back. Check for discount trips up to Jungfraujoch;
three trips a day (one early, two late, tel. 264111, weather
551022). Jungfraujoch crowds can be frightening. Until
the new rolling stock is in place (late 1992), expect long
waits and unruly mobs at the top on sunny days. The
price has been jacked up to reduce the crowd problems
and it's still a mess.

From Kleine Scheidegg, enjoy the ever-changing
Alpine panorama of the north face of the Eiger, Jungfrau,

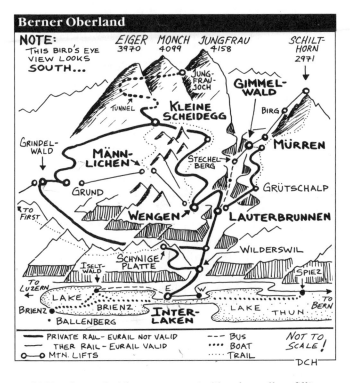

Berner Oberland

NOTE: THIS BIRD'S EYE VIEW LOOKS SOUTH...

EIGER 3970   MONCH 4099   JUNGFRAU 4158   SCHILTHORN 2971

JUNGFRAUJOCH

TUNNEL

KLEINE SCHEIDEGG

GIMMELWALD

BIRG

GRINDELWALD

MÄNNLICHEN

STECHELBERG

MÜRREN

GRUND

TO FIRST

WENGEN

GRÜTSCHALP

LAUTERBRUNNEN

WILDERSWIL

SCHYNIGE PLATTE

ISELTWALD

SPIEZ

TO LUZERN

LAKE BRIENZ

BRIENZ • BALLENBERG

LAKE BRIENZ

INTERLAKEN

E   W

LAKE THUN

TO BERN

— PRIVATE RAIL – EURAIL NOT VALID   --- BUS
— THER RAIL – EURAIL VALID   •••• BOAT
o—o MTN. LIFTS   ••••• TRAIL

NOT TO SCALE!

DCH

and Mönch, probably accompanied by the valley-filling mellow sound of alp horns and distant avalanches as you ride the train or hike downhill (30 minutes gorgeously to Wengenalp, 90 more minutes steeply from there) into the town of Wengen. If the weather turns bad or you run out of steam, catch the train early at the little Wengenalp station along the way. After Wengenalp, the trail is steep and, while not dangerous, requires a good set of knees. Wengen is a fine shopping town. The boring final descent is knee-killer steep, so catch the train from Wengen to Lauterbrunnen. Trails are often snowbound into early summer; ask about conditions at lift stations. If the Männlichen lift is closed, take the train straight from Lauterbrunnen to Kleine Scheidegg. Many enjoy the Kleine–Scheidegg–Wengenalp walk even on the snow.

▲▲▲ **Hike 3: Schynige Platte to First**—The best day I've had hiking in the Berner Oberland is the 6-hour

ridge walk high above Lake Brienz on one side and all
that Jungfrau beauty on the other. Start at Wilderswil
where you catch the little train up to Schynige Platte
(6,500 feet). Walk through the alpine flower display garden and into the wild alpine yonder. The high point is
Faulhorn (8,700 feet), with its famous mountaintop hotel.
Your destination is a chair lift called First (7,050 feet)
where you descend to Grindelwald and catch a train back
to your starting point, Wilderswil (or if you have no car, a
regional train pass, or endless money, return to Lauterbrunnen from Grindelwald over Kleine Scheidegg).

▲ **Other Hikes from Gimmelwald**—For a level
3-hour walk with great Jungfrau views and some mountain farm action, ride the funicular from Mürren to
Allmenhübel (6,300 feet), walk to Marchegg, Saustal, and
Grütschalp (4,900 feet) where you catch the panorama
train back to Mürren.

An easy go-as-far-as-you-like trail from Gimmelwald is
up the Sefinen Valley. Or, you can wind from there down
to Stechelberg. Don von Gimmelwald is writing a small
Gimmelwald guidebook with more details and other
good hikes (available at Hotel Mittaghorn).

Rainy Day Options
Trümmelbach Falls (7 SF, on the Lauterbrunnen-
Stechelberg road, 9:00-18:00 daily, April-October) is the
valley's most powerful one. You can sneak a behind-the-
scenes look at it. You'll ride an elevator up through the
mountain and climb through several caves to see the melt
of the Eiger, Mönch, and Jungfrau grinding like God's
bandsaw through the mountain at the rate of up to 20,000
liters a second (that's faster than the beer is consumed at
Oktoberfest!). The upper area, "chutes 6 to 10," is best.

Lauterbrunnen's Heimatmuseum (3 SF, 14:00-17:30,
Tuesday, Thursday, Saturday, and Sunday, mid-June
through September, just over the bridge) shows off the
local folk culture.

Mürren's slick **Sports Center** (mid-June through
mid-September) offers a world of indoor activities. 7 SF
gets you into the swimming pool and the whirlpool.

WEST TO FRENCH SWITZERLAND

This morning, get your last fill of the Alps. Take a quick look at the Swiss capital of Bern, and set up in the medieval walled town of Murten, or should I call it Morat, since we're now in French Switzerland.

Suggested Schedule	
7:30	Breakfast.
8:00	Lift to car, drive to Lauterbrunnen. Lift to Männlichen (via Wengen), hike down to Wengen.
12:00	Lunch in Wengen, train to car.
13:00	Drive to Bern.
14:00	Explore downtown Bern.
18:00	Drive into Murten.

Transportation: Interlaken to Murten (50 miles)
From Lauterbrunnen, drive toward Interlaken and catch the autobahn (direction Spiez, Thun, Bern). After Spiez, the autobahn will take you right to Bern. Circle the city on the autobahn, taking the (fourth) Bern exit, Neufeld Bern, into the center. Signs to Zentrum will take you to the Bahnhof. Turn right just before the station into the Bahnhof Parkplatz (2-hour meter parking outside, all-day lot inside, 2 SF per hour). You're just an escalator ride away from a great tourist information center and Switzerland's compact, user-friendly capital. From the station, drive out of Bern following blue Lausanne signs, then green signs to Neuchatel and Murten. Notice the big gray Jacob Suchard Tobler chocolate factory overlooking the autobahn at the Bern-Brunnen autobahn exit. This is the home of Toblerone, recently purchased by Philip Morris and no longer giving tours. In about 20 minutes you'll be in Murten.

Parking within Murten's walls is medieval. If you have a dashboard clock (free at TIs and banks) you can try the

BERN — INTERLAKEN   1 HOUR

blue spots near the Ringmauer Hotel, but it's best to settle for the large free lots just outside either gate and walk in. It's a tiny town.

Bern

The charming Swiss capital fills a peninsula bounded by the Aare River, giving you the most (maybe even only) enjoyable look at urban Switzerland. Just an hour from Interlaken, directly on your way to Murten, it's worth a stop, especially if disappointing weather cuts your mountain time short.

For a quick, well-organized visit, park your car at the train station, visit the tourist office inside (open 8:00-20:30 daily, until 18:30 in winter, tel. 031/227676), pick up a map, a list of city sights, and info on the parliament, the clock, or whatever you're interested in, confirm your plans, and get a Murten map. "This Week in Bern" lists

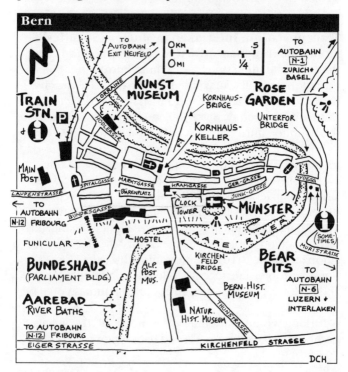

Bern

TO AUTOBAHN Exit NEUFELD

0 KM _____ .5
0 MI _____ ¼

TO AUTOBAHN N-1 ZURICH + BASEL

TRAIN STN. P

LORRAINE

KUNST MUSEUM

KORNHAUS-BRIDGE

ROSE GARDEN

UNTERFOR BRIDGE

KORNHAUS-KELLER

NYDEGG

MAIN POST

SPITALGASSE MARKTGASSE KRAMGASSE GER-GASSE

JUNK-GASSE

BÄRENPLATZ

LAUPENSTRASSE

TO AUTOBAHN N-12 FRIBOURG

BUNDESGASSE

Clock Tower

MÜNSTER

AARE RIVER

(SOME-TIMES)

MURISTRASSE

FUNICULAR →

HOSTEL

KIRCHEN-FELD BRIDGE

BEAR PITS

TO AUTOBAHN N-6 LUZERN + INTERLAKEN

BUNDESHAUS (PARLIAMENT BLDG.)

ALP. POST MUS.

BERN. HIST. MUSEUM

AAREBAD RIVER BATHS

NATUR. HIST. MUSEUM

THUNSTRASSE

TO AUTOBAHN N-12 FRIBOURG

EIGER STRASSE

KIRCHENFELD STRASSE

DCH

museum hours and a calendar of events. Follow the walking tour explained in the handy city map while browsing your way downhill. Visit Einstein's house. Finish with a look at the bear pits (*Bärengraben*) and a city view from the Rose Garden across the river, and catch trolley 12 back up to the station (buy the cheapest, yellow-button ticket from the machine at the stop).

Sightseeing Highlights—Bern
▲▲ **The Old Town**—Window-shopping and people-watching through the lovely arcaded streets and busy market squares are Bern's top attractions. This is my favorite shopping town: the prices are so high, there's no danger of buying. Great browsing. The clock tower (*Zytgloggeturm*) performs at 4 minutes before each hour. Apparently this 5-minute slowest-moving nonevent in Europe was considered entertaining in 1530. To pass the time during the performance, read the TI's brochure explaining what's so interesting about the fancy old clock. Enthusiasts can tour the medieval mechanics daily at 16:30 (May through October, tickets 4 SF at the TI or on the spot).

The 1421 Swiss late Gothic Münster Cathedral, is worth a look (closed 12:00-14:00). Climb the spiral staircase 100 yards above the town for a great view, good exercise, and a chance to meet a live church watchman. Peter Probst and his wife, Sigi, live way up there watching over the church, answering questions, and charging tourists for the view.

Nearby is the imposing Parliament building (Bundeshaus) of Switzerland (free 45-minute tours most days at 9:00, 10:00, 11:00, 14:00, 15:00, and 16:00, tel. 031/618522 to confirm; closed about March, June, September, and December; five people minimum group size). Don't miss the view from the Parliament terrace. You may see some national legislators, but you wouldn't know it. Everything looks very casual for a national capital.

Einstein did much of his most important thinking while living in a house on the old town's main drag. It was just another house to me, but I guess everything's relative (free, Kramgasse 49, 10:00-17:00, Saturday until 16:00, closed Sunday, Monday, December, and January).

▲ **Bear Pits and Rose Garden**—The symbol of Bern is the bear, and some lively ones frolic their days away (7:00-18:00) to the delight of locals and tourists alike in the big barren concrete pits, or Graben. Up the paved pathway is the Rosengarten, worth the walk for the great city view. The Rosengarten restaurant (tel. 413206) has a great view and serves a fine 16 SF lunch special.

▲▲▲ **The Berner Swim**—For something to write home about, join the local merchants, legislators, publishers, carp, and students in a lunchtime float down the Aare River. The Bernese, proud of their very clean river and their basic ruddiness, have a tradition—sort of a wet, urban paseo—of hiking upstream 5 to 30 minutes and floating playfully or relaxed back down to the excellent (and free) riverside baths and pools (Aarebad) just below the Parliament building. If the river is a bit much, you're welcome to enjoy just the Aarebad. If the river is not enough, a popular day trip is to raft all the way from Thun to Bern.

▲▲ **Museum of Fine Arts (Kunstmuseum)**—Located four blocks from the station, it features 1,000 years of local art and some Impressionism, but the real hit is its fabulous collection of Paul Klee's playful and colorful paintings. If you don't know Klee, I'd love to introduce you (4 SF, #12 Holdergasse, open 10:00-17:00, Tuesday until 21:00, closed Monday).

Other Bern Museums—Across the bridge from the Parliament on Helvetiaplatz are several museums (Alpine, Bern History, Postal) that sound more interesting than they are. Nearly all are closed on Monday.

Sleeping and Eating in Bern

Each of these places is in the old town within a 15-minute walk of the station. Except for the hostel, there are no alternatives to good, comfortable, clean, and expensive hotels in the entire city. The places listed are right in the old center. Since they are not modernized, and the only ones offering rooms with showers down the hall, they are far cheaper than other places. Get parking advice

Southwest Switzerland

locally. Supposedly, out-of-country cars aren't given parking tickets.

Hotel Hospiz zur Heimat (84 SF small doubles without showers, 110 SF big doubles with showers, Gerechtigkeitsgasse 50, on the main street near the bridge and bears, 15-minute walk from the station or tram 12, tel. 031/220436, fax 213386) is Bern's best budget hotel value. Its restaurant, next door, serves a good 11 SF lunch special (daily, except Sunday, 11:30-14:00).

Hotel Goldener Schlüssel (95-120 SF doubles, Rathausgasse 72, CH-3011 Bern, tel. 031/220216, fax 031/225688) is a sleepable basic, crank-em-out old hotel in the center.

Bern's newly renovated big, sterile, well-run IYHF **hostel** (14 SF beds, nonmembers 21 SF, Weihergasse 4, 3005 Bern, tel. 031/226316) has 8- to 26-bed rooms about a 10-minute walk from the station down the stairs from the Parliament building, by the river. It provides an all-day lounge, laundry machines, cheap meals (office open 7:00-9:30 and 17:00-23:00).

For a decent and affordable meal in the center, try the
Migros restaurant on Marktgasse, **Gratineria** at #44
Rathausgasse, **Café Brunne** at #18 Rathausgasse, or
Barenhöfli on Zeughausgasse.

Murten

The finest medieval ramparts in Switzerland surround the
4,600 people of Murten, or Morat in French (we're on the
lingua-cusp of Switzerland here, 25% of Murten speaks
French; a few miles to the south nearly everyone does).
The town is a mini-Bern with three parallel streets, the
middle one nicely arcaded with elegant shops and breezy
outdoor cafés. Its castle is romantically set overlooking
the tiny Murtensee and the rolling vineyards of gentle
Mount Vully in the distance. Try some Vully wine.

The town history museum in an old mill (closed Monday) is not quite worth a look. The only required sightseeing is to do the rampart ramble (free, always open,
easy stairway access on east side of town). You can rent a
bike just outside the town wall for a lakeside ride.

The TI (tel. 037/715112, 9:00-12:00, 14:00-17:30,
closed Saturday afternoon and Sunday) is very helpful,
but there's not much to say. They organize free town
walks (10:00, Fridays in July and August). Murten is touristic but seems to be enjoyed mostly by its own people.

Sleeping and Eating in Murten

Hotel Ringmauer (that's German for ramparts, 80 SF
doubles, 50 SF singles, 2 Deutsche Kirchgasse, near the
wall on the side farthest from the lake, tel. 037/711101) is
Murten's only good accommodations deal, and this place
is great. Run by Frau Gutknecht (who speaks enough
English), the Ringmauer is friendly, very characteristic, a
block from the town center, clean as a croissant, and has
showers and toilets within a naked dash of each room. It's
my nominee for the "best modern hallway art in an old
hotel" and the "best bathroom hardware" awards. It's a
bowl of apples and homemade marmalade kind of place
with a good restaurant (try the tasty 10 SF *Rösti*).

Hotel Murtenhof (120-180 SF doubles, next to the castle on Rathausgasse, tel. 037/715656, fax 715059), a full-fledged hotel, is a worthwhile splurge with all the comforts and a lake view. I go here every night for their salad bar (summer only, closed Monday, 7 SF small plate, 12 SF for the big one, the small one heaped high is plenty, comes with wonderful bread and a sunset over the lake). The terrace setting here is romantic, and it's a good place to try the wine—just point to the vineyards across the lake. (Handy toddlers' play area next to restaurant.)

Avenches
About four miles south of Murten is Avenches. It was Aventicum, the Roman capital of the Confederation Helvetica. Back then its population was 50,000. Today it could barely fill the well-worn ruins of its 15,000-seat Roman amphitheater. You can tour the Roman museum and an evocative Roman theater in the fields, a short walk out of town. Avenches, with a pleasant small French town feel, is a quiet alternative to Murten for the night (TI tel. 037/751159).

Sleeping in Avenches
The Avenches IYHF **hostel** (15 SF for bed, sheets, and breakfast, 22 SF for nonmembers, Rue du Lavoir 5, two blocks out of the old center at the medieval *lavoir,* or laundry) is the only hostel in the area, and it's a beauty. It's run by the Dhyaf family, with 4- to 8-bed rooms, a homey TV room, Ping-Pong, a big backyard, and a very quiet setting near the Roman theater (open 7:00-9:00 and 17:00-22:00, tel. 037/752666, fax 752717, English spoken).

Hotel de L'Union (75 SF doubles and triples, rue Centrale 23, tel. 037/751384) is a simple old place, mostly a restaurant with a few 2- and 3-bed rooms upstairs, shower down the hall, right on the central square of Avenches, two blocks from the Roman amphitheater. It's nothing special except for its price and location. There are no Zimmer in this part of Switzerland.

FRENCH SWITZERLAND HIGHLIGHTS

A third of Switzerland is French, and, as you'll see in today's circle south, that means more than language. While the highest mountains in Europe are just over the border in France, you've seen the Alps, so now it's time for Roman ruins, a folk museum, cheese making, a chocolate tour, a visit to one of Europe's most romantic castles and a taste of the Swiss Riviera along Lake Geneva (Lac Leman) in an area so beautiful that Charlie Chaplin and Idi Amin both chose it as their second home.

Suggested Schedule	
7:45	Breakfast.
8:15	Depart.
9:00	Chocolate tour in Broc.
10:30	Gruérien folk museum in Bulle.
12:00	Picnic in Gruyères.
13:30	Cheese demonstration in Gruyères, autobahn to Lake Geneva, or go home to relax.
15:00	Château Chillon.
16:00	Quick drive through Montreux, Vevey, and the Corniche de Laveau, before returning to Murten.

Transportation Tips—Murten to Lake Geneva (50 miles)

The autobahn corridor from Bern to Lausanne/Lake Geneva makes everything very speedy. Murten and Avenches are about 10 minutes from the autobahn. Broc, Bulle, and Gruyères are within sight of each other and the autobahn. It takes about an hour to drive from Murten to Montreux. Towns are well sign-posted.

By public transportation, you'll find plenty of cross-country trolleys and buses using Fribourg and Bulle as hubs. For example: Bulle–Gruyères (15 minutes, 7 a day), Bulle–Broc Fabrique (12 minutes, hourly), Fribourg–Bulle (45 minutes, hourly), Avenches–Fribourg (30

minutes, 7 a day), Murten–Fribourg (30 minutes, hourly).
Buses connect towns along Lake Geneva every 15 minutes.

Sightseeing Highlights—Southwest Switzerland
▲▲ **Caillers Chocolate Factory**—Okay, time to drool
in front of a molten river of your favorite chocolate. The
nearby town of Broc is dominated by a huge chocolate
factory. While you're in Switzerland, it's fun to see how
all that great chocolate is actually made. This factory gives
free one-hour tours with samples Monday afternoons to
Friday mornings with tours departing from 9:00 to 10:00
and from 13:30 to 14:45 (closed July and from November
to February, tel. 029/65 151 to confirm plans). Drivers follow the chocolate brown signs to Nestle and Broc Fabrique. Train travelers can stay on all the way to the factory
stop, Broc-Fabrique.

Broc town is just the sleepy home of the chocolate
makers. It has a small typical hotel, the Auberge des Mon-
tagnards (64 SF doubles with breakfast and a great Gruyères
view and an elegant dining room, tel. 029/61526).
▲▲ **Musée Gruèrien**—Somehow the unassuming little
town of Bulle built a refreshing, cheery folk museum that
manages to teach you all about life in these parts and
leave you feeling very good. It's small and easy (open
10:00-12:00 and 14:00-17:00, closed Sunday morning
and Monday, 4 SF plus 1 SF for the excellent English
guide). When it's over, the guide reminds you, "The
Golden Book of Visitors awaits your signature and com-
ments. Don't you think this museum deserves another
visit? Thank you!"
▲ **Gruyères**—This ultra-touristy town fills its fortified
little hilltop like a bouquet. Its ramparts are a park, and
the ancient buildings serve the tourist crowds. The castle
is mediocre, and you don't need to stay long, but make a
short stop for the setting.

The home of Gruyères cheese, the modern production
center in the valley at the foot of the town (signs to
Fromagerie) gives a worthwhile look at how it is made
with a good continuous English audiovisual presentation
(free, 8:00-18:30 daily). Cheese is actually being made,

usually from 10:00 to 11:00 and from 14:00 to 15:00. The cute cheese shop has lunches and picnic stuff (closed from 12:00-13:30). Minimize your walk by driving up to the second parking lot. Hotels in Gruyères are expensive.

▲▲ **Lake Geneva (Lac Leman)**—Separating France and Switzerland, surrounded by Alps, and lined with a collage of castles, towns, museums, and vineyards, Lac Leman's crowds are understandable.

Boats carry its visitors comfortably to all sights of importance, and Eurailers sail free. The 15 SF ride from Lausanne to Chillon takes 90 minutes with stops in Vevey and Montreux (6 trips daily in each direction). Get the full story from any hotel, hostel, or TI on the lake. The 10-minute Montreux–Château Chillon cruise is fun even for those with a car.

Montreux is an expensive resort with a famous jazz festival each July. The casino is an entertainment center with a wimpy gaming room and the Bar du Festival, which plays great videos of the latest jazz festival. A beer here makes for an enjoyable evening. Vevey nearby is a smaller and more comfortable resort town.

The Corniche de Lavaux, the Swiss Wine Road, winds ruggedly through picturesque towns and the stingy vineyards that produce most of Switzerland's tasty but expensive wine, Fendant. Hikers can take the boat to Cully and explore on foot from there. A car tour is quick and frightening (from Montreux go west along the lake, through Vevey, following blue signs to Lausanne along the waterfront, taking the Moudon/Chexbres exit). Explore some of the smaller roads before you get to Chexbres where the green autobahn signs (to Bern) get you on the fast road home. It's 45 minutes from Chexbres to Murten.

Lausanne is the most interesting city on the lake. You can park near its impressive cathedral and walk through the colorful old town. The Collection de l'Art Brut (11 Avenue des Bergieres, 10:00-12:00, 14:00-18:00, closed Saturday and Sunday mornings and Monday, follow signs to Palais de Beaulieu) is a fascinating and thought-provoking collection of art by those who have been labeled criminal or crazy by society.

Geneva bores me. This big city is sterile, cosmopolitan, expensive, and full of executives, diplomats, and tourists looking for profits, peace, cheap rooms, and other worthy but elusive goals.

▲▲▲ **Château Chillon**—A wonderfully preserved thirteenth-century castle set wistfully at the edge of Lac Leman and a joy. Follow the free English map brochure from one fascinating room to the next (or freeload on one of the many English group tours)—tingly views, a dank prison, battle-scarred weapons, interesting furniture, and even 700-year-old toilets. The long climb to the top of the keep (#25 in the brochure) isn't worth the time or sweat. Curl up on a window sill to enjoy the lake (9:00-18:30 daily, less off-season, 5 SF, easy parking, tel. 021/963 3912).

Sleeping near Château Chillon and Montreux
Since Switzerland is so small with such fast roads, I'd side-trip down to the lake from Murten. But if you want to sleep on the lake, there are a few options. Montreux is expensive, but the town of Villeneuve, three miles east, has the same palmy lakeside setting without the crowds or glitz. Its main drag runs parallel to the shore, one block in. The waterfront promenade leads to the château and to Montreux. Villeneuve is the first exit east of Montreux on the autobahn.

Le Romantica (60 SF doubles, Grand-Rue 34, 1844 Villeneuve, tel. 021/960 1540) is a rare value with frumpy, very French atmosphere. Even the stools are overstuffed. **Hotel du Soleil** (100 SF doubles, Grand-Rue 20, tel. 021/960 4206) is renovated with all the comforts, an expensive but likable place. **Hotel de l'Aigle** (80 SF doubles, Grand-Rue 48, tel. 021/960 1004) is depressing; it has only location and price going for it.

Haut Lac youth hostel (18 SF for sheets, bed, and breakfast in bleak dorms, 55 SF for doubles, Passage de l'Auberge 8, 1820 Territet, tel. 021/963 4934) in the town of Territet at the edge of Montreux is right on the lake, a 10-minute stroll north of the château and a short walk from the fun of Montreux. It's a well-run place with cheap

meals, cursed by a noisy train that seems to run over its
roof through the night. (English spoken, members only,
closed 9:00-17:00, will hold a bed until 18:00 if you call.)

More Alp Sights between Interlaken and Lake Geneva

▲ **Simmental**—The Simmen Valley (*tal* means valley) is
famous in the United States for its great milk cows. It's
known locally for its fine medieval churches (the most in
the Berner Oberland) and for the American farmers who
come to see the cows. The Erlenbach Church (park at the
market square) is worth a look. An English brochure
explains that, as in most local churches, the beautiful
paintings decorating the interior have survived, ironically,
because they were whitewashed over by baroque people.

▲▲ **Glacier des Diablerets**—For another grand Alpine
trip to the tip of a 10,000-foot peak, take the three-part
lift from Reusch or Col du Pillon. A quick trip takes about
90 minutes and costs 38 SF. You can stay for lunch. From
the top, on a clear day, you can see the Matterhorn and
even a bit of Mont Blanc, Europe's highest mountain. This
is your only good chance to do or watch some summer
skiing. Normally expensive and a major headache, it isn't
bad here. Lift ticket, rental skis, poles, boots, and a heavy
coat cost about 65 SF. Since the slopes close at 14:00 and
it's a 2-hour drive from Murten or Gimmelwald, you'll
need to leave early.

▲▲ **Taveyanne**—One of the most enchanting and
remote hamlets in Switzerland, Taveyanne is 2 miles off
the main road between Col de la Croix and Villars. A
small sign points down a tiny road to a jumble of log
cabins and snoozing cows stranded at 5,000 feet. The
only inn in town is the Refuge de Taveyanne (1882
Gryon), where the Seibenthal family serves hearty meals
in a prize-winning rustic setting—no electricity, low ceilings, huge charred fireplace. This is French Switzerland,
but these people speak some English. For a back-on-the-
farm experience, consider sleeping in their primitive loft.
It's never full (5 mattresses, access by a ladder outside, 8
SF, tel. 025/681947).

FRENCH SWITZERLAND TO GERMANY'S BLACK FOREST

Take an easy morning, enjoy the bubbly streets of Murten, consider a short side trip to Avenches to see the Roman ruins. Then drive 3 or 4 hours to Germany's Black Forest to set up in the town of Staufen.

Suggested Schedule	
9:00	Free morning in Murten or Avenches.
11:00	Drive north into Germany.
3:00	Set up in Staufen. Sort through your options.

Transportation: Murten to the Black Forest (130 miles)

From Murten, follow signs to Bern, then Basel/Zürich. Before Basel you'll go through a tunnel and come to Raststätte Pratteln Nord, a strange orange shopping mall that looks like a huge submarine laying eggs on the freeway. Take a break here for a look around one of Europe's greatest freeway stops. You'll find a bakery and grocery store for picnickers, a restaurant, showers, and a change desk open daily until 21:00 with rates about 2 percent worse than banks. Change or spend your last francs. Eat the samples, get your glasses cleaned, then carry on.

At Basel, follow the signs to Karlsruhe and Deutschland. Once in Germany (bank at the border station is fair, open 7:00-20:00), the autobahn will take you along the French border, which, for now, is the Rhine River. Exit at Bad Krotzingen, just before Freiburg, and cut down to Staufen. Park along the little river (near the Sparkasse bank) and you're just a bridge away from your hotel.

Train travelers will catch the milk-run train from Murten into Bern, where an hourly train zips to Basel in 75 minutes and then on into Germany. At least one train per hour makes the 40-minute trip from Basel to Freiburg.

Sightseeing Highlights

▲ **Badenweiler**—If ever a town was a park, Baden-weiler is it; an idyllic, poodle-elegant, and finicky-clean spa town known only to the wealthy Germans who soak there. Its Markgrafen-*bad* (bath) is next to the ruins of a Roman mineral bath in a park of imported and exotic trees (including a California redwood). This prize-winning piece of architecture perfectly mixes trees and peace with an elegant indoor-outdoor swimming pool (open 8:00-18:00, Monday, Wednesday, and Friday until 20:00, but the glory of the place, its outdoor section, is closed for renovation until 1993). The locker procedure combined with the language barrier makes getting to the pool more memorable than you'd expect (3 hours for 10 DM, towels, required caps, and suits are rentable). Baden-weiler is a 20-minute drive south of Staufen, or get off at the Badenweiler autobahn exit on your way north. (Bad Krozingen, just a couple of miles from Staufen, has a fancy new spa pool if Badenweiler is too much work.)

Badische Weinstrasse—The wine road of this part of Germany staggers through the tiny towns (Britzingen, Sulzburg, Dottingen, Grunern) between Staufen and Badenweiler. If you're in the mood for some tasting, look for the *Winzergnossenshaft* signs, which invite visitors in to taste, buy, and often tour the winery. There is a Win-zergnossenshaft in Staufen at the base of the castle hill at the edge of the old town.

Staufen in Breisgau—This is a cute (the standard Black Forest adjective) town in the Black Forest. It's a mini-Freiburg, a perfect combination of smallness and off-the-beaten-path-ness with a quiet pedestrian zone of colorful old buildings bounded by a happy creek that actually babbles. There's nothing to do here but enjoy the market-place atmosphere. Hike through the vineyards to the ruined castle overlooking the town and savor a good dinner with local wine.

Sleeping in Staufen

The Black Forest has lots of hotels and enough visitors to keep them busy. It's wise to call ahead. Staufen makes a good overnight stop. The TI (on the main square in the Rathaus, Monday-Friday 8:00-16:30, closed Saturday afternoon and Sunday, tel. 07633/80536) has a long list of private Zimmer, but most don't like to take one-nighters. They post a photo board outside showing each place.

Hotel Kreuz Post (75-95 DM, right in the pedestrian zone just over the bridge at Hauptstrasse 65, 7813 Staufen/Breisgau, tel. 07633/5240, call in advance for Wednesday and Thursday arrivals when the restaurant is closed), run by the Heckle family, is friendly and immaculate and has lots of character, cute rooms, cute sisters, and good food.

Gasthaus Bahnhof (60 DM doubles, across from the sleepy station, tel. 07633/61900) is colorful in a ruddy way. This is the cheapest place in town, with a castle out back, no breakfast, self-cooking facilities, and great food at the café. It can seem a little depressing during the day, but at night, master of ceremonies Lotte makes it the heartbeat of Staufen. People come from miles around to party with Lotte whenever they need a lift. Even if you don't sleep at Lotte's, try to eat here. She serves just one meal, the daily menu, and it's great.

Gasthaus Hirschen (100 DM doubles, #19 on main pedestrian street, 7813 Staufen, tel. 07633/5297), which has a storybook location in the old pedestrian center and a characteristic restaurant, is run by the hardworking Kerber family. Its rooms come with more facilities, less warmth, and a higher price than the Kreuz Post. I wasn't sure whether or not to list them here, but they gave me a bottle of homemade "cherry firewater" (which I gave to the Bulgarian accordionist at Lotte's).

Freiburg Youth Hostel (23 DM per bed with sheets and breakfast, Kartäuserstr. 151, tram 1 to Römerhof, tel. 0761/67656) is the nearest hostel. Train travelers may choose to stay in Freiburg. This big, modern hostel is just outside of Freiburg on the recommended road into the Black Forest.

THE BLACK FOREST—GERMANY'S SCHWARZWALD

Spend the day exploring the best of this most romantic of German forests. By late afternoon you'll be set up in Germany's greatest nineteenth-century spa resort and ready for a stroll through its elegant streets and casino, finishing the day with a *kur*—sauna, massage, and utter restfulness.

Suggested Schedule

9:00	Enjoy Freiburg's pedestrian zone, Münster Platz, Augustiner Museum. Buy picnic.
11:30	Drive into Black Forest, village picnic.
14:00	Drive north to Baden-Baden.
15:00	Baden-Baden, set up, browse the elegant town center.
17:00	Take the kur (or go swimming).
20:00	Dine downtown.
22:00	Stroll Lichtentaler Allee.

Transportation: Staufen–Freiburg–Baden Baden (70 miles)

From Staufen drive into Freiburg, follow signs to Stadtmitte until you see the TI (near the Bahnhof, on your right a few blocks after you cross the train tracks). The center of town is a pedestrian zone circled by the ring road with lots of parking. (For the scenic Black Forest detour, see below.) The autobahn goes from Freiburg north toward Karlsruhe and into Baden-Baden. Follow signs to Oos (Bahnhof) or drive straight into town. Enter the tunnel and take the first exit. The "i" signs will lead you close to the tourist office. It's well hidden so ask for help. If you're going straight to the baths, look for the left turn marked "Thermen, parking" and follow that road around town and into the underground parking place at the baths (first two hours free if going to Caracalla Baths). Parking is very tight in Baden-Baden. Use a garage (12 DM a day).

Train travelers will need to simplify. After probably sleeping in Freiburg, let the TI recommend the most scenic public transportation route to get to Baden-Baden. Your Eurailpass works on some Black Forest buses. Consider the Schauinsland excursion and the hourly 90-minute Freiburg to Baden-Baden train. The Baden-Oos station is 5 miles from the center. Bus 1 to Augustaplatz (hostelers get off long before the center at Grosse Dollen Strasse) connects the Oos station with the center every ten minutes.

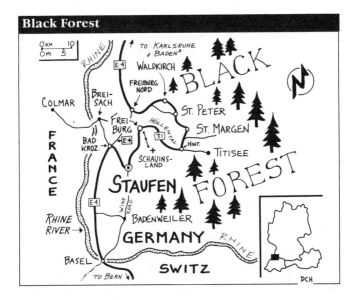

Black Forest

The Black Forest

Called the Schwarzwald in German, this is a range of hills stretching north-south along the French border from Karlsruhe to Switzerland. It's so thickly wooded, the people called it black. Today it's popular for its clean air, cheery villages, hiking possibilities, and cuckoo clocks. The area is impressively Catholic and traditional. On any Sunday, you'll find volks marches and traditional costumes coloring the Black Forest.

While parts of the Black Forest are a commercial jungle, your proposed route gives you a quick and painless look at this famous chunk of Germany.

Sightseeing Highlights—Black Forest
▲▲ **Freiburg im Breisgau**—The "sunniest town in Germany" feels like the university town it is (with 22,000 students). It feels like it had a chance to start all over and do it right (it was bombed almost flat in 1944). And it feels cozy, almost Austrian (it was Habsburg territory for 500 years). It's the "capital" of the Schwarzwald, surrounded by lush forests. Freiburg's worth a quick look, but it's nothing to fax home about.

Enjoy the pedestrian-only old center. Freiburg's trademark is its system of *Bächle*, tiny streams running down each street. They are fresh and cute today, but imagine back 500 years when these were the town's sewer system. Enjoy the ice cream and street-singing ambience of the cathedral square.

The church and its towering tower (not worth the 116-meter ascent) are impressive. Don't miss the Augustiner Museum for a fine look at local culture and a great closeup look at some of the Münster's medieval stained glass downstairs (open 9:30-17:00, Wednesday 10:00-20:00, closed Monday). All of Freiburg's museums are free.

The TI (between old center and station, 9:00-21:30, Sunday 10:00-12:00, less off-season, tel. 0761/3689090) has a fine 4 DM city guidebook, room-finding service, twice daily guided walks, and information on the entire Black Forest region. Bounce your plan for the day off these people.

Schauinsland—Freiburg's own mountain is the handiest quick look at the Schwarzwald for those without wheels. A gondola system, one of Germany's oldest, was designed for Freiburgers relying on public transportation. At the 4,000-foot summit are a panorama restaurant, pleasant circular walks, a tower on a nearby peak offering a commanding Black Forest view, and the Schniederli—a 1592 farmhouse museum. Ask at the TI for the bus-tram-gondola package ticket. About 14 DM will get you there and back including the tram ride from the town center to the lift.

▲▲ **The Short and Scenic Black Forest Joyride**—
This pleasant loop from Freiburg takes you through the
most representative chunk of the area, avoiding the
touristy and overcrowded Titisee. Leave Freiburg on
Schwarzwaldstrasse, which becomes scenic road 31
down the dark and fertile-with-fairy tales Höhental
(Hell's Valley) toward Titisee. Turn left at Hinterzarten
onto road 500, follow signs to St. Margen, then to St.
Peter—one of the healthy, go-take-a-walk-in-the-clean-
air places that doctors actually prescribe for people from
all over Germany. Its TI, just next to the fine Benedictine
abbey (open Monday-Friday 7:30-12:00, 13:30- 17:00, tel.
07660/274), can recommend a walk. If you're feeling like
an overnight here might just do you some good, the
traditional old Gasthof Hirschen (85-95 DM doubles,
7811 St. Peter/Hochschwarzwald, tel. 07660/204) is on
the main square. Pension Schwär (52 DM doubles,
Schweighofweg 4, tel. 07660/219) is basic and friendly.

From St. Peter, take the winding road (closed on summer weekends) through idyllic Black Forest scenery up to
Kandelhof. At the summit is the Berghotel Kandel, where
you can park and take a short walk to the peak at 4,000
feet for a commanding view. Then the road winds steeply
through a dense forest to Waldkirch, where a fast road
will take you to the Freiburg Nord autobahn entrance.
With no long stops, this route will get you from Freiburg
to Baden-Baden in 3 hours.

▲▲ **The Extended Black Forest Drive**—Of course,
you could spend much more time in the land of cuckoo
clocks and healthy hikes. For a more thorough visit, still
connecting Freiburg and Baden-Baden, try this drive. As
described above, drive from Freiburg down Höhental,
but skip St. Peter and stay on road 500 to Furtwangen,
which has an impressive cuckoo clock museum (daily
9:00-17:00, less off-season).

Triberg, surrounded by great Black Forest scenery, has
the famous Gutach Waterfall (500-foot fall in several
bounces, 3 DM to see it) and more important, the Heimat
Museum (4 DM, daily 8:00-18:00, fewer hours off-season),
which gives a fine look at the costumes, carvings, and tra-

ditions of the local culture. Touristy as Triberg is, it offers the easiest way for travelers without a car to enjoy the Black Forest. The youth hostel (a steep hike above the train station, Rohrbacherstrasse 35, tel. 07722/4110, hostel card required, 16 DM per bed) is beautifully situated with some great get-away-from-it-all walks out its back door.

If you want to learn more about Schwarzwald life, drive 20 kilometers farther north to Gutach to visit the open-air museum (Schwarzwälder Freilichtermuseum, 7 DM, daily 9:00-18:00, summer only, tel. 07831/230), where you can wander through several old farms and see local crafts in action. The road continues through the scenic town of Schiltach to Freudenstadt, the capital of the northern Black Forest. This town is also a delight, but drive through it, onto the Schwarzwald-Hochstrasse, which takes you in 35 miles to Baden-Baden.

Baden-Baden

Of all the high-class resort towns I've seen, Baden-Baden is the easiest to enjoy on a budget, in blue jeans. One hundred fifty years ago, this was the playground of Europe's elite and had the world's top casino. Royalty and aristocracy would come from all corners to take the kur—soak in the curative (or at least they feel that way) mineral waters. Today this town of 55,000 attracts a more middle-class crowd, both tourists and Germans enjoying the fruits of their generous health care system. Baden-Baden has a tremendous tourist office complete with lounge and library (right in the center near the riverside park at Augustaplatz 8, open 9:00-22:00, Sunday 10:00-22:00; tel. 07221/275200).

The best approach to Baden-Baden, given your tight schedule, is to get set up by 16:00 and spend one hour just browsing through the center, enjoying ritzy window displays, gardens, street fairs, and fountains. After taking a kur at 17:00, dine at 20:00 and finish the evening bestowing on yourself a royal title and promenading down the famous Lichtentaler Allee, a pleasant lane through a park along a stream and past old mansions. (This is lit until

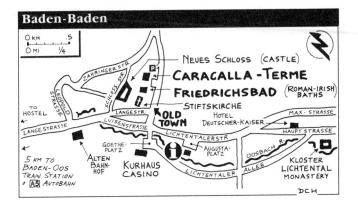

Baden-Baden

22:00. During the day consider taking city bus 1 or 3 to Klosterplatz and walking its entire length back into town.)

Tomorrow morning, even if you don't gamble, tour the casino. It's open for gambling from 14:00 to 2:00 (5 DM entry, 5 DM minimum bet, tie and coat required) but gives dicey 30-minute German-language tours of its Versailles-rivaling interior every morning from 9:30 to 12:00, 10:00 to 12:00 in winter (tours start on the half hour, last one at 11:30, 3 DM, and no ties, tel. 07221/1060).

The Germans who come to Baden-Baden generally stay put for two weeks, and the TI has enough recommended walks and organized excursions to keep even the most energetic vacationers happy. Telephone code: 07221.

▲▲ **The Roman-Irish Bath, Friedrichsbad**—The highlight of most Baden-Baden visits is a sober two-hour ritual called the Roman-Irish Bath. Friedrichsbad, on Römerplatz 1, pampered the rich and famous in its elegant surroundings when it opened 120 years ago. Today, this steamy world of marble, brass columns, tropical tiles, herons, lily pads, and graceful nudity welcomes gawky tourists as well as locals.

For 32 DM, you get the works (27 DM without the massage). The complex routine is explained in the blue English brochure and on the walls, following the numbered arrows: shower to clean; warm air bath for 15 minutes; hot air bath for 5 minutes; shower; soap brush massage—rough, slippery, and finished with a spank;

play gumby in the shower; lounge under sunbeams and caryatids in one of five different thermal steam baths; cold plunge; dry in warmed towels; wrapped like a cocoon on a bed for 30 minutes; clean; and almost new-born in the silent room.

You'll get a key, locker, and towel (open daily except Sunday from 9:00-22:00, men and women together all day Wednesday and Saturday and from 16:00-22:00 on Tuesday and Friday, last admissions two hours before closing, tel. 02271/2751). The nearby, more modern Caracalla Baths are open Sundays. The dress code is always nude. During separate times, men and women use parallel and nearly identical facilities. "Mixed" means men and women using the whole place together. Being your average American, I'm not used to nude. But naked, bewildered, and surrounded by beautiful people with no tan lines is a feeling Woody Allen could write a movie about.

You don't appreciate how really clean you are after this experience until you put your dirty socks back on.

Afterward, browse through the special exhibits and Roman artifacts in the Renaissance Hall, sip just a little ter-rible but "magic" water from the elegant fountain with old ladies who don't seem to be getting much out of it, and stroll down the broad royal stairway feeling, as they say, five years younger—or at least no older.

▲▲ **Caracalla Therme**—For more of a glorified swim-ming pool experience, spend a few hours at the Baths of Caracalla (open daily 8:00-22:00, last entry at 20:00). This huge palace of water, steam, and relaxed people is just past the Friedrichsbad.

Bring a towel (5 DM rental) and swimsuit (any shorts are okay), pick up the blue English instruction sheet and buy a card (18 DM for the first two hours, 5 DM per half-hour after that), put the card in the locker room lock to get a key, change, strap the key around your wrist, and go play. (Your key gets you into a poolside locker if you want money for a tan or a drink. You can park under the *Ther-men* for free for 2 hours if you validate your ticket at the Caracalla turnstile.)

It's a seemingly infinite indoor/outdoor wonderland of huge steamy pools, waterfalls, neck showers, Jacuzzis, hot springs, cold pools, lounge chairs, exercise instructors, saunas, cafeteria, and bar. One area has a current simulating a river. The steamy "inhalation" room seems like purgatory's waiting room, with 6 misty inches of visibility, filled with strange, silent bodies.

Climb the spiral staircase into a naked world of saunas, tanning lights, cold plunges, and sunbathing. There are three eucalyptus-smelling saunas: 80, 90, and 95 degrees. Read and follow the instructions on the wall. Towels are required, not for modesty but to separate your body from the wood that every other body sits on. The highlight for me was the great cold bucket in the shower room. Only rarely will you feel so good.

As you leave, take a look at the old Roman bath that Emperor Caracalla himself soaked in to conquer his rheumatism nearly 2,000 years ago.

Sleeping in Baden-Baden (1.5 DM = about US$1)
Except for its hostel, rooms in Baden-Baden are fairly expensive. But the TI can always find you a room if you arrive by 17:00 (doubles from 80 DM, more expensive in the center, a few Zimmer for 30-35 DM per person). If you can find a room without private plumbing, you'll save a lot. In Baden-Baden, of all places, you should be able to manage without a private bath.

The easiest budget strategy is to use the great bus line #1, connecting Baden-Baden's Oos train station (cheap hotels, easy parking) with the center (Augustaplatz, TI, baths, casino) and continuing to cheap hotels on the east end of town (runs every 10 minutes, 2 DM per ride, or 5 DM for 24 hours, buy tickets on the bus).

There are three hotels right in the nearly traffic-free old town, 2 minutes from the TI, baths, and casino. **Gästehaus Löhr** (40 DM singles, 70-100 DM doubles, office at Cafe Löhr at 19 Lichtentaler Strasse, on the main drag across the street from the TI, tel. 07221/26204 or 31370) is basic, comfortable, clean enough, and a good deal if you don't mind the mickey mouse setup of the reception being in a café two blocks from the hotel. I'd take their cheap showerless rooms over the hostel. **Hotel am Markt** (85-115 DM doubles, Marktplatz 18, 7570 Baden-Baden, tel. 07221/22747 or 22743) is the best splurge for a warm family-run small hotel with all the comforts a commoner could want in a very quiet and central location, two cobbled blocks from the baths. **Hotel Bischoff** (120 DM doubles, Römerplatz 2, 7570 Baden-Baden, tel. 07221/22378) embraces the conform-ist values of elevators and private showers at all cost. It's a rather plain place facing the baths.

Train travelers will get only as close as the suburb of Oos. Those driving in from the autobahn will hit Oos first also. Connoisseurs of simplicity will check into one of the following three accommodations, save money, park easy, and ride the bus. Each of these places is on Ooser Hauptstrasse, with easy parking, just a few minutes walk in front of the station. **Gasthof Adler** (75-95 DM doubles, Ooser Hauptstrasse 1, 7570 Baden-Baden Oos, tel. 07221/61858 or 61811) is plain, comfortable, and friendly. **Hotel Goldener Stern** (85-100 DM doubles, Ooser Hauptstrasse 16, 7570 Baden-Baden, tel. 07221/61509) has big, bright rooms. **Gasthaus zum Engel** (65 DM doubles and a few cheap singles, Ooser Hauptstrasse 20, tel. 07221/61610) is in all the guidebooks, cheap, and a bit depressing.

Baden-Baden's great new **Werner Dietz Youth Hos-tel** (24 DM for bed, sheets, and breakfast, Hardbergstr. 34, bus 1 to Grosse Dollenstr. from the station or down-town, tel. 07221/52223, open 8:00-23:30, but doesn't answer phone in midday) is your budget ace in the hole. They always save 25 beds to be doled out to "travelers" at 17:00, have an overflow hall when all beds are taken, give 3 DM discount coupons for both city baths, and serve cheap meals. (Those driving, turn left at the first light after the freeway into Baden-Baden ends, and follow the signs winding uphill to the big modern hostel next to a public swimming pool.)

There are good budget beds, and easy parking, down Lichtentaler Allee. **Deutscher Kaiser** (70-100 DM doubles, Hauptstr. 35, 7570 Baden-Baden-Lichtental, tel. 07221/72152, fax 72154), with 4 cheap doubles, offers the best rooms in town for the money. This big traditional guest house is in a down-to-earth suburb town right on bus 1 line about a 15-minute walk down polite Lichtentaler Allee. **Gasthof Cäcilienberg** (70-85 DM, Geroldsauer Strasse 2, tel. 07221/72297) is even farther out in a quiet area at the end of Lichtentaler Allee and the end of bus 1 line, behind the Kloster Lichtental.

Pension La Sila (90 DM doubles, Fremersbergstr. 23, bus 1, then 5 or 16, tel. 07221/22642) is about a 10-minute walk from the casino in a woodsy residential area beyond the Lichtentaler Allee.

DAY 19
BADEN-BADEN TO THE MOSEL VALLEY

After touring one of the world's most lavish casinos, leave Baden-Baden for a look at Germany's oldest town, Roman Trier, and an afternoon meandering through the village vineyards and soothing views of the Mosel River Valley.

Suggested Schedule	
9:30	Tour Baden-Baden casino.
11:00	Drive to Trier.
15:00	Mosey up the Mosel Valley.
17:00	Find a Zimmer in Zell.

Transportation: Baden-Baden to the Mosel (180 miles)

From Baden-Baden, there's no direct road to Trier. Remember that in Germany, the shortest distance between any two points is the autobahn. Follow autobahn signs to Karlsruhe and hook around past Karlsruhe, Ludwigshafen, and Kaiserslautern. From Trier, follow the signs to the Mosel Valley, letting scenic riverside route 53 wind you north past Bernkastel-Kues to Zell am Mosel.

Eurailers should rearrange things a bit, taking the express to Koblenz (Baden-Baden to Koblenz, changing in Mannheim, 2 per hour, 2-hour ride) and then another down the Mosel to Trier (hourly, 75-minute rides) or skipping Trier and setting up in Cochem (on the Koblenz–Trier line) or in nearby Zell.

For sightseeing along the Mosel, Eurailers have some interesting transportation options. While the train can take you along much of the river, consider riding the K-D (Köln–Düsseldorf) line, which sails once a day in the summer from Trier to Bernkastel–Kues and from Cochem to Koblenz (free with Eurail). You can also rent bikes at some stations and leave them at others, or rent a bike from Zenz at Enderstrasse 3 in Cochem. If you find yourself stranded in some town, hitching isn't bad.

Sightseeing Highlights

Heidelberg—This famous old university town attracts hordes of Americans, and any former charm is stained almost beyond recognition by commercialism. Skip it— you've seen much better on this trip.

Speyer—You'll be going right by it; if you'd like to see Germany's most impressive Romanesque cathedral, drop in. You'll see the Speyer spires in the distance from the autobahn.

▲▲ **Trier**—Germany's oldest city lies at the head of the scenic Mosel Valley, near the border with Luxembourg. Founded by Augustus in 15 B.C., it was 80,000 strong when Emperor Constantine's father used the town as the capital of the fading western Roman Empire. A short stop here offers you a look at Germany's oldest Christian church and its oldest Gothic church (Dom and Liebfrau churches, open 7:00-18:00). Also, you'll find Karl Marx's house (fascinating to Marx fans, 15-minute film at 20 past each hour, 10:00-18:00, Monday 13:00-18:00).

Trier has a lovely park featuring the remains of a Roman bath and the striking fourth-century relics of the Roman emperor's summer residence now built into a palace and church. The famous and huge Porta Nigra (best Roman fortifications in Germany, climb to the top) is noteworthy, but skip the city museum in the adjacent courtyard.

The Hauptmarkt square is a pleasant swirl of fruit stands, flowers, painted facades, and fountains—with a handy public W.C. Trier's tourist office is next to the Porta Nigra (open 9:00-18:45, Sunday 9:00-15:30, tel. 0651/48071; when it's closed, a coin-op machine may dispense maps and room lists).

▲▲ **Mosel Valley**—The Mosel is what many visitors hoped the Rhine would be—peaceful, sleepy, romantic, with fine wine, plenty of castles, hospitable little towns, and lots of Zimmer. Boat, train, and car traffic here is a trickle compared to the roaring Rhine. While the Mosel moseys from France to Koblenz, where it dumps into the Rhine, the most scenic piece of the valley lies between the towns of Bernkastel-Kues and Cochem. I'd savor only this section.

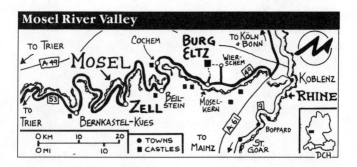

Bernkastel, while pretty, is overrated and overcrowded, but the vine-draped, castle-studded hills and the meandering Mosel north of there are lovely.

The town of Zell is best for an overnight stop—peaceful, with a fine riverside promenade, a pedestrian bridge over the river, plenty of Zimmer, colorful shops, restaurants, and winestubes.

Beilstein, farther downstream, is the quaintest of all Mosel towns. Check out its narrow lanes, ancient wine cellar, resident (and very territorial) swans, and ruined castle.

Cochem, with a majestic castle and picturesque medieval streets, is the touristic hub of this part of the river. Even with the tourist crowds, it's worth a stop. The Cochem castle is spectacular—even if it is the work of over-imaginative nineteenth-century restorers (mid-March-October, 9:00-17:00, tours on the hour, 3 DM). Consider a boat ride from Cochem to Beilstein (1 hour) or to Zell (3 hours). The peaceful thirteenth-century Winneburg ruins up the valley, a pleasant 2-mile hike behind Cochem, are lonely and worth the hike only to a castle connoisseur.

Throughout the region on summer weekends, you'll find wine festivals with oompah bands, dancing, colorful costumes, and lots of good food and wine. Any local TI can give you a schedule.

Sleeping in Zell on the Mosel

Zell is my choice for the Mosel evening. By car, this is a natural. By train, you'll need to go to Bullay (hourly

40-minute rides from Trier, four 10-minute rides per hour from Cochem) where the hourly 10-minute bus ride takes you to little Zell. The tourist office (next to the Rathaus, 8:00-12:30, 13:30-16:30, tel. 06542/4031) posts room vacancies after hours. Zell's hotels are a disappointment, but its private homes are great. The owners speak almost no English and discount their rates if you stay more than one night. My favorites are on the south end of town, a 2-minute walk from the town hall square and the bus stop.

The comfortable and modern home of Fritz and Susanne **Mesenich** is quiet, friendly, clean, central, and across from a good winestube (50 DM doubles, Oberstr. 3, 5583 Zell/Mosel, tel. 06542/4753). Frau Mesenich can find you a room if she's full. Herr Mesenich can take you into his cellar for a look at the haus wine. Notice the flood marks on the wall across the street and flood photos in her breakfast room and hope it doesn't rain.

Gästhaus Gertrud Thiesen (60 DM doubles, Balduinstr. 1, 5583 Zell/Mosel, tel. 06542/4453) is across the street with less laughs but classier TV/living/breakfast room and a river view. The Thiesen house has big bright rooms and is on the town's first corner overlooking the Mosel from a great terrace.

If you've got to have room service and an elevator, sleep at **Hotel Grüner Kranz** (140 DM doubles with Mosel views, 5583 Zell/Mosel, tel. 06542/4549 or 4276). Their rooms in the older building, farther off the river, are more reasonable and traditional, as is the restaurant in that section.

Sleeping in Cinderella Land, Beilstein on the Mosel

Cozier and farther north, Beilstein is very small and quiet, with no train nearby and almost no cars (but several daily bus connections to Cochem). The TI (tel. 02673/1417, or 7912 in the winter) is open daily 7:00 to 19:00 in the Café Klapperburg.

Hotel Haus Lipmann (95 DM doubles, D-5591 Beilstein/Mosel, tel. 02673/1573) is your chance to live in a medieval mansion with hot showers and TVs. This place, with only 5 rooms, is a prize winner for atmosphere. It's

been in the Lipmann family for 200 years. The creaky
wooden staircase and the elegant dining hall with long
wooden tables surrounded by antlers, chandeliers, and
feudal weapons will get you in the mood for your castle
sightseeing. The riverside terrace may mace your
momentum.

Gasthaus Winzerschenke an der Klostertreppe
(60 DM doubles with shower, tel. 02673/1354) is comfortable, right in the tiny heart of town but not as memorable
as the Haus Lipmann. There are plenty of cheaper rooms
in Beilstein's gaggle of private homes.

Sleeping in Cochem

If you have a car, use it to stay out of Cochem. Train
travelers have permission to be lazy and sleep in Cochem.
It has plenty of Zimmer on Oberbachstrasse and Endert-
strasse and a youth **hostel** over the bridge and left half a
mile down Bergstrasse (21 DM per bed with sheets and
breakfast, members only, Klottener Str. 9, tel. 02671/8633).
The Cochem TI (open Monday-Friday 9:00-13:00,
14:00-17:00, Saturday 10:00-15:00, tel. 02671/3971)
books rooms and keeps a thorough 24-hour listing in its
window. **Gästezimmer Götz** (60 DM doubles,
Ravenestr. 34, next to the station, tel. 02671/8438) is a
good and handy value. Decent budget beds can also be
found at **Gasthaus Onkel Willi** (70-90 DM doubles,
Endertstr. 39, tel. 02671/7305) and **Gasthaus Dohler**
(50-70 DM doubles, Valwigerstr. 41, tel. 02671/7696).

MOSEL VALLEY TO BONN

Tour the town of Cochem and the great Eltz Castle before traveling up to the Rhine and over to Bonn, the former home of Germany's post-World War II government and Beethoven.

Suggested Schedule	
9:00	Cochem, skip the castle, buy a picnic.
10:30	Burg Eltz, lunch at castle's budget cafeteria or picnic.
13:30	Drive rest of Mosel Valley. Autobahn from Koblenz to Bonn.
16:00	Park near station, visit TI, get set up in Bonn.

Transportation: Mosel to Bonn (90 miles)

You can't get lost if you stick to the river. For Burg Eltz, drive to the car park at the end of the road above Moselkern, or if you'd like to skip the enchanting but long 30-minute walk to the castle, drive around through Lasserg and Wiersheim, where it's a 15-minute walk or a quick, cheap shuttle bus ride to the castle. By train, walk one steep hour from Moselkern station, midway between Cochem and Koblenz.

The quickest way to Bonn is to enter the autobahn where it crosses the Mosel (Koblenz-Dieblich) and head north following the signs to Köln and Bonn. For a look at Koblenz, Remagen, and the capital buildings in Bonn-Bad Godesberg, follow the Mosel into Koblenz, work your way to the Deutsches-Eck where the rivers touch, then leave town on highway 9 along the Rhine through Mulheim, Andernach, and Remagen.

In Bonn, take the Bonn-Endenich exit and follow signs to Zentrum, Stadtmitte, Bahnhof, and TI. Park near the Bahnhof; there's a big lot just north on Thomastrasse.

By train, simply change in Koblenz, catching one of

many expresses to Bonn and Köln (don't get off in Bonn-
Bad Godesberg).

Sightseeing
▲▲▲ **Burg Eltz**—My favorite castle in all of Europe is
set in a mysterious forest, left intact for 700 years, and furnished throughout as it was 500 years ago. Even with its
German-only tours, it's a must. (April-October, Monday-
Saturday, 9:00-17:30, Sunday 10:00-17:30, tel. 02672/
1300, 7 DM.)

Bonn
See tomorrow.

BONN, KÖLN, AND THE RHINELAND

Today you get a good dose of no-nonsense urban German muscle, visit its greatest Gothic cathedral along with one of Germany's finest art museums, and drive back into the fairy-tale world of Rhine legends and castles.

Suggested Schedule	
9:00	Catch boat to Köln, see its cathedral and museums, take train back to Bonn.
13:00	Lunch, afternoon free in Bonn.
16:00	Drive south to Bacharach.
Sleep	Bacharach.

Transportation: Bonn to Bacharach (90 miles)
Big city driving is something most normal people try to minimize. Today you can avoid it entirely by riding the boat up to Köln and returning by train (or vice versa, the 20-minute train ride costs 8 DM). Ask at the TI for boat schedules. All the important sights in each town are within comfortable walking distance between the train and boat stations. Plan this upon arrival in Bonn at the TI. If you decide to drive to Köln, park in the pay lot under the cathedral, go upstairs, and thank the Lord you survived.

From Bonn, catch the autobahn south (direction Frankfurt), getting off in downtown Koblenz and following the highway 9 signs in the direction of Mainz. (*Umleitung*, a common road sign around here, means detour.) Highway 9 will put you right on the Rhine's west bank. Now the castle fun begins.

Eurailers should take the train from Bonn through Koblenz to Boppard, a good place to catch one of the K-D boats. If you're rushed, stay on the train to whatever Rhine village you choose to call home. Express trains don't stop in small towns, so you'll probably be changing trains in Koblenz. The walk from the Koblenz Bahnhof to the boat dock is much longer (30 minutes, or catch bus #1) than in the smaller towns farther south.

Sightseeing Highlights—Unromantic Rhine
▲▲ **Bonn**—Bonn was chosen for its sleepy, cultured, and peaceful nature as a good place to plant Germany's first post-Hitler government. Now that Germany is one again, Berlin will retake its position as capital of Germany. Apart from the tremendous cost of switching the seat of government, over 100,000 jobs are involved, and lots of Bonn families will have some difficult decisions to make.

Today Bonn is sleek, modern, and, by big city standards, remarkably pleasant and easygoing. Stop here not only to see Beethoven's house (open 10:00-17:00, Sunday 10:00-13:00, 5 DM, tel. 0228/635188) but to come up for a smoggy breath of the real world before diving into the misty, romantic Rhine.

The excellent TI is directly in front of the station (open 8:00-21:00, Sunday 9:30-12:30, tel. 0228/773466, free room-finding service). Stop here for information, to confirm tomorrow's plans, and to get advice on overnight parking.

The pedestrian-only old town stretches out from the station and makes you wonder why the United States can't trade its malls in on real, people-friendly cities. The market square and Münsterplatz are a joy, as are the local shopping and people-watching.

Hotels are expensive in Bonn, but the TI is helpful. A good value is the Hotel Eschweiler (95-110 DM doubles, Bonngasse 7, 5300 Bonn 1, tel. 0228/631760 or 631769, fax 694904). It's plain, but perfectly located just off the market square on a pedestrian street next to Beethoven's place (10-minute walk from the station—don't drive). The Bonn youth hostel (cheap, way out of town in the woods on Venusberg, bus 621, tel. 0228/281200) is clean and modern.

Bonn-Bad Godesberg—This suburb of Bonn was the home of Germany's government. Very little is open to the public, but if you drive into Bonn on highway 9, you'll go right by the parks, monuments, embassies, and important

buildings that made up West Germany's sleepy capital.
▲▲ **Köln (Cologne)**—A big, no-nonsense city, Germany's fourth largest, it has a compact and fascinating center. Since the Rhine was the northern boundary of the Roman Empire, Köln, like most of these towns, goes back 2,000 years. It was an important cultural and religious center throughout the Middle Ages. Even after World War II bombs destroyed 95 percent of it, Köln has remained, after a remarkable recovery, a cultural and commercial center as well as a fun, colorful, and pleasant-smelling city.

Its Dom, or cathedral, is far and away Germany's most exciting Gothic church (100 yards from the station, open 7:00-19:00, free tours in German only). Next to the Dom is the outstanding Römisch-Germanisches Museum, Germany's best Roman museum (Tuesday-Sunday 10:00-17:00, Wednesday and Thursday until 20:00; you can view its prize piece, a fine mosaic floor, free from the front window). Sadly, the displays are in German only. The fine Wallraf-Richartz Museum has a new home next to the Roman museum and the cathedral. It has a great collection of paintings by the European masters with a modern and pop art bonus. Don't miss Kienholz's "Portable War Memorial." (Friday-Sunday 10:00-18:00, Tuesday-Thursday 10:00-20:00, closed Monday, tel. 0221/221 2379.) The helpful TI is near the station, opposite the Dom's main entry (tel. 0221/221 3345, daily 8:00-22:30, closes early in winter).

Other Sights
Charlemagne's Capital, Open-Air Folk Life, and Phantasialand—If you have an extra day, a number of interesting sights are within easy striking distance of Bonn and Köln. Aachen was the capital of Europe in A.D. 800, when Charles the Great (Charlemagne) called it Aix-la-Chapelle. The remains of his rule are there, including a very impressive Byzantine/Ravenna-inspired church with his sarcophagus and throne. The city also has a headliner newspaper museum and great fountains including a clever arrange-'em-yourself version.

To learn more about regional folk life, visit the

Rheinisches Freilichtmuseum (open-air museum) in a lovely natural setting near Kommern (take the Euskirchen-Wisskirchen autobahn exit southwest of Bonn).

For a chance to fight the lowbrow local crowds at a tacky second-rate local Disneyland, visit Phantasialand. It's popular enough to have its very own autobahn exit south of Brühl between Bonn and Köln.

Remagen—North of Koblenz is what's left of the Bridge at Remagen, the "Bridge Too Far" of World War II fame. Little remains, but the memorial and the bridge stubs are enough to stir the emotions of Americans who remember when it was the only bridge that remained, allowing the Allies to cross the Rhine and race to Berlin in 1945. It's never closed. Just follow the signs through the small town.

THE RHINE AND ITS CASTLES, FLY HOME FROM FRANKFURT

A fitting finale for this tour is a day on the romantic Rhine. Cruise the most exciting stretch and climb through the Rhineland's greatest castle before returning to the Frankfurt airport to fly home.

Suggested Schedule

9:00	Train to St. Goar, explore Rheinfels Castle, buy picnic.
11:55	Boat back to Bacharach.
13:00	Picnic in park. Afternoon free.

Return to Frankfurt, turn in car, and fly home.

Transportation on the Rhine

While the Rhine flows hundreds of miles from Switzerland to Holland, the chunk from Mainz to Koblenz is by far the most interesting. This stretch, studded with the crenellated cream of Germany's castles, is busy with boats, trains, and highway traffic. It's easy to explore. While many do the whole trip by boat, I'd tour the area by train or car and cruise just the most scenic hour, from St. Goar to Bacharach. Sit on the top deck with your handy Rhine map-guide and enjoy the parade of castles, towns, boats, and vineyards. Note that the Rhine boats only cruise from Easter through October. Off-season, the Rhine is so quiet that many hotels close down.

There are several boat companies, but most travelers sail on the bigger, more expensive but more romantic Köln–Düsseldorf line (free with Eurail, tel. 0221/2088). Boats run daily in both directions (the "fast" boat doesn't go on Monday) from May through September with fewer boats off-season. Complete, up-to-date, and more complicated schedules are posted at any station, Rhineland hotel, or TI. Or check a current Thomas Cook Timetable.

Rhine Steamer Schedule (Köln-Düsseldorf Line)

Daily/dates	Koblenz	Boppard	St. Goar	Bacharach	Bingen
May-Sept	—	9:00	10:15	11:20	12:55
Apr-Oct	9:00	10:40	11:55	12:55	14:20
May-Sept	11:00	12:40	13:55	14:55	16:20
Apr-Oct	14:00	15:40	16:55	17:55	19:20
		⟶			
fast, May-Oct	11:05	11:30	11:50	12:08	12:28
July-Aug	12:30	14:10	15:25	16:25	17:50
May-Oct	12:20	11:20	10:35	9:55	9:10
July-Aug	15:50	14:40	13:35	12:45	12:00
		⟵			
fast, May-Oct	16:17	15:55	—	—	15:05
Apr-Sept	20:00	18:50	18:00	17:20	16:35

Koblenz–Bingen tickets cost 50 DM, St. Goar–Bacharach 12
DM, free with Eurail; groups of 15 get a 20 percent discount.
The fast boat is not free with Eurail.

In St. Goar, the Köln–Düsseldorf dock is at the far end
of Main Street. If you rush doing the castle, you can catch
the 10:15 boat and picnic in Bacharach. Or take it easy
and picnic on the 11:55 boat. Purchase tickets at the dock
5 minutes before departure. The boat is never full. (Confirm times at your hotel the night before.)

The smaller Bingen–Rüdesheimer line (tel. 06721/14140,
Eurail not valid, tickets at St. Goar TI) is 25 percent
cheaper than K-D with three 2-hour St. Goar–Bacharach
round-trips daily in summer (departing St. Goar at 11:00,
14:15, and 16:10; departing Bacharach at 10:10, 12:30,
15:00; 10 DM one way, 13 DM round-trip).

If you're driving, the boat ride can present a problem.
Your choices: (1) skip the boat; (2) take a round-trip
Bingen–Rüdesheimer ride from St. Goar; (3) draw pretzels and let the loser of your group drive to Bacharach,
prepare the picnic, and meet the boat; (4) take the boat to
Bacharach and return by train, spending your waiting
time exploring that old half-timbered town; (5) bring a

bike on the boat (free) and bike back; or (6) decide it's an insurmountable problem, get depressed, and stay in the hotel all day.

Taking the boat one way and returning by train works well. Milk-run Rhine Valley trains leave major towns every two hours, and rides are very quick (St. Goar–Bacharach 12 min., Bacharach–Mainz 30 min., Mainz–Frankfurt 30 min.)

There's a lovely riverside bike path from St. Goar to Bacharach, and you can rent bikes at the St. Goar TI or at several Bacharach Zimmer. Those with more time and energy can sail to Bingen and bike back, visiting Rheinstein Castle and Reichenstein Castle and maybe even taking a ferry across the river to Kaub. While there are no bridges between Koblenz and Mainz, several small ferries do their job constantly and cheaply.

For train travelers, if you're rushed, the speediest schedule is to tour Rheinfels Castle from 9:00 to 10:00, cruise from St. Goar to Bacharach from 10:15 to 11:20, picnic in Bacharach, and catch the early afternoon train to Frankfurt (via Mainz) and on to Rothenburg.

Sightseeing Highlights—The Romantic Rhine (working south from Koblenz to Bingen)

▲▲▲ **Der Romantische Rhine Blitz Zug Fahrt** (fast train tour, north to south, from Koblenz to Mainz)—One of Europe's great train thrills is zipping along the Rhine. Here's a quick and easy, from-the-train-window tour (works for car, boat, or bike also) that skips the syrupy myths and the life story of Dieter V von Katzenelnbogen that fill normal Rhine guides.

The stretch from St. Goar to Bacharach is best by boat, but you could argue it's the same river by 50-mph train. For more information than necessary, buy the handy *Rhine Guide from Mainz to Cologne* (5 DM book with foldout map, at most shops). Sit on the left (river) side of the train going south from Koblenz. While nearly all the castles listed are viewed from this side, clear a path to the right window for the times I yell, "Crossover."

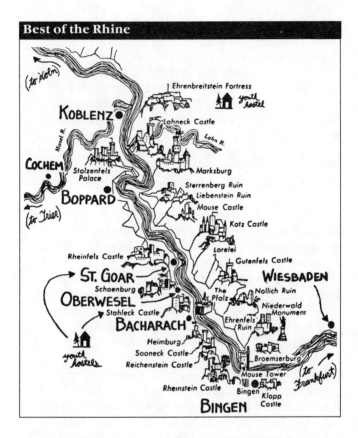

Best of the Rhine

Rhine Overview

You'll notice large black and white kilometer markers
along the riverbank. I put those up years ago just to help
with this tour. They tell the distance from the Rhinefalls
where the Rhine leaves Switzerland and becomes navigable.
Now the boats have learned to accept these as navigational aids as well.

We're tackling just 36 miles of the 820-mile-long Rhine.
Ever since Roman times, when this was the Empire's northern boundary, the Rhine has been one of the world's busiest shipping rivers. You'll see a steady flow of barges
with 1,000- to 2,000-ton loads. Along both banks are tour
buses with 48 people, very busy train tracks, and highways.

Many of the castles you see today were "robber baron"

castles, put there by petty rulers (there were 300 independent little countries in medieval Germany) to levy tolls on
all the passing river traffic. There were ten customs stops
between Koblenz and Mainz alone (no wonder merchants
were proponents of the creation of larger nation-states).

A robber baron would put his castle on, or even in, the
river and, often with the help of chains, stop each ship
and get his toll. Other castles were built to control and
protect settlements. Some were the residences of kings.
As times changed, so did the life-styles of the rich and
feudal. Many castles were abandoned for comfortable
mansions in the towns.

Most of the Rhine castles were originally built in the
eleventh, twelfth, and thirteenth centuries. Since the
pope successfully asserted his power over the German
emperor in 1076, local princes ran wild over the rule of
their emperor. The castles saw military action in the
1300s and 1400s as emperors began trying to reassert
control over Germany's many silly kingdoms.

The castles were also involved in the Reformation wars
that saw Europe's Catholic and "protesting" dynasties
fight it out using a fragmented Germany as their battle-
ground. These wars, known as the Hundred Years War,
the Thirty Years War, and even the first World War (since
so many countries participated), devastated Germany for
100 years until 1648.

The French destroyed most of the castles prophylacti-
cally (Louis XIV in the 1680s, the Revolutionary army in
the 1790s, and Napoleon in 1806). They were often
rebuilt in neo-Gothic style in the romantic age—the late
1800s—and today are enjoyed as restaurants, hotels,
youth hostels, and museums.

Km 590: Koblenz—This Rhine tour starts at Koblenz
city with Ehrenbreitstein Castle fortress across the river
(described below).

Km 585: Burg Lahneck (above the modern autobahn
bridge over the Lahn river) was built in 1240 to defend
local silver mines, ruined by the French in 1688, and
rebuilt in the 1850s in neo-Gothic style. Burg Lahneck
faces the yellow Schloss Stolzenfels (out of view above

the train, worth touring, a 10-minute climb from the tiny car park, closed Monday).

Km 580: Marksburg (with the three modern chimneys behind it) is the best looking of all the Rhine castles and the only surviving medieval castle on the Rhine. Because of its commanding position, it was never attacked. It was once a state prison. Now the bars help keep English-speaking visitors suffering through the mandatory German language tours of its fascinating interior.

Km 570: Boppard—After a broad horseshoe bend in the river, you come to Boppard, a Roman town with some impressive remains of fourth-century walls. Notice the Roman tower just before the Boppard station and the substantial chunk of Roman wall just after (stop-worthy, see below).

Km 567: The "Hostile Brothers" castles (with the white square tower)—Take the wall between Burg Sterrenberg and Burg Liebenstein (actually designed to improve the defenses of both castles), add two greedy and jealous brothers and a fair maiden, and create your own legend. They are restaurants today.

Km 559: Burg Maus got its name because the next castle was owned by the Katzenelnbogen family. In the 1300s, it was considered a state-of-the-art fortification. It was no longer state of the art when Napoleon had it blown up in 1806. It was rebuilt true to its original plans around 1900.

Km 557: Rheinfels and St. Goar—See below.

Km 556: Burg Katz—From the town of St. Goar, you'll see Burg Katz (Katzenelnbogen) across the river. Look back on your side of the river to see the mighty Rheinfels castle over St. Goar. Be quick, there's a tunnel and it's gone.

Together, Burg Katz (b. 1371) and Rheinfels had a clear view up and down the river and effectively controlled traffic. There was absolutely no duty-free shopping on the medieval Rhine. Katz got Napoleoned in 1806 and rebuilt around 1900; today it's a convalescent home.

St. Goar (a recommended stop, see below) was named for a sixth-century hometown monk. It originated in

Celtic times (really old) as a place where sailors would stop, catch their breath, send home a postcard, and give thanks after surviving the seductive and treacherous Loreley crossing (see km 554).

Burg Rheinfels (b. 1245) withstood a siege of 28,000 French troops in 1692, but was creamed by the same country in 1797. It was huge, biggest on the Rhine, then used as a quarry. Today it's a hollow but interesting museum (your best single hands-on castle experience on the river; see below).

Km 554: The Loreley—Steep a big slate rock in centuries of legend and it becomes a tourist attraction, the ultimate Rhinestone. The Loreley (two flags on top, name painted near shoreline) rises 450 feet over the narrowest and deepest point of the Rhine. (The fine echoes were thought to be ghostly voices in the old days, fertilizing the legendary soil.)

Because of the reefs just upstream (called the "Seven Maidens"), many ships never made it to St. Goar. Sailors (after days on the river) blamed their misfortune on a wunderbar Fräulein whose long blond hair almost covered her body. Heinrich Heine's *Song of Loreley* (Cliff Notes version on local postcards) tells the story of how a count sent his men to kill or capture this siren after his son was killed because of her. When the soldiers cornered the nymph in her cave, she called her father (Father Rhine) for help. Huge waves, the likes of which you'll never see today, rose out of the river and carried her to safety. And she has never been seen since.

But alas, when the moon shines brightly and the tour buses are parked, a soft, playful Rhine whine can still be heard from the Loreley. As you pass, listen carefully ("Sailors. . .sailors. . .over our bounding waves"). You'll be saved by two medieval train tunnels and then, unless the river's high, see the killer reefs (km 552).

Km 550 (cross to other side of train): Oberwesel —A Celtic town in 400 B.C., then a Roman military station, it has some of the best Roman wall and tower remains on the Rhine. Near the Schönburg Castle there's a fine modern youth hostel (tel. 06744/7046). Okay, back to the river side.

Lower Rhine

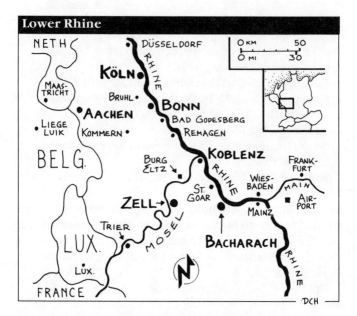

Km 546: Burg Gutenfels (white painted hotel sign) and the ship-shape **Pfalz Castle** (built in the river in the 1300s) worked very effectively to tax medieval river traffic. The town of Kaub grew rich as Pfalz raised its chains when boats came and lowered them only when the merchants had paid their duty. Those who didn't spent time touring its fascinating prison with a floor that went up and down with the river level. In 1504, a pope called for the destruction of Pfalz, but a six-week siege failed. Pfalz is tourable, accessible by ferry from the other side.

Km 543 (cross to other side of train): Bacharach is a great stop (see below) with fourteenth-century fortifications preserved throughout the town. One of the old towers is my favorite Rhine hotel. The train screams within 10 yards of Hotel Kranenturm. Bacharach prospered from its wood and wine trade. The thirteenth-century Berg Stahleck above the town is now a youth hostel.

Km 540: Lorch—is a pathetic stub of a castle (barely visible by car). Notice the small car ferry, one of several between Koblenz and Mainz, where there are no bridges.

Km 538 (cross to other side of train): Castle Sooneck, built in the eleventh century, was twice destroyed by people sick and tired of robber barons. On the same side (at km 534), you'll see Burg Reichenstein and (at km 533) Burg Rheinstein, which was one of the first to be rebuilt in the romantic era (both are tourable and are connected by a pleasant trail, info at TI).

Km 530: Ehrenfels Castle—Opposite the Bingerbrück station, you'll see the ghostly Ehrenfels Castle (clobbered by the Swedes in 1636 and by the French in 1689). Since it had no view of the river traffic to the north, it built the cute little Mäuseturm (Mouse Tower) on an island (the yellow tower you'll see near the station today). Rebuilt in the 1800s in neo-Gothic style, today it's used as a Rhine navigation signal station.

Km 528: Niederwald monument—Across from the Bingen station on a hilltop is the 120-foot-high Niederwald monument, a memorial built with 32 tons of bronze in 1877 to commemorate "the reestablishment of the German Empire." A lift takes tourists to this statue from the famous and extremely touristic wine town of Rüdesheim. At this point, your train or car leaves the Rhine and your blitz tour is over.

Recommended Stops along the Rhine Gorge

Koblenz—Not a nice city, it was really hit hard in World War II, but its place as the historic *Deutsches-Eck* (German corner), the tip of land where the Mosel joins the Rhine, gives it a certain magnetism. Koblenz has Roman origins (its name is Latin for "confluence"). Walk through the park, noticing the blackened base of what was once a huge memorial to the kaiser. Across the river, the yellow Ehrenbreitstein fortress is now a youth hostel. It's a long hike from the station to the Koblenz boat dock.

▲ **Boppard**—This is a more substantial town than St. Goar or Bacharach. Park near the center (or at the DB train station and walk). Just above the market square are the remains of a Roman wall. Below the square is a fascinating church. Notice the carved Romanesque crazies at the doorway. Inside, to the right of the entrance, you'll

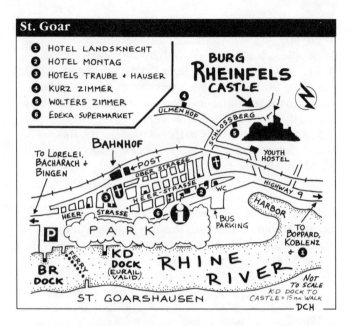

see Christian symbols from Roman times. Also notice the
painted arches and vaults—originally most Romanesque
churches were painted this way. Down by the river,
notice the high water (*Hochwasser*) marks on the arches
from various flood years.

▲ **St. Goar**—A pleasant town, established as a place
where sailors who survived the Loreley could stop and
thank the gods, St. Goar has good shops (steins and
cuckoo clocks, of course), a waterfront park, and a helpful TI. It's worth a stop for its Rheinfels castle. The small
supermarket (EDEKA) on Main Street is fine for picnic
fixins. The friendly and helpful Montag family in the
shop under the Hotel Montag has Koblenz–to–Mainz
Rhine guidebooks, fine steins, and copies of this Germany, Austria, Switzerland guidebook. And across the
street, you'll see what must be the biggest cuckoo clock
in the world.

The St. Goar TI (8:00-12:30, 14:00-17:00, Saturday
9:30-12:00, closed Sunday and earlier in winter, tel.
06741/383) now functions as the town's train station (free
left-luggage service, 5 DM per half day bike rentals). They

have information on which local wineries do tours and tastings in English for individuals.

▲▲ **Bacharach**—Just a very pleasant old town that misses most of the tourist glitz. Next to the K-D dock is a great park for a picnic. The friendly TI is helpful (open Monday-Friday 9:00-12:30 and 13:30-17:00, tel. 06743/1297, on the hill side of the main street you'll see the "i." Open the big door, go up the stairs, and down the squeaky hall). Some of the Rhine's best wine is from this town. Those in search of a stein should stop by the huge Jost beer stein "factory outlet" just a block north of the church.

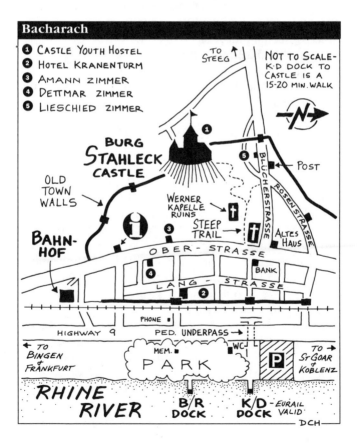

▲▲ **Rheinfels Castle**—This mightiest of Rhine castles is an intriguing ruin today. Follow the castle map with English instructions (.50 DM from the ticket window). If you follow the castle's perimeter, circling counterclockwise, and downward, you'll find a few of the several miles of spooky tunnels. Explore. Bring your flashlight (and bayonet). These tunnels were used to lure in and entomb enemy troops. You'll be walking over the remains (from 1626) of 300 unfortunate Spanish soldiers. Be sure to see the reconstruction of the castle in the museum showing how much bigger it was before Louis XIV destroyed it. And climb to the castle's summit for the Rhine view (4 DM, daily 9:00-18:00, in October until 17:00, winter only Saturday and Sunday, free English tours at 11:00 and 16:00, fifteen minutes' steep hike up from St. Goar).

Mainz, Wiesbaden, Rüdesheim, and Frankfurt—These towns are all too big or too famous. They're not worth your time. Mainz's Gutenberg Museum is also a disappointment.

Sleeping on the Rhine in St. Goar (1.5 DM = about $1)

Rhine Zimmer and Gasthäuser abound, offering beds for 25 to 30 DM per person. For cheaper beds, there are several exceptional Rhine-area youth hostels. And each town has a helpful TI eager to set you up. Finding a room should be easy any time of year. St. Goar and Bacharach are the best towns for an overnight stop. They are about 10 minutes apart, and both are served by the same milk-run trains and the same boats and are connected by a fine riverside bike path. Bacharach is a little less touristic; St. Goar has the famous castle.

In town, and easier for those without wheels, is **Hotel Montag** (100 DM doubles, Heerstr. 128, just across the street from the world's largest free-hanging cuckoo clock, tel. 06741/1629, fax 2086). Mannfred Montag and his family speak English and run a good crafts shop (especially for steins) adjacent. Even though Montag gets a lot of bus tours, it is friendly, laid back, and very comfortable.

Hotel Hauser (95 DM doubles with shower and Rhine view balconies, Heerstr. 77, tel. 06741/333, fax 1464) is newly redone, very central, and a good value.

Hotel Traube (80 DM doubles all with showers, breakfast, and a great Rhine view, Heerstr. 75, 5401 St. Goar, tel. 06741/7511) goes beyond antlers. The dining room is fluttering with stuffed birds of prey. The carpets are depressing and the rooms are plain, but the location, across the street from the boat dock, is great. Just down the street, the **Jägerhaus** (70 DM doubles with shower, Heerstr. 61, tel. 06741/1665) doesn't appreciate one-night stays but will work in a pinch.

Hotel Landsknecht (110 DM doubles, one mile north of town, 5401 St. Goar, tel. 06741/2011, fax 06741/7499) is a ritzy place with a great Rhine terrace and top-notch dining.

St. Goar's best Zimmer are the homes of **Frau Kurz** (56 DM doubles, 32 DM single, Ulmenhof 11, 5401 St. Goar/Rhein, tel. 06741/459, 2-minute walk above the station) and similarly priced **Frau Wolters** (Schlossberg 24, tel. 06741/1695, on the road to the castle). Both charge less for longer stays and are cozier and more comfortable than hotels, with homey TV rooms and great river and castle views.

The very Germanly run **St. Goar hostel** (15 DM beds, Bismarckweg 17, tel. 06741/388 morning and after 17:00), the big beige building under the castle, is a good value with cheap dorm beds, a few smaller rooms, a 22:00 curfew, and hearty 8 DM dinners.

Sleeping and Eating on the Rhine in Bacharach

Overlooking Bacharach is **Jugendherberge Stahleck**, Germany's most impregnable youth hostel. This twelfth-century castle on the hilltop with a royal Rhine view (IYHF members of all ages welcome, 20 DM dorm beds, 5 DM for sheets, normally places available but call and leave your name, tel. 06743/1266, English spoken) is a gem but very much a youth hostel—with dorms crowded with metal bunk beds, showers in the basement, and often filled with school groups. It's a 15-minute climb on the trail from the town church, or you can drive up. It is energetically run by Evelyn and Bernhard Falke (pron. fall-kay), who serve up hearty and very cheap meals.

Hotel Kranenturm (70 DM doubles with this book and a discount for staying several nights, Langstr. 30, tel. 06743/1308, fax 1021) gives you the feeling of a castle without the hostel-ity or the climb. This is my choice for the best combination of comfort and hotel privacy with Zimmer warmth, central location, and medieval atmosphere. Run by hardworking Kurt and Fatima Engel, this is actually part of the medieval fortification. Its former Kranen (crane) towers are now round rooms. Centuries ago when the riverbank was higher, cranes on this tower loaded barrels of wine onto Rhine boats. Hotel Kranenturm is located virtually on the train tracks (from the river, just under the medieval gate at the left end of town), but a combination of medieval sturdiness and triple-pane windows makes sleeping no problem. The current of materialism has no eyes, and the Kranenturm really stretches it to get toilets and showers in each room. Kurt is a great cook, and his Kranenturm ice cream special may ruin you (8.50 DM, one is enough for two). For a taste of Polynesia in a medieval German cellar, check out Kurt's tropical bar.

Frau Amann (44-50 DM doubles, Oberstr. 13, in the old center on a side lane a few yards off the main street, tel. 06743/1271) rents 4 rooms in her quiet, homey, traditional place. Guests get a cushy living room and a self-serve kitchen and the free use of bikes. You'll laugh right through the language barrier with this lovely woman. Zimmer normally discount their prices if you're staying longer.

Annelie and Hans Dettmar (55-60 DM doubles, Oberstr. 8, on the main drag in the center, tel. 06743/2661 or 2979) are a young couple who rent 6 rooms (one is a huge family-of-four room, several have kitchenettes) in a modern house above their craft shop. They speak English well and rent bikes for 8 DM per day.

Frau Erna Leischied (50 DM doubles, Blucherstr. 39, 6533 Bacharach, tel. 06743/1510, speaks German fluently) shares her ancient higgledy-piggledy half-timbered house, 3 blocks from the church uphill, next to the medieval town gate, with travelers. The rooms are very comfortable.

For inexpensive and atmospheric dining in Bacharach, try the **Hotel Kranenturm**, **Altes Haus** (15-25 DM dinners in the oldest building in town), or the less expensive but still atmospheric **Weinstuben Münze** (open daily, tel. 1375), across the street.

Departure

If you're flying home from Frankfurt, be sure to telephone your airline (phone numbers in Practical Extras) three days in advance to confirm your seat. Also, call the morning of your departure to check the departure time.

To get to the airport by autobahn, head toward Frankfurt. After you cross the Rhine, follow signs to the airport (*Flughafen*), which is right on the autobahn. There are plenty of little airplane signs to direct you.

By train, it's even easier. The airport has its own train station, and many of the trains from the Rhine stop there on their way into Frankfurt. A 12-minute shuttle train connects the city's central station and its airport six times an hour.

As you charge down the runway and then fasten your seat belt, I hope you'll enjoy thinking back over a smooth and exciting 2 to 22 days in Germany, Austria, and Switzerland.

POSTTOUR OPTION: BERLIN

No tour of Germany is complete without a look at its historic and newly united capital, Berlin. My greatest frustration in putting this 22-day plan together was my inability to work Berlin in. If you have a couple of extra days, plug in Berlin. It's connected by easy overnight trains to Frankfurt, Köln, Munich, and Vienna.

Suggested Schedule—Berlin in 2 Days

Day 1

7:00	Arrive (overnight trains arrive early), at Berlin's Zoo Bahnhof.
8:00	Stop by TI, move in to your hotel room.
9:00	Ku'damm—visit Memorial church, tour KaDeWe Department Store (late breakfast?).
10:30	Do bus 100 circuit: climb Siegessaule for the view, visit Reichstag History Museum, walk over Brandenburg Gate, stroll down Unter den Linden, tour German History Museum, munch lunch on Alexanderplatz, the heart of eastern Berlin.
14:00	Tour Pergamon Museum.
16:00	Walk down Friedrichstrasse to what was Checkpoint Charlie, walk west a few blocks to see the remains of the wall, then tour the Museum of the Wall. Possible venture into Kreuzberg.
19:00	Dinner near Savignyplatz or on Ku'damm.
21:00	Sample Berlin nightlife (or watch it) on Ku'damm.

Day 2

8:00	Breakfast, consider checking out of hotel, store bag at station.
9:00	Tour Charlottenburg Schloss, cross the street for Egyptian Museum, see Nefertiti.
14:00	Dahlem Museum complex, tour picture gallery.
21:00	Catch night train west.

Berlin is wrapping up one tumultuous 50-year chapter in its 750 years of history. After being flattened in World War II, it was divided by the Allied powers, with the American, British, and French sectors comprising what we knew as West Berlin and the Russian sector comprising East Berlin. The division was set in stone when the East built the infamous Berlin Wall between the two in 1961. On November 9, 1989, the wall fell, and about a year later Germany was formally united. Today the newly healed city is like a man who had a terrible accident and half the body was given the best of care and the other was denied therapy. The West, benefiting from a generation of government schemes to keep the city vital (tax breaks, draft deferments, transportation subsidies, business incentives), provides a striking contrast to the East, which still looks dreary with ersatz jeans, new Fiats made from antiquated factory molds, war-scarred buildings, and people still gawky in their new capitalist lives. Berlin offers a

unique look at urban Deutschland, offering more contrast, culture, hedonism, and history than any city in this
guide. Slowly, the differences will fade, but for now, Berlin is still, in many ways, two cities.

Transportation—Frankfurt to Berlin (330 miles), Munich to Berlin (340 miles)

Drivers will find autobahn signs from most of Germany
to Berlin. By train, it's an easy overnight trip from Frankfurt (15 per day, around 8 hours, 2 direct overnight trains;
e.g., 22:20-7:10, about 85 DM second class) or from
Munich (8 per day, 2 direct overnight trains; e.g.,
21:00-7:00, about 110 DM second class). A *Liege-platz*, or
bunk bed, on the train is 20 DM well spent.

Orientation

Berlin's central station is called Bahnhof Zoo (near Berlin's famous zoo). It has a sickly little TI (open 8:00-23:00
daily), but the main Verkehrsamt Berlin (TI info tel.
262-6031) is two minutes east of the station, in the
Europa Center (the skyscraper with the Mercedes-Benz
symbol on top, on Budapesterstr., open 8:00-22:30
daily). Pick up "Berlin Berlin" for a listing of all the sights
and hours, a town map, the latest events listing, and the
bus 100 flyer, and consider buying the 3 DM transit map.
They can find rooms, but only after scolding you for not
booking in advance. Also next to the station is the Infor-
mationzentrum Berlin (Hardenbergstr. 20, second floor,
open Monday-Friday 8:30-19:00 and Saturday 8:30-16:00,
closed Sunday), which has political and historical information. It also has the best youth information and a very
good city map. Telephone code: 030.

Transportation within Berlin

Even if you drove to Berlin, park your car and use the fine
public transit system (U-bahn, S-bahn, and buses). Ask at
the TI for specifics. A basic buy-as-you-board 3 DM
ticket gives you two hours of travel. The Berlin Ticket
gives you 24 hours of transportation through the entire
city on all the buses and both subway systems for 12 DM.

Buy this pass on arrival at any subway station. The 3 DM transit (*Liniennetz*) map gives you the city by the tail. The double-decker buses are a joy to ride, and the subway is a snap. Bus 100, circling past most major sights from Zoo to Alexanderplatz, is great for sightseeing. Taxis are easy to catch but not cheap.

Sightseeing Highlights—Berlin

▲ **Kurfürstendamm**—The glitter of the crazy 1920s still echoes here in neon. During the Cold War, economic subsidies from the West made sure that the full flashy vibrancy of capitalism thrived on Ku'damm (its popular nickname). This hamburgerized Champs-Elysées of Berlin is still the place to feel the pulse of the city. Near the head of Ku'damm are the main train station, Europa Center, Kaiser Wilhelm memorial church, and Savignyplatz.

Europa Center—An impressive high-rise shopping center you're bound to bump into. It's the skyscraper where you'll find the city tourist information, lots of shops and restaurants, a special Berlin movie, and a great view from the top. If your overnight train arrives before the TI opens, the café (open at 7:30) inside on the ground floor is a much more pleasant place to brush your teeth and start your day than the Bahnhof Zoo.

▲ **Kaiser-Wilhelm Gedachtniskirche (Memorial Church)**—This most important World War II memorial, with charred and gutted ruins of the old bombed-out church, has great ceiling mosaics. Next to it is the very impressive new church. Go inside for a world of blue glass. You'll see why they call this complex the broken tooth, the lipstick, and the powder compact.

Siegessaüle—This tower was built to commemorate the Prussian defeat of France in 1870. You can climb its 285 steps for a fine Berlin-wide view (on the bus 100 line).

▲ **The Reichstag**—The old parliament building, burned by Hitler to frame the communists, now houses a fine modern German history exhibit (open 10:00-17:00 Tuesday-Sunday, free, take bus 100 from Zoo). History buffs will enjoy comparing this version with a perspective from the political left shown in East Berlin's counterpart. Now that Berlin is one, the final chapter in the story will be told (by the winner). The Reichstag may soon be reinstated as Germany's parliament building.

▲▲ **Brandenburg Gate**—The historic Brandenburg Gate was the symbol of Berlin and then the symbol of divided Berlin. It sat sad and quiet in a no-man's-land, part of the wall, for over 25 years. Now the postcards show the ecstatic day, November 9, 1989, when the world enjoyed the sight of happy Berliners jamming the gate like flowers on a parade float. A carnival atmosphere continues as tourists stroll, past hawkers with "authentic" pieces of the wall and DDR flags and uniform parts, to the traditional rhythm of an organ grinder. Berlin has lived and died through so much, and it is still distinctly Berlin. As you walk over Brandenburg Gate, look down the vacant swath of formerly fortified land, breathe in the freedom . . . and remember those who fought and still fight for it.

▲▲ **The Museum of the Wall (Haus am Checkpoint Charlie) and the last bit of the Wall**—The 100-mile "Anti-Fascist Protective Rampart," as it was called by the DDR, was erected almost overnight by East Germany (and friends) in 1961. It was 13 feet high with a 16-foot tank ditch and 160 feet of no-man's-land. The opposite of a medieval rampart, this wall kept people in. When it fell it was literally carried away by the euphoria. Only a small stretch remains, between Friedrichstrasse and the Museum of the Wall and Potsdamer Platz. Potsdamer Platz was the Times Square of Berlin and at one time, the busiest square in Europe. Since East and West grew facing away from each other, Potsdamer Platz today is strangely vacant.

Don't miss the fascinating Haus am Checkpoint Charlie, the little museum that tells the gripping history of the wall and countless imaginative escape attempts. It has become a much happier place, and a visit will include plenty of video and film coverage of those heady days when people power beat the wall (U-Bahn to Kochstr., daily 9:00-22:00, 5 DM).

The "Topography of Terror" exhibit (walk along Zim-

Eastern Berlin

WHAT WAS THE WALL 1961–1989

FRIEDRICHSTRASSE BAHNHOF

PERGAMON MUSEUM

TV TOWER & i

N

TIER·

REICHS-TAG

BRANDENBURG GATE

GER.HIST. MUSEUM

MUSEUM ISLAND

MARIEN CHURCH

ALEX-ANDER PLATZ

← Bus 100 TO ZOO

VICTIMS MEMORIAL

DOM

PALACE OF REP.

RATHAUS

BERLIN HBF

STR. DES 17 JUNI

UNTER DEN LINDEN

MARX-ENGELS PLATZ

← TO SIEGSSÄULE

GARTEN·

TIERGARTENSTRASSE

PHIL-HARMONIE

NAT'L. GALL.

PORTION OF WALL STILL STANDING

LEIPZIGER- STRASSE

FRIEDRICHSTRASSE

↑ NIKOLAI CHURCH + OLD TOWN

TO SOVIET WAR MEMORIAL ↓

SPREE R.

"EAST"

POTSDAMER STRASSE

POTSDAMER "PLATZ"

CITY LIBRARY

FORMER "CHECKPOINT CHARLIE"

■ MUSEUM OF THE WALL

KOCHSTRASSE

"WEST"

ORANIEN STR.

LINDENSTR.

BUS 129

SCHÖNEBERGSTRASSE

ANHALTER BAHNHOF (RUINS)

KOCH-STRASSE

← BUS 129 TO KU'DAMM

KREUZBERG

S S-BAHN
U U-BAHN
NOT ALL STATIONS ARE SHOWN

NOTE: MAP NOT TO SCALE BRAND. GATE TO T.V. TOWER IS A **15**-MIN. WALK

merstrasse to the end of the last piece of wall from the Museum of the Wall), on a former site of the Gestapo, shows the story of Nazism in Germany.

▲▲▲ **A Walk through Eastern Berlin**—Unter den Linden was one of Europe's grand boulevards in Berlin's good old days. Still a fine stroll is the walk from Brandenburg Gate to Alexanderplatz. Along the way, visit the neoclassical, temple-like Memorial to the Victims of Fascism and Militarism and the fascinating German History Museum just a few steps farther toward the river. This museum (Unter den Linden 2, open Monday-Thursday 8:00-18:00, Saturday and Sunday 10:00-17:00) is a thought-provoking look at the history of Germany (and the world) from a socialist perspective (the other side is currently updating the museum with the latest chapter).

Formerly the proud showpiece of East Berlin, the boxy glass Palace of the Republic is now closed and probably

slated for the wrecking ball. Continue east over the Spree
River and browse through the (happy to be free but yet to
be rich) people, fountains, and flowers to the TV tower
(fine view, TI below). Farther east, pass under the S-Bahn
station into the mod Alexanderplatz with fast-food stalls
and a huge and proud Centrum Warenhaus department
store on the left. This was the East Berlin consumer's
paradise. It still is the heart of eastern Berlin.

▲▲ **Museum Island (Museuminsel)**—Berlin's top
museums are concentrated on the Museuminsel, just off
Unter den Linden, in the eastern section. The Pergamon
Museum is a must. There you can see the fantastic Pergamon Altar, the Babylonian Ishtar Gate, and many more
treasures from the classical world (open 10:00-18:00, but
only the main section with the altar is open on Mon. and
Tues.).

▲ **Treptower Park Soviet War Memorial**—Consider
an S-Bahn trip (get on trains heading for either Flughafen
Bin-Schönefeld or Königs Wusterhausen to the Treptower Park stop) to the Soviet War Memorial, a vast green
and somber park with giant evocative statues. From the
subway, walk 10 minutes through the park and across the
big street to Ehrenmal für die Gefallenen Sowjetischen
Helden. Return on the S-bahn to Alexanderplatz. Walk
past the Rathaus (city hall, good, handy restaurant downstairs) toward the double spires of the St. Nikolai Church
to the fine shops and cafes of the pleasantly restored old
Berlin. Cross the bridge and walk or catch a bus back to
Friedrichstrasse and the Museum of the Wall (sight of
Checkpoint Charlie).

Schloss Charlottenburg—This is the only surviving
Hohenzollern Palace and Berlin's top baroque palace
(Tuesday-Sunday 10:00-17:00, Thursday until 20:00, U-1
to Sophie-Charlotte Platz, then bus 204 from Zoo). If
you've seen the great palaces of Europe, this is really
mediocre, especially since its center is tourable only with
a German guide. For a quick look, the Knöbelsdorff Wing
is set up to let you wander on your own, a substantial
hike through restored (since the war) gold-crusted white
rooms filled with no-name baroque paintings.

▲ **The Egyptian Museum**—Across the street from the palace is a fine little museum filled with Egyptian treasures. It's free and offers one of the great thrills in the world of art appreciation—gazing into the beautiful face of 3,000-year-old Queen Nefertiti, the wife of King Akhnaton (Monday-Thursday 9:00-17:00, Saturday and Sunday 10:00-17:00).

The Bröhan Museum (5 DM, next to the Egyptian Museum, across the street from the Charlottenburg Palace, 10:00-18:00, closed Monday) is like walking through a dozen beautifully furnished Art Nouveau (Jugendstil) and Art Deco living rooms. The final rooms are not worth the six flights of stairs.

▲▲ **Dahlem Museums**—Dahlem is actually a cluster of important museums that, one by one over the next decade, will be moved to the new museum complex in the Tiergarten (all are free and open Tuesday-Sunday 9:00-17:00, U-bahn to Dahlem-Dorf). The *Gemälde-galerie* (picture gallery) is the only essential stop here. It has over 600 canvases by the likes of Dürer, Titian, Botticelli, Rubens, Vermeer, and Bruegel and the world's greatest collection of Rembrandts, including the *Man with the Golden Helmet* (which, though recently determined not to have been painted by Rembrandt, is still engrossing).

Zoo—Berlin's famous zoo (with more species than any other) stretches out from Berlin's central station (9:00-17:00, summer evenings until 19:00, entrance fee, feeding times posted at entry, morning is the best visiting time). Next to the zoo is Berlin's biggest and most pleasant city park, the Tiergarten.

Gedenkstätte Plötzensee Memorial—Powerful memorial to Nazi victims in Hitler's former execution chambers (daily 8:00-18:00, fewer hours off-season, free).

Kreuzberg—This poorer district along the wall, with old restored and unrestored buildings and plenty of student and Turkish street life, is the best look at melting pot Berlin in a city where original Berliners are as rare as old buildings. This is the "downtown" of the fourth-largest

Turkish city, but to call it a little Istanbul insults the big
one. While the area around Kottbusser Tor and Orianien-
strasse is the place for "alternative" entertainment, my
experience was dominated by the obnoxious graffiti, broken bottles, skinheads, and punks. A browse around the
Mehringdamm U-bahn station is a little milder.

Evenings in Berlin
Several magazines sold at kiosks tell you what's on. *Zitty*
is your guide to alternative culture, *Tip* is also hip, and
Berlin Program lists more traditional culture. There are
endless concerts, plays, exhibits, and cultural events. And
when that fails you, Berlin has thousands of night spots
for drinking, dancing, and making the local scene. If you
just wander around Savignyplatz, Olivaerplatz, Leniner-
platz, and Ludwigskirchplatz (all near Ku'damm), you'll
find plenty of action. The famous drag revues are as out-
rageous as you've heard. Contributing to Berlin's wild
late-night scene is the fact that while the rest of Germany
must close down at midnight or 1:00, Berlin night spots
must close only one hour a day.

Sleeping in Berlin
Arriving early, on the overnight train, I've found room-
finding in Berlin is easy. But the TI says it's often booked
solid and you should call ahead. For about 3 DM, they'll
find you a room.

The following listings are near the Ku'damm, within a
10-minute walk of the Zoo Bahnhof, and listed in order
of comfort and efficiency per dollar. For Berlin, they are
central and cheap but not seedy, a rare combination.
Beds in Berlin are expensive, and there are some incredi-
bly bad values out there.

Pension Heide am Zoo (110-130 DM doubles,
Fasanenstr. 12, 1000 Berlin 12, tel. 030/310496) is stylish
but homey on a quiet street a 5-minute walk from the station. Call first; no rooms are given to drop-ins.

Pension Fischer (60-100 DM doubles, Nürnberger

Strasse 24a, 1000 Berlin 30, tel. 030/218 6808) has simple
quiet rooms.

Hotel Bogota (100-170 DM doubles, Schlüterstr. 45,
1000 Berlin 15, tel. 030/881 5001, fax 883 5887) has big
bright modern rooms in a safe-feeling, spacious old
building half a block off Ku'damm. The service is brisk
and hotelesque. This is the best no-nonsense hotel-
type listing.

Hotel Pension Majesty (120-130 DM doubles,
Mommsenstr. 55, D-1000 Berlin 12, tel. 030/323 2061,
fax 32 32 063) is like an old inn, stylish but sparse.

Those on a tight budget should find a hostel. Hostels
are often packed with West German school groups field-
tripping to Berlin. Of Berlin's four fine hostels, the
Jugendgastehaus Berlin (31 DM beds with sheets and
breakfast in 4- to 8-bed rooms, Kluckstr. 3, take bus 129
in front of Wertheim department store, tel. 030/261 1097
or 261 1098, over 400 beds, but often filled with groups
so call up to two weeks in advance and leave your name,
members only) is most central. It serves 8 DM lunches
and dinners. The **Studenten Hotel Berlin** (32-36 DM
per bed in doubles and quads with breakfast, Meinin-
gerstr. 10, tel. 030/7846720, near the city hall on JFK
Platz or U-Bahn to Rathaus Schoneberg) is also decent.

Eating in Berlin

Berlin has plenty of fun food places, both German and
imported. If you're tired of kraut and wurst, try one of
the many Turkish, Italian, or Balkan restaurants. Those
counting pennies fill up on a hearty stew at a funky pub
called **Dicke Wirtin** (4 DM per bowl, 9 Carmerstr., a
5-minute walk off Ku'damm at Savignyplatz) or at one of
several ethnic eateries near Savignyplatz (check the small
lane under the S-bahn, Knesebeck and Bleibtreu streets,
and the area west of the Platz). Kurfürstendamm's **Wertheim** has cheap basement food counters and a second
floor self-service cafeteria.

Don't miss the huge KaDeWe (Kaufhaus des Westens)
department store on Tauentzenstrasse, corner of Witten-

bergplatz. While its self-service Zille-stube is a fine value, the sixth-floor food department, Europe's largest, is a picnicker's nirvana. Drool your way through over 1,000 kinds of sausage and 1,500 types of cheese. You can even get peanut butter here! Put together a picnic and grab a sunny bench.

Students with ISIC cards should try to enjoy the cheap food and local crowds at a Berlin *mensa* (university cafeteria). And there are plenty of decent fast-food (*schnell imbiss*) joints along Ku'damm. For cheap and substantial kebabs, feast with the Turks in the Kreuzberg area.

The local pubs, called *Kneipe*, are colorful places for a light meal and to try out the local beer, Berliner Weiss. Ask for it *mit Schuss* and you'll get a shot of syrup in your suds.

TRANSPORTATION

The chart below lists the major train segments you may use with average duration of journey, cost in U.S. dollars for a one-way second-class ticket (for first class, just add 50 percent, and spit out your gum), and about how many trips are made per day. Any journey of six or more hours can be done overnight. To figure fares yourself, remember second-class ticket prices are based on 20 DM for 100 km (about $12 for 60 miles).

Train Almanac for Germany, Austria, and Switzerland

From-To	Length of Trip	Approx 1993 cost in $, o/w, 2nd class	Trips/Day
Frankfurt-Würzburg	1 hr. 20 min.	20	20
Frankfurt-Berlin	8 hrs.	66	7
Frankfurt-Munich (train)	4 hrs.	55	17
Frankfurt-Munich (bus tour)	11 hrs.	55	1
Frankfurt-Köln	2 hrs. 10 min.	30	20
Frankfurt-Amsterdam	5 hrs. 30 min.	60	11
Würzburg-Rothenburg, via Steinach	1 hr.	8	20
Rothenburg-Munich (bus)	5 hrs.	30	1
Rothenburg-Füssen	6 hrs.	35	1
Füssen-Reutte in Tirol (bus)	45 min.	3	11
Reutte-Munich, via Garmisch	3 hrs.	20	8
Munich-Füssen	1 hr.	16	12
Munich-Salzburg	2 hrs.	20	15
Munich-Vienna	5 hrs. 30 min.	54	7
Munich-Venice	9 hrs.	52	2
Vienna-Venice	10 hrs.	58	5
Salzburg-Vienna	3 hrs. 20 min.	34	16
Vienna-Mauthausen	2 hrs.	17	20
Vienna-Innsbruck	5 hrs. 30 min.	60	8
Vienna-Zürich	9 hrs. 30 min.	90	5
Vienna-Budapest	3 hrs. 30 min.	25	4
Vienna-Prague	6 hrs.	31	4
Innsbruck-Zürich	4 hrs.	42	7
Zürich-Munich	4 hrs. 30 min.	51	5
Zürich-Paris	6 hrs. 30 min.	70	5
Zürich-Luzern	50 min.	13	20
Luzern-Interlaken	2 hrs.	13	20

Train Almanac (cont.)

From-To	Length of Trip	Approx 1993 cost in $, o/w, 2nd class	Trips/Day
Interlaken Ost-Gimmelwald	1 hr. 30 min.	7	20
Interlaken-Montreux	3 hrs.	30	16
Interlaken-Bern	1 hr.	13	20
Montreux-Lausanne	20 min.	5	30
Lausanne-Murten	1 hr.	13	12
Murten-Bern	1 hr.	13	12
Bern-Freiburg (Germany)	3 hrs.	30	4
Freiburg-Baden-Baden	1 hr. 20 min.	13	30
Baden-Baden-Koblenz	2 hrs. 30 min.	35	20
Koblenz-Cochem	40 min.	7	17
Cochem-Trier	45 min.	8	17
Koblenz-Mainz, train	50 min.	13	40
Koblenz-Mainz, boat	6 hrs.	30	5
Koblenz-Bonn	30 min.	7	40
Bonn-Köln	30 min.	5	40
Koblenz-Frankfurt	1 hr. 30 min.	17	20
Frankfurt-Frankfurt Airport	15 min.	3	50
Berlin-Munich	10 hrs.	85	3
Berlin-Vienna	12 hrs.	68	1
Berlin-Amsterdam	10 hrs.	85	5
Berlin-Copenhagen	10 hrs.	54	2

Train Itinerary

Day		Overnight in
1	Arrive Frankfurt, train to Rothenburg	Rothenburg
2	Sightsee Rothenburg	Rothenburg
3	Morning in Rothenburg, afternoon Romantic Road bus tour	Munich
4	All day sightsee in Munich	Munich
5	Munich, sidetrip to Bavaria, castles, towns	Munich
6	All day in Munich, plenty to do	Night train
7	Sightsee in Vienna	Vienna
8	Sightsee in Vienna	Vienna
9	Cruise the Danube, Salzburg	Salzburg
10	Sightsee Salzburg, Salzkammergut Lakes trip	Night train
11	Bern, Interlaken, Grindelwald, hike to. . .	Gimmelwald
12	Free to frolic in the heart of the Alps	Gimmelwald
13	Château Chillon, Montreux, Lake Geneva	Montreux
14	French Switzerland, Murten, Bern	Murten or Bern

Train Itinerary (cont.)

Day		Overnight in
15	Explore Germany's Black Forest, Freiburg	Baden-Baden
16	Free day in old spa town, soak, massage. . .	Baden-Baden
17	Train up Rhine to castle country	St. Goar
18	Mosel River, Cochem, Bonn, or Köln	St. Goar
19	Rhine cruise, explore castles	Night train
20	Berlin	Berlin
21	Berlin	Night train
22	Frankfurt, tour over, fly home	

Train Lines, Germany, Austria, Switzerland

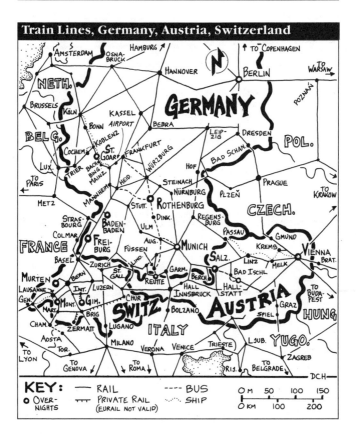

TELEPHONING

Country Codes
U.S.A.—1
Canada—1
France—33
Belgium—32
German—49
Italy—39
Netherlands—31
Switzerland—41
Austria—43
Great Britain—44

International Code to Call Out of:
Germany—00; Switzerland—00; Austria—050; USA—011

USA Direct toll-free access numbers for calling home from Europe (your credit card will be billed about $2.50 plus the cheaper USA to Europe long-distance rate.)

	ATT	MCI	SPRINT
Germany	0130-0010	0130-0012	0130-0013
Austria	022-903-011	022-903-012	022-903-014
Switzerland	155-00-11	155-02-22	155-97-77

Climate Chart

1st line: average daily low; 2nd: average daily high; 3rd: days of no rain

	J	F	M	A	M	J	J	A	S	O	N	D
GERMANY	29	31	35	41	48	53	56	55	51	43	36	31
Frankfurt	37	42	49	58	67	72	75	74	67	56	45	39
	22	19	22	21	22	21	21	21	21	22	21	20
AUSTRIA	26	28	34	41	50	56	59	58	52	44	36	30
Vienna	34	38	47	57	66	71	75	73	66	55	44	37
	23	21	24	21	22	21	22	21	23	23	22	22
SWITZER-	29	30	35	41	48	55	58	57	52	44	37	31
LAND	39	43	51	58	66	73	77	76	69	58	47	40
Geneva	20	19	21	19	19	19	22	21	20	20	19	21

INDEX

Rick Steves' BACK DOOR CATALOG

All items field tested, highly recommended, completely guaranteed, discounted below retail and ideal for independent, mobile travelers. Prices include tax (if applicable), handling, and postage.

The Back Door Suitcase / Rucksack $70.00

At 9"x22"x14" this specially designed, sturdy functional bag is maximum carry-on-the-plane size (fits under the seat) and your key to foot-loose and fancy-free travel. Made of rugged water resistant Cordura nylon, it converts easily from a smart-looking suitcase to a handy rucksack. It has hide-away padded shoulder straps, top and side handles and a detachable shoulder strap (for toting as a suitcase). Lockable perimeter zippers allow easy access to the roomy (2,700 cubic inches) central compartment. Two large outside pockets are perfect for frequently used items. Also included is one nylon stuff bag. Over 40,000 Back Door travelers have used these bags around the world. Rick Steves helped design and lives out of this bag for 3 months at a time. Comparable bags cost much more. Available in navy blue, black, or grey.

Moneybelt $8.00

This required, ultra-light, sturdy, under-the-pants, nylon pouch just big enough to carry the essentials (passport, airline ticket, travelers checks, and so on) comfortably. I'll never travel without one and I hope you won't either. Beige, nylon zipper, one size fits nearly all, with "manual."

Catalog FREE

For a complete listing of all the books, travel videos, products and services Rick Steves and Europe Through the Back Door offer you, ask us for our 64-page catalog.

Eurailpasses . . .

...cost the same everywhere. We carefully examine each order and include for no extra charge a 90-minute Rick Steves VHS video Train User's Guide, helpful itinerary advice, Eurail train schedule booklet and map, plus a free 22 Days book of your choice! Send us a check for the cost of the pass(es) you want along with your legal name (as it appears on your passport), a proposed itinerary (including dates and places of entry and exit if known), choice of 22 Days book (Europe, Brit, Spain/Port, Scand, France, or Germ/Switz/Aust) and a list of questions. Within 2 weeks of receiving your order we'll send you your pass(es) and any other information pertinent to your trip. Due to this unique service Rick Steves sells more passes than anyone on the West Coast and you'll have an efficient and expertly-organized Eurail trip.

Back Door Tours

We encourage independent travel, but for those who want a tour in the Back Door style, we do offer a 22-day "Best of Europe" tour. For complete details, send for our free 64 page tour booklet/catalog.

All orders will be processed within 2 weeks and include tax (where applicable), shipping and a one year's subscription to our Back Door Travel newsletter. Prices good through 1993. Rush orders add $5. Sorry, no credit cards. Send checks to:

Europe Through The Back Door ● 120 Fourth Ave. N.
Box   2009 ● Edmonds, WA 98020 ● (206) 771-8303

Other Books from John Muir Publications

Adventure Vacations: From Trekking in New Guinea to Swimming in Siberia, Bangs 256 pp. $17.95

Asia Through the Back Door, 3rd ed., Steves and Gottberg 326 pp. $15.95

Belize: A Natural Destination, Mahler, Wotkyns, Schafer 304 pp. $16.95

Bus Touring: Charter Vacations, U.S.A., Warren with Bloch 168 pp. $9.95

California Public Gardens: A Visitor's Guide, Sigg 304 pp. $16.95

Catholic America: Self-Renewal Centers and Retreats, Christian-Meyer 325 pp. $13.95

Costa Rica: A Natural Destination, 2nd ed., Sheck 288 pp. $16.95

Elderhostels: The Students' Choice, 2nd ed., Hyman 312 pp. $15.95

Environmental Vacations: Volunteer Projects to Save the Planet, 2nd ed., Ocko 248 pp. $16.95

Europe 101: History & Art for the Traveler, 4th ed., Steves and Openshaw 372 pp. $15.95

Europe Through the Back Door, 10th ed., Steves 448 pp. $16.95

A Foreign Visitor's Guide to America, Baldwin and Levine 200 pp. $10.95 (avail. 9/92)

Floating Vacations: River, Lake, and Ocean Adventures, White 256 pp. $17.95

Great Cities of Eastern Europe, Rapoport 256 pp. $16.95

Gypsying After 40: A Guide to Adventure and Self-Discovery, Harris 264 pp. $14.95

The Heart of Jerusalem, Nellhaus 336 pp. $12.95

Indian America: A Traveler's Companion, 2nd ed., Eagle/Walking Turtle 448 pp. $17.95

Interior Furnishings Southwest: The Sourcebook of the Best Production Craftspeople, Deats and Villani 256 pp. $19.95 (avail. 9/92)

Mona Winks: Self-Guided Tours of Europe's Top Museums, Steves and Openshaw 456 pp. $14.95

Opera! The Guide to Western Europe's Great Houses, Zietz 296 pp. $18.95

Paintbrushes and Pistols: How the Taos Artists Sold the West, Taggett and Schwarz 280 pp. $17.95

The People's Guide to Mexico, 8th ed., Franz 608 pp. $17.95

The People's Guide to RV Camping in Mexico, Franz with Rogers 320 pp. $13.95

Ranch Vacations: The Complete Guide to Guest and Resort, Fly-Fishing, and Cross-Country Skiing Ranches, 2nd ed., Kilgore 396 pp. $18.95

The Shopper's Guide to Art and Crafts in the Hawaiian Islands, Schuchter 272 pp. $13.95

The Shopper's Guide to Mexico, Rogers and Rosa 224 pp. $9.95

Ski Tech's Guide to Equipment, Skiwear, and Accessories, ed. Tanler 144 pp. $11.95

Ski Tech's Guide to Maintenance and Repair, ed. Tanler 160 pp. $11.95

A Traveler's Guide to Asian Culture, Chambers 224 pp. $13.95

Traveler's Guide to Healing Centers and Retreats in North America, Rudee and Blease 240 pp. $11.95

Understanding Europeans, Miller 272 pp. $14.95

Undiscovered Islands of the Caribbean, 2nd ed., Willes 232 pp. $14.95

Undiscovered Islands of the Mediterranean, 2nd ed., Moyer and Willes 256 pp. $13.95

Undiscovered Islands of the U.S. and Canadian West Coast, Moyer and Willes 208 pp. $12.95

A Viewer's Guide to Art: A Glossary of Gods, People, and Creatures, Shaw and Warren 144 pp. $10.95

2 to 22 Days Series

Each title offers 22 flexible daily itineraries that can be used to get the most out of vacations of any length. Included are not only "must see" attractions but also little-known villages and hidden "jewels" as well as valuable general information.

22 Days Around the World, 1992 ed., Rapoport and Willes 256 pp. $12.95 (**1993 ed.** avail. 8/92)

2 to 22 Days Around the Great Lakes, 1992 ed., Schuchter 192 pp. $9.95

22 Days in Alaska, Lanier 128 pp. $7.95
2 to 22 Days in the American Southwest, 1992 ed., Harris 176 pp. $9.95
2 to 22 Days in Asia, 1992 ed., Rapoport and Willes 176 pp. $9.95 (**1993 ed.** avail. 8/92)
2 to 22 Days in Australia, 1992 ed., Gottberg 192 pp. $9.95 (**1993 ed.** avail. 8/92)
2 to 22 Days in California, 1992 ed., Rapoport 192 pp. $9.95 (**1993 ed.** avail. 8/92)
22 Days in China, Duke and Victor 144 pp. $7.95
2 to 22 Days in Europe, 1992 ed., Steves 276 pp. $12.95
2 to 22 Days in Florida, 1992 ed., Harris 192 pp. $9.95 (**1993 ed.** avail. 8/92)
2 to 22 Days in France, 1992 ed., Steves 192 pp. $9.95
2 to 22 Days in Germany, Austria, & Switzerland, 1992 ed., Steves 224 pp. $9.95
2 to 22 Days in Great Britain, 1992 ed., Steves 192 pp. $9.95
2 to 22 Days in Hawaii, 1992 ed., Schuchter 176 pp. $9.95 (**1993 ed.** avail. 8/92)
22 Days in India, Mathur 136 pp. $7.95
22 Days in Japan, Old 136 pp. $7.95
22 Days in Mexico, 2nd ed., Rogers and Rosa 128 pp. $7.95
2 to 22 Days in New England, 1992 ed., Wright 192 pp. $9.95
2 to 22 Days in New Zealand, 1992 ed., Schuchter 176 pp. $9.95 (**1993 ed.** avail. 8/92)
2 to 22 Days in Norway, Sweden, & Denmark, 1992 ed., Steves 192 pp. $9.95
2 to 22 Days in the Pacific Northwest, 1992 ed., Harris 192 pp. $9.95
2 to 22 Days in the Rockies, 1992 ed., Rapoport 176 pp. $9.95
2 to 22 Days in Spain & Portugal, 1992 ed., Steves 192 pp. $9.95
2 to 22 Days in Texas, 1992 ed., Harris 192 pp. $9.95 (**1993 ed.** avail. 8/92)
2 to 22 Days in Thailand, 1992 ed., Richardson 176 pp. $9.95 (**1993 ed.** avail. 8/92)
22 Days in the West Indies, Morreale and Morreale 136 pp. $7.95

Parenting Series

Being a Father: Family, Work, and Self, *Mothering* Magazine 176 pp. $12.95
Preconception: A Woman's Guide to Preparing for Pregnancy and Parenthood, Aikey-Keller 232 pp. $14.95
Schooling at Home: Parents, Kids, and Learning, *Mothering* Magazine 264 pp. $14.95
Teens: A Fresh Look, *Mothering* Magazine 240 pp. $14.95

"Kidding Around" Travel Guides for Young Readers
Written for kids eight years of age and older.

Kidding Around Atlanta, Pedersen 64 pp. $9.95
Kidding Around Boston, Byers 64 pp. $9.95
Kidding Around Chicago, Davis 64 pp. $9.95
Kidding Around the Hawaiian Islands, Lovett 64 pp. $9.95
Kidding Around London, Lovett 64 pp. $9.95
Kidding Around Los Angeles, Cash 64 pp. $9.95
Kidding Around the National Parks of the Southwest, Lovett 108 pp. $12.95
Kidding Around New York City, Lovett 64 pp. $9.95
Kidding Around Paris, Clay 64 pp. $9.95
Kidding Around Philadelphia, Clay 64 pp. $9.95
Kidding Around San Diego, Luhrs 64 pp. $9.95
Kidding Around San Francisco, Zibart 64 pp. $9.95
Kidding Around Santa Fe, York 64 pp. $9.95
Kidding Around Seattle, Steves 64 pp. $9.95
Kidding Around Spain, Biggs 108 pp. $12.95
Kidding Around Washington, D.C., Pedersen 64 pp. $9.95

"Extremely Weird" Series for Young Readers
Written for kids eight years of age and older.

Extremely Weird Bats, Lovett 48 pp. $9.95
Extremely Weird Birds, Lovett 48 pp. $9.95
Extremely Weird Endangered Species, Lovett 48 pp. $9.95
Extremely Weird Fishes, Lovett 48 pp. $9.95
Extremely Weird Frogs, Lovett 48 pp. $9.95
Extremely Weird Primates, Lovett 48 pp. $9.95
Extremely Weird Reptiles, Lovett 48 pp. $9.95
Extremely Weird Spiders, Lovett 48 pp. $9.95

Masters of Motion Series

For kids eight years and older.

How to Drive an Indy Race Car, Rubel 48 pages $9.95 paper (avail. 8/92)
How to Fly a 747, Paulson 48 pages $9.95 (avail. 9/92)
How to Fly the Space Shuttle, Shorto 48 pages $9.95 paper (avail. 10/92)

Quill Hedgehog Adventures Series

Green fiction for kids. Written for kids eight years of age and older.

Quill's Adventures in the Great Beyond. Waddington-Feather 96 pp. $5.95
Quill's Adventures in Wasteland, Waddington-Feather 132 pp. $5.95
Quill's Adventures in Grozzieland, Waddington-Feather 132 pp. $5.95

X-ray Vision Series

For kids eight years and older.

Looking Inside Cartoon Animation, Schultz 48 pages $9.95 paper (avail. 9/92)
Looking Inside Sports Aerodynamics, Schultz 48 pages $9.95 paper
(avail. 9/92)
Looking Inside the Brain, Schultz 48 pages $9.95 paper

Other Young Readers Titles

The Indian Way: Learning to Communicate with Mother Earth, McLain 114 pp.
$9.95
The Kids' Environment Book: What's Awry and Why, Pedersen 192 pp. $13.95
Kids Explore America's Hispanic Heritage, Westridge Young Writers Workshop
112 pp. $7.95
**Rads, Ergs, and Cheeseburgers: The Kids' Guide to Energy and the Environ-
ment,** Yanda 108 pp. $12.95

Automotive Titles

How to Keep Your VW Alive, 14th ed., 440 pp. $21.95
How to Keep Your Subaru Alive 480 pp. $21.95
How to Keep Your Toyota Pickup Alive 392 pp. $21.95
How to Keep Your Datsun/Nissan Alive 544 pp. $21.95
**The Greaseless Guide to Car Care Confidence: Take the Terror Out of Talking
to Your Mechanic,** Jackson 224 pp. $14.95
Off-Road Emergency Repair & Survival, Ristow 160 pp. $9.95

Ordering Information

If you cannot find our books in your local bookstore, you can order directly from us.
Please check the "Available" date above. If you send us money for a book not yet
available, we will hold your money until we can ship you the book. Your books will
be sent to you via UPS (for U.S. destinations). UPS will not deliver to a P.O. Box;
please give us a street address. Include $3.75 for the first item ordered and $.50 for
each additional item to cover shipping and handling costs. For airmail within the
U.S., enclose $4.00. All foreign orders will be shipped surface rate; please enclose
$3.00 for the first item and $1.00 for each additional item. Please inquire about
foreign airmail rates.

Method of Payment

Your order may be paid by check, money order, or credit card. We cannot be
responsible for cash sent through the mail. All payments must be made in U.S.
dollars drawn on a U.S. bank. Canadian postal money orders in U.S. dollars are
acceptable. For VISA, MasterCard, or American Express orders, include your card
number, expiration date, and your signature, or call (800) 888-7504. Books ordered
on American Express cards can be shipped only to the billing address of the card-
holder. Sorry, no C.O.D.'s. Residents of sunny New Mexico, add 5.875% tax to the
total.

Address all orders and inquiries to:
John Muir Publications
P.O. Box 613
Santa Fe, NM 87504
(505) 982-4078
(800) 888-7504